Robert T. Eberwein

FILM &

THE DREAM

SCREEN

A Sleep and a Forgetting

Princeton University Press
Princeton, New Jersey

Published by Princeton University Press, 41 William Street,
Princeton, New Jersey 08540
In the United Kingdom: Princeton University Press, Guildford, Surrey

Library of Congress Cataloging in Publication Data will be
found on the last printed page of this book

ISBN 0-691-06619-1

Publication of this book has been aided by a grant from the Paul Mellon
Fund of Princeton University Press

This book has been composed in Linotron Bodoni

Clothbound editions of Princeton University Press books
are printed on acid-free paper, and binding materials are
chosen for strength and durability. Paperbacks, although satisfactory
for personal collections, are not usually suitable for library rebinding.

Printed in the United States of America by Princeton University Press
Princeton, New Jersey

for Jane

Contents

List of Illustrations

Acknowledgments

I AM HAPPY to acknowledge the assistance of several friends and associates and a number of kind people known to me only through their correspondence and cheerful voices on the telephone.

At Oakland University, Anne Lalas, Editorial Associate of the College of Arts and Sciences, asked pointed questions which resulted in clarification of the book's conception and design; she also introduced me to the mysteries of the word processor. Dolores M. Burdick, Director of the Concentration in Film Aesthetics and History, offered thoughtful advice and welcome encouragement. Other colleagues supplied useful information: Herbert Appleman, Nigel Hampton, Brian F. Murphy, and Helen J. Schwartz (English); Carl F. Barnes and Charlotte V. Stokes (Art and Art History); Harold Zepelin (Psychology); and Jane Briggs-Bunting (Rhetoric, Communications, and Journalism). Ruth A. Eberle and June A. Fisher, Secretaries of the Department of English, volunteered their helpful, effective assistance in many ways. Richard L. Pettengill, Elizabeth A. Titus, and the staff of the Inter-Library Loan division of the Kresge Library found all the materials I requested. Patrick D. McNeill, Tina Persha, and George T. Preisinger of the Instructional Technology Center of the Library responded to my audio-visual needs. I am also grateful to Beverly J. Darrenkamp, Executive Secretary of the Director of Computer Services, and to Suzanne Gillich and Joan Pistonetti of that office. Thomas A. Aston, Director of the Student Enterprise Theatre, deserves thanks for allowing me to view one of his films. In addition, members of my Cinema Studies 450 Seminar in Film and Dream proved to be a challenging audience as I developed various parts of my argument.

I am forever grateful for the extraordinary guidance and support offered by members of the Princeton University Press, especially Joanna Hitchcock, Executive Editor, who has been a genial and loyal mentor. I value her excellent suggestions about revisions, her assistance in the polishing of the manuscript, and her faith in the value of the project. Marilyn Campbell, Editor, has offered moral support, listened patiently to my endless questions and responded unfailingly with clear, calming answers and advice. Loren Hoekzema, Reprints and Paperbacks Manager, was kind enough to suggest I send my manuscript to the Press initially. And Phil Leclerc, Associate Plant Manager, has helped with the computer-related aspects of the book's production.

Peter Lehman (University of Arizona) merits special credit for providing me an opportunity to test my hypothesis at the 1980 Ohio University Film Conference in Athens, Ohio. In a somewhat different form, part of this book appeared in *Wide Angle*, which he edits, and I acknowledge with pleasure the first appearance of that material in his journal.

I received assistance from film scholars outside my university. John C. Stubbs (University of Illinois) responded to my queries about Federico Fellini by generously committing a substantial amount of time verifying data. Robert T. Self (Northern Illinois University) shared his considerable knowledge of Robert Altman. Victoria Araña-Robinson (Howard University) and William G. Luhr (St. Peter's College) stimulated my thinking on questions raised by the films of Ingmar Bergman and R. W. Fassbinder. And Marshall Deutelbaum

(Purdue University) introduced me to some relevent silent films I might otherwise have missed.

I appreciated very much the comments of those who read my study in manuscript form: Marsha Kinder (University of Southern California); Frank D. McConnell (University of California at Santa Barbara); and Dennis Turner (Wayne State University).

I also wish to thank several individuals for their special kindness: Ivan Bender, Mary Grimley, and Leslie Lowe Woodfin at Films Incorporated; Walter Calmette and Kenneth Low of Embassy Pictures; Howard Feinstein, Film Stills Archive, Museum of Modern Art; George Pratt, International Museum of Photography at George Eastman House; Val Almendarez, Academy of Motion Picture Arts and Sciences; and Jeff Dighton, Larry Edmonds Bookshop, Inc.

The still from *The Temptations of Dr. Antonio* appears courtesy of Embassy Pictures. The stills from *Spellbound* are used courtesy of ABC Pictures International, Inc. I offer special thanks to Christina Kuhn, Export Manager of AB Svensk Filmindustrie for her informative, useful assistance and for the cooperation of the company. I am particularly grateful to Ingmar Bergman for granting me permission to use stills from *Persona*.

FILM &
THE DREAM SCREEN

Our birth is but a sleep and a forgetting:
The Soul that rises with us, our life's Star,
    Hath had elsewhere its setting,
    And cometh from afar:
    Not in entire forgetfulness,
    And not in utter nakedness,
But trailing clouds of glory do we come
    From God, who is our home:
Heaven lies about us in our infancy!
Shades of the prison-house begin to close
    Upon the growing Boy,
But he beholds the light, and whence it flows,
    He sees it in his joy;
The Youth, who daily farther from the east
    Must travel, still is Nature's priest,
    And by the vision splendid
    Is on his way attended;
At length the Man perceives it die away,
And fade into the light of common day.

    —William Wordsworth
    from "Ode: Intimations of Immortality
    from Recollections of Early Childhood"

Introduction

MANY PEOPLE have noticed that watching a film is like having a dream. Narrative elements sometimes seem to be outside spatial and temporal laws. The viewing conditions in the theater (such as the darkened room and the relative sense of isolation) are reminiscent of our solitary existence as dreamers alone in the night. The overpowering images on the screen sometimes frighten us and make us feel the same kind of paralysis we know in nightmares. In addition, films seem "real" in the way dreams do; in fact, their ability to make us believe we are a part of the action is for many one of film's most important achievements as a form of art.

In the following work, I propose a hypothesis to explain how our experience as dreamers affects our relationship to the cinematic screen. I hope such an endeavor will make it possible to talk more specifically about how dreams in film have been presented and why we react to them in various ways.

The hypothesis, presented in detail in the first part, posits a connection between our experiences as dreamers and as viewers of film. Seated in the darkened theater, observing a film on the cinematic screen, we find ourselves thrust back in time to infancy. At some point in our development, when we drifted off to sleep after feeding, we began to dream. In our mind's eye, we sensed those first oneiric images as being somewhere, projected on a field that provided the screen for the dream. Adopting and modifying the theory of Bertram Lewin, I argue that this field is a complex psychic structure, a "dream screen" comprised of two elements: the mother's breast, or a surrogate for it, and our own sense of self, the ego. These elements merge to form a dream screen where dreams appear to the sleeper.

As we grow older, we continue to feel the same sense of unity with the oneiric universe that we knew as infants. Our belief that what we "see" in dreams is real and actually present to us, no matter how unreal and illogical, derives from our first experience as dreamers, whenever that may have occurred. For in those earliest dreams, there was no "other," only ourselves and our hallucinated perceptions. Such a state of fusion, in which perceiver and perceived are one, suggests a primal state of visionary unity. This fusion is similar to the condition William Wordsworth describes in infants who, "trailing clouds of glory" from their prior existence, are still able to feel a sense of complete unity with the universe they perceive. According to the poet, growth into adulthood robs us of our ability to maintain a sense of oneness with our perceptions. Thus, for Wordsworth, our "birth" is inevitably "a sleep and a forgetting"—an entrance into a world that will deprive us of the integrative vision we have as infants and as children.

I shall adapt Wordsworth's language in order to argue that our experience of film permits us to return to the state of perceptual unity that we first participated in as infants and that we can know as dreamers. The "sleep" in our experience of film, that is, will be seen to return us to the primal sense of unity with our dreams. As a result, we are able to watch and feel a sense of involvement in the images on the screen, the distinction between *res cogitans* and *res extensa* having dissolved as we enter into the oneiric world of film.

The "forgetting" that Wordsworth laments is thus precluded—at least for the duration of our experience before the screen. Nonetheless, even though we can continue to recall the sense of unity, and the feeling that what we saw seemed very real to us during the experience of viewing, we have trouble remembering various events and details in the narrative. The longer we are away from the film, the more confused our memories of it become. In fact, the difficulty that presents itself as we try to recall the events and details of a film seems similar to that which we encounter as we try to remember dreams. A cause common to both is the very condition of the experience. Our sense of being present to the events of films and dreams is a result of the revived feeling of oneness; the filmic and oneiric worlds are extensions of ourselves and we seem to inhabit the same space. But when the worlds disappear from our mind's eye, we not only lose the immediacy of the events and characters; we also let go of the space in which these appeared, a space that emanates, in part, out of our linkage with the dream and cinematic screens. When we attempt to recall, we find ourselves positioning events and characters in a space that no longer exists. To revive that space requires more than a mere act of memory; it demands an act of the imagination, an endeavor that involves us inevitably as creators of the scene we wish to recapture. In other words, in trying to recall events, we are also attempting to reconstruct the manner in which they were present to us. Lacking a firm anchor in actual perceptual experience, we must rely on our own minds.

I have divided the study into two parts. In the first, which is limited to theoretical considerations, I offer a brief overview of dream theory from a psychoanalytic and physiological perspective, and then develop the hypothesis of the dream screen in order to explain how our experiences as dreamers affect us as viewers.

In the second part, I apply the hypothesis of the dream screen to particular films within a framework of three sections.

First, I develop a taxonomy of dreams, generally identified as belonging to particular characters. The filmmaker may sometimes introduce these with narrative cues, or with cinematic effects, or with a combination of these. When the dreams occur, no matter how they are introduced, the cinematic screen to which we are now linked by virtue of the revival of the dream screen of our infancy becomes charged with the dream screen of the dreaming character. It is as if the character were projecting his or her dream on the cinematic screen that we provide for the dreamer.

Next, I examine films that not only present dreams, but, more significantly, manifest the actual dream screens of the characters. In such works, we see the screen or its surrogate, on which a character projects a dream. Detailed analysis of *Sherlock, Jr.*, *Spellbound*, *The Temptations of Dr. Antonio*, and *Persona* will reveal that the presence of the characters' dream screens directly on the cinematic screen positions us and our screen in varying complex ways. Particularly with *Persona*, we will find that the merging of visible dream screens effects an unusual and hitherto unexplored linkage of artist, creation, and viewer.

Finally, I consider films that present dreams in what I shall call the retroactive mode. Essentially two subgroups belong here. In the first are works such as *The Avenging Conscience*, *8 1/2*, *Providence*, *Fireworks*, and *City of Women*, in which the film offers a dream that we recover retroactively. Either filmmakers withhold explicit narrative and cinematic cues which would alert us to the fact that we have begun to watch a dream, or else they disguise or limit these indicators considerably. The second subgroup includes *Dead of Night*, *Belle de Jour*, and *The Discreet Charm of the Bourgeoisie*. These films are constituted *entirely* as dreams, but we learn only at their conclusions that the worlds we have inhabited imaginatively are totally closed oneiric structures.

Depending on the particular retroactive mode they choose,

filmmakers can succeed in implicating us in the consciousness of the individual dreamers. We discover that *our* dream
screen has been the site of another's dream screen. In contrast
to our experience with the first two categories, when we know
that we provide or share a dream screen, we are overtaken
by the revelation that we have been linked to another consciousness, not only to the cinematic screen. Whatever sense
of ironic detachment or distance we may have felt as we
experienced the events is retroactively weakened. We will
see that filmmakers can use the retroactive mode to create
works that affect us in powerful ways.

Part One

THE DREAM
SCREEN

I N PART ONE, I present an overview of major dream
theories before developing my hypothesis. Perhaps the desire
for a sense of unity with the external world, like that unity
established in our earliest experiences as dreamers, explains
the motive for the birth of cinema. What Bertram Lewin calls
the dream screen, the psychic structure that represents the
mother's breast, affords us a primal screen on which we
perceive our oneiric world. The viewing of film on the cinematic screen when we are older revives the sensation of the
dream screen, a structure that is in part a product of our own
ego. This discussion concludes with the consideration that
one reason we forget dreams and films lies in the nature of
the space in which we experience cinematic and oneiric narratives.

Dream Theories

Since I will be referring to important psychoanalytic and
physiological theories of dreams throughout this work and
analyzing some of the films in the light of these theories, it
seems appropriate to provide a brief summary of the major
positions.

The most important theory of the origin and nature of dreams has come from Sigmund Freud, particularly in *The Interpretation of Dreams.* His work has exerted a tremendous influence on the way we approach dreams in films and on the practice of various filmmakers. Except for some of the silent films, all of the works I discuss were created after Freud's ideas were known and, with varying degrees, understood. But the fact that Freud's ideas were generally known does not mean that any of them were *necessarily* being applied consciously or accurately.[1]

Essentially, Freud believes that a dream is ultimately an infantile wish that emerges during sleep. The dream's apparent lack of coherence is a result of the dream-work, which performs the following operations: condensation, or the merging of persons and places; displacement, the shifting of psychic attention from important to apparently irrelevant or minor details; secondary revision, the means by which connections and structure are built into the disjointed memories of the dream; and considerations of representability, by which the abstract materials of the dream are given the form of pictorial language.

The dream incorporates material from the most recent events of the dreamer's life, the "day's residue." Since its real motive, an infantile wish, contains erotic material of an unacceptable nature, the operation of the dream-work creates a disguise. In such a covert form, the dream can pass the censor which during the day has succeeded in repressing the wish. But at night, the dream itself leads us back regressively to childhood. All the unfulfilled impulses and desires associated with what Freud calls primary process thinking, primal forces emerging from the id, begin to assert themselves and struggle up through the unconscious, seeking release.

The final dream as we remember it presents only its manifest content to us. The task of analysis of the dream is to discover the latent content, a revelation achieved by examining all the associations that the analysand has in reference to the dream and to daily life. Ultimately, the elements in the dream are seen to be overdetermined; that is, many features are the products of a number of influences, memories, and forces. The analyst attempts to interpret the dream's meaning by sorting through the pictorial puzzle, or rebus, recalled by the dreamer. A successful interpretation will lead both doctor and patient into the buried life of the individual, since dreams are, as Freud sees it, "the royal road" leading back into the unconscious.

Yet another feature of the dream is its importance as a preserver of sleep. To achieve that end, the dream-work will attempt to integrate any external stimuli (ringing alarms, for example) into the narrative so that the dreamer can continue to maintain a state in which the satisfying of a wish is possible.

Freud acknowledges two kinds of dreams that seem to contradict the argument that the dream satisfies an infantile wish. First, nightmares about flunking examinations in particular do not fulfill a wish but allow the dreamer to construct a dream for which no *real* cause for anxiety in the past was justified. Second, dreams about horrible experiences, such as those reported by war prisoners who actually endured them, occur when the dreamer is attempting to master disturbing traumatic events.

With the exception of examination or traumatic dreams, though, dreams are disguised infantile wishes. As such, they are not the results of somatic influences. Although Freud admits that bodily pressures can play a minor part in dream formation, the thrust of his theory is against the idea that a dream is, in effect, the result of something one ate.[2]

Perhaps the greatest challenge to Freud's theory of dream formation has come as the result of dream research done recently by physiologists, psychologists, and psychiatrists. Earlier psychoanalysts sometimes challenged Freud's views and offered alternative theories to explain the nature of the dream. For example, Carl G. Jung argues that the dream is a compensatory activity on the part of the individual rather than a disguised wish. Dreams themselves emerge from the buried psychic life of the dreamer as well as of the human race and display in their content archetypal elements common to all cultures.[3] Still, for Jung (and for Alfred Adler, who also qualifies Freud's theory of dreams), the dream is understood to be a psychic event emerging from the unconscious mind of the dreamer. But, with the discovery of empirical data about the nature of the dreaming process, Freud's view has been severely tested.

The motivating impulse for this revision of Freudian theory has come out of clinical observation of dreamers. Freud himself mentions the work of G. Trumbull Ladd. In 1892, Ladd had noticed that the eyes of someone asleep can be seen to move beneath the eyelids, presumably in the course of a dream.[4] But it was not until the 1950s that the implications of Ladd's discovery became important for dream theory.

By that time, the electroencephalograph (EEG), invented in 1929 by Hans Berger, was being used to measure the activity of the brain under various circumstances, including that of sleep. Eugene Aserinsky and Nathaniel Kleitman, who had conducted experiments on the effects of sleep deprivation, attached electrodes from the EEG to a sleeper and discovered that the traces of brain activity vary in the course of the night; this suggested that a sleeper passes through different stages of mental activity.[5]

The periods of sleep in which eye movement appeared beneath the eyelids were seen to correlate with a particular pattern of brain waves. When we are awake, our brain waves generate a distinct configuration on the EEG. As we fall asleep, we move through four stages, each signaled by a specific kind of brain wave, before entering the stage of sleep characterized by rapid eye movement, which is accompanied by its own unique pattern on the EEG. In REM (rapid eye movement) sleep, the low intensity waves are fast and produce a sawtoothed design.

Analysis of the EEG data indicates that dreaming is a phasic activity linked to REM sleep and occurs five or six times during a night as part of a general pattern of brain activity. Each movement from stages one through four, followed by an REM period, takes approximately sixty to ninety minutes. Then the dreamer repeats the passage through the stages again. Toward the end of the night's sleep, more time is spent in dreaming periods (REM sleep).

As a result of these and related discoveries, scientists found themselves reversing Freud's claim that the function of the dream was to preserve sleep. In fact, the opposite seemed to be true: the function of sleep was to permit individuals to dream. Studies of sleep deprivation revealed that dreaming is a necessary part of our activities as human beings.

In addition, by watching for indications of when the dreamer had entered REM sleep, the researchers could waken the dreamer and ask for the content of the dream. This permitted them (and the dreamer as well) to recover dreams that might otherwise have been lost from memory. Moreover, it allowed them and later researchers who employed their methodology to follow the course of dreams in a given night. Some studies revealed that the dreams of a single night may even have a unifying theme or pattern. Also, some experimenters used this technique to test the influence of recently experienced phenomena on the content of dreams. For example, researchers tried to see if particular dream images could be induced by depriving the sleepers of certain things (water) or by exposing them to others (pornographic films).

By the end of the 1950s, it was generally agreed that dreams occurred in the REM phase of sleep. Moreover, as a result of various experiments conducted by such scientists as William C. Dement (who coined the term REM sleep) and Howard P. Roffwarg, sleep researchers suggested that the rapid eye movements were themselves ocular actions on the part of the dreamer "watching" the dream. For example, a high percentage of vertical eye movement was determined to be related to the content of a dream about shooting basketballs. Other patterns of eye movements appeared to be related to such dream actions as climbing stairs.[6]

But these conclusions—REM sleep is dreaming sleep; eye movements during this period reflect the dreamer's activity in the dream—came under scrutiny for a number of reasons. First, scientists pointed to the fact that newborn infants display an extremely high percentage of REM sleep. But it could hardly be imagined that neonatals were "dreaming." Second, sleep researchers conducting experiments similar to those which had been used to defend the initial hypotheses argued that the correlations observed in earlier research were inadequate. W. David Foulkes, for example, found that sleepers awakened during periods of sleep other than the REM stage also reported having dreams. These dreams were not as vivid as those reported in the REM stage and were characterized more by reflective thinking; but they were still dreams, if a dream is understood as a hallucinatory experience in which some kind of visual or linguistic activity occurs.[7] Some researchers suggest that the distinction between REM and NREM (non-rapid eye movement sleep) is similar to that which Freud posits between primary process and secondary process thought—primal, libidinal urges as opposed to intellectualized activity. The claim that the eye movements could be correlated with the events seen by the dreamer was also challenged by several other scientists. For example, Ralph J. Berger and Eric Moscowitz ran similar experiments and arrived at much less convincing and statistically reliable data.[8]

One of the most significant arguments raised against the conclusion that the eye movements necessarily followed the material being observed in the dream has come in relation to studies of the neurophysiology of dreaming. These studies have also been the most influential in calling Freud's theory of dreams into question. A number of scientists have explored the neurophysiological aspects of dreaming, among them William C. Dement, Mardi Jon Horowitz, Richard M. Jones, Michel Jouvet, and Frederick Snyder.[9]

Although not the first to discuss dreaming from a neurophysiological perspective, Robert W. McCarley and J. Allan Hobson have received perhaps the greatest amount of attention lately. Essentially they argue that the phasic nature of dreams and our entrance periodically throughout the night into the D (desynchronized) state are primarily results of the operations of our neurophysiological systems. The technical aspects of their theory are extremely complex, but, without simplifying too much, the following summary fairly captures their argument. At various times during the night, the dreamer's system undergoes a completely involuntary series of reactions involving chemical and neuronal activity. Discharges of neurons occasioned by the action of the Pontine reticular cells stimulate various parts of the lower brain, particularly the section of the cortex controlling visual activities. In effect, the periodic firings through the system provide a jolt that causes eye movements. These, in turn, issue "commands" to the entire brain and lead to the calling up of various sensations and perceptions which the brain offers as correlates to the neuronal impulses.

Thus the images we "see" during dreams are our brain's response to the endogenous stimulations that occur every ninety minutes during sleep. Rather than offering an index of how we follow the action of what we watch as dreamers, the rapid eye movements *precede* the hallucinated images in our brain, and, in effect, call up visual elements that match them. Hobson and McCarley see the brain as a vast computer, processing an abundance of commands and information. Not surprisingly, the dream is a jumbled and confused affair, composed as it is out of a series of unrelated commands issued in the course of the rapid eye movement phase of sleep. The brain does what it can to effect some linkage in the information confronting it: its response is the dream.

Although they do not deny that a dreamer's characteristic feelings and desires can be elements in such dreams, they do reject the thesis that a wish is the motivating force for the dream. Since the dream is understood as consisting of images isomorphically related to a series of events in the brain, it can hardly be approached as an infantile wish.[10]

Recently Hobson has applied their activation-synthesis theory to film and suggested a number of physiological and psychological parallels between dreaming and the experience of film.[11] In addition, he specifically argues that their theory corrects not only the psychoanalytic shortcomings of Freud's theory but also what they see as its negative and deterministic effects on criticism. Thus he says: "Activation-synthesis frees the investigation of dream cognition . . . from the Freudian strait jacket of historical and pathogenic determination by viewing dream synthesis as both original and conflict-free." Freudianism generally "has misled both psychiatry and film-making."[12]

Readers will see that in the following pages I attempt to maintain an eclectic rather than an exclusive approach to this complex material. Hobson's objections notwithstanding, I believe that our considerations of dreams and their appearance in films can be enriched by cautious application of the psychoanalytic theory he questions. In addition, when appropriate, I incorporate the findings and suggestions of researchers and theorists in other disciplines such as linguistics and child development.

The Desire for Cinema

When the Lumière brothers first showed their film of a train coming into a railroad station, many in the Parisian audience

1. Unable to distinguish the image from reality, Uncle Josh pulls down the screen.

of 1895 fled out onto the street, terrified of the engine that seemed about to enter their three-dimensional space. Their inability to distinguish the appearance of the flat but moving image from reality is mirrored in a short film made by Edwin S. Porter in 1902, *Uncle Josh at the Moving Picture Show.* The hero, obviously attending his first motion picture, watches the screen in amazement. He too sees a train coming at him; rather than running from the theater, though, he simply ducks, and then peeks behind one edge of the screen. Earlier in the film, when a dancing girl appears on the screen, he steps to the stage and attempts to dance along with her. When he sees a farm boy courting a girl, Uncle Josh tries to interfere with the romance by entering into the action he sees before him. But he succeeds only in pulling down the screen, re-

vealing a projectionist behind it. The men grapple, in slap-
stick fashion, and the film ends.

Yet another example of the inability to distinguish appearance from reality occurs in Jean-Luc Godard's *Les Carabiniers* (1963). Michelangelo, a young soldier, equally un-
familiar with the nature of film, enters a theater for the first
time. He too is disturbed by the sight of a train, but the most
interesting response that the viewing experience elicits from
him comes as he sees a girl taking a bath. He explores the
screen, trying to effect a better, more comprehensive view;
only by mastering the space of the screen will he be able to
see the complete body of the woman. But his actions fail to
achieve his voyeuristic aim, and, instead, he pulls down the
screen.

The citizens of Paris, Uncle Josh, and Michelangelo all
think that they share the space of the objects and people seen
on the screen. In fact, the screen seems to exist not as a
separate "field" for them but, rather, as an extension of their
own space. The images presented to them as iconic traces
seem to be realities, for, like dreamers, all have lost the
ability to distinguish between hallucination and reality.

When Uncle Josh and the soldier touch the screen, it
crumbles and collapses, perhaps in the way that the field of
our dreams disappears when we awake. Their attempts to
investigate the field on which the images taken for realities
appear only result in frustration. As we will see later, the
only way to enter into and master the screen is through a
dream; in fact, Buster Keaton's Sherlock, Jr. will literally
dream himself into the screen.

Like dreams, the screen resists physical scrutiny; touch it
and it breaks. If we want to retrieve the images from dreams
or cinema, we must rely on memory. In both cases, we must
be content with fragments—the images left in our minds of
what we experienced.

Speaking of another kind of loss, in "Ode: Intimations of

Immortality from Recollections of Early Childhood," William Wordsworth describes our birth as "a sleep and a forgetting." Modifying a Platonic conception, he suggests that prior to our birth and early in our development as children, we exist in a realm of pure vision and unity. As we grow older, we begin to forget all we knew in the earlier blissful state, and, unfortunately, we lose the ability to experience the world with the same wonder and delight. "Shades of the prison-house" close in around us as we mature; eventually, we lose our sense of oneness with the universe and see life only in "the light of common day."

Partially modifying Wordsworth's conception here, I suggest that each experience of film provides a kind of "birth" into a new world. Instead of causing a loss of unity, this birth leads to a "sleep" which returns us to something like the perceptual world Wordsworth says we inhabit before birth and as children. In this sleep of film, as in our dreams, we escape the dichotomy between subject and object which has haunted philosophy since the seventeenth century. In film and dream, we are at one with our perceptions.

But, after the film ends and we try to remember what we experienced, we become like the sleeper who is unable to recall all of a dream; we have only pieces of our experience left over. Dreams and films elude us when we try to reconstruct them, in part because of the way they were present to us as we experienced them. Film and dreams offer us a momentary triumph over our isolation from the world. But reentry into reality after we awake from the dream or conclude our viewing of the film plunges us back into our alienation from our perceptions.

Various critics have described the special appeal of the world into which film leads us and the specific nature of our desire for the cinema. In one of the best-known commentaries, "The Myth of Total Cinema," André Bazin argues that the motive for the development of cinema was the desire for "integral realism, a recreation of the world in its own image."[13] Ironically, the very desire to have complete realism all at once impeded the invention of the medium; that is, because its creators were striving for a total cinema to begin with, the medium was actually *delayed* in its appearance.[14]

But we not only want "the world in its own image"; we also desire the kind of presence that film affords us. Underlying the desire for total cinema is an unconscious and unarticulated longing to be unified with what one sees—an impulse that figures again and again in Romantic aesthetics, particularly in the criticism of Immanuel Kant and Samuel Taylor Coleridge. The integration of sound, color, and image Bazin speaks of would be less a primary goal than a necessary condition for realizing a more pressing need—giving to the viewer the sense of being present in the fictionalized world to which, for the moment, one belongs.

Such a feeling is captured in dreams. The dreamer's world, whether or not the dreamer is visible in the narrative, positions the dreaming subject and integrates vision and the scene (seen) in a continuous bond. To be sure, the narrative is filled with disruptions, gaps, irrational junctures, and bizarre content. Still, the mind's montage seems integrated at the time insofar as the experienced dream is felt to be continuous and totally part of the dreamer. We are the dream to the extent that it seems to emanate from our being.

Film puts us in contact with the aesthetic object in a similar manner. With no other form of narrative and visual art do we experience such a sense of oneness. F. E. Sparshott suggests that our experience as dreamers may have prepared us for the style and operation of film.[15] But the medium "imitates" more than the dreaming mode. By replicating the conditions of sleep and dream, film returns us to a condition of being in which the kind of subject-object integration I spoke of is possible.

One of the chief reasons we feel such a sense of integration has to do with the screen on which we watch the images. The screen seems to be a kind of extension of ourselves; we feel as if we have enclosed what we see in the private theater of our own minds, rather in the way one possesses the images in dreams.

Consider in this connection what Sigmund Freud says about human potential. Echoing Hamlet's "What a piece of work is man!" Freud speaks of humanity's power to extend and project itself with tools and machines: "[B]y means of the telescope [man] sees into the far distance; and by means of the microscope he overcomes the limits of visibility set by the structure of his retina. In the photographic camera he has created an instrument which retains the fleeting visual impressions, just as a gramophone disc retains the equally fleeting auditory ones; both are at bottom materializations of the power he possesses of recollection, his memory."[16] He observes that "all the forms of auxiliary apparatus which we have invented for the improvement or intensification of our sensory functions are built on the same model as the sense organs themselves or portions of them: for instance, spectacles, photographic cameras, ear-trumpets."[17] In this light, he exclaims: "Man has, as it were, become a kind of prosthetic God. When he puts on all his auxiliary organs he is truly magnificent. . . ."[18]

Bertram Lewin also speaks of the ways in which humans extend themselves and their potential for action with tools: "A rake is an imitation of the fingers or a scoop of the cupped palm of the hand." He suggests that the first such extension of human attributes occurred in Lascaux. Some fifteen thousand years ago, the primitive beings who drew images of animals and men on the walls of their caves were, in fact, presenting a model of what they sensed was the inside of their heads and, in addition, the images *in* the head: "The cave at Lascaux portrayed the head, particularly the visually receptive head image. It was an externalized replica of the internal cephalic image, where our 'pictures' are stored and concealed. If this is so, the cave not only holds the earliest visual images, but is also the first model of memory and the mind."[19]

The primitive beings' use of the cave as a model of the mind antedates Plato's myth of the cave in *The Republic* by thousands of years. In that familiar allegory, Plato describes prisoners chained to walls within a cave in such a way that they experience all the elements of the world as shadows. Plato uses the allegory of the cave to explain the nature of reality and our perception of it. Like all human beings, the prisoners, who must be content with shadowy appearances, cannot experience the ideal forms constituting the ultimate reality.

Jean-Louis Baudry and Frank D. McConnell consider the relationship of the prisoners to film viewers.[20] Baudry in particular suggests that the prisoners are similar to dreamers and to those watching a film—constrained, immobile, caught up in illusions. After noting the obvious relation of the cave to the "maternal womb," he explores a more complex relationship. Plato's cave represents and prefigures the human desire for "an apparatus capable . . . of fabricating an impression of reality."[21] The viewing subjects are part of the very "apparatus" of the cave; so too are those watching the cinema.

Baudry sees cinema as "the answer to a desire inherent in our psychical structure." It is possible, moreover, to consider "the allegory of the cave [as] the text of a signifier of desire which haunts the invention of cinema and the history of its invention."[22] The cinema leads one into a dreamlike world where regression is possible and where one senses a unity with the external world: "Return towards a relative narcissism, and even more towards a mode of relating to reality which could be defined as enveloping and in which the separation between one's own body and the exterior world is not well defined."[23] The prisoners' experience living with shadows, and their apparent willingness to take the appearance for the reality, thus adumbrate our own desire for cinema: "This wish . . . prepares the long history of cinema: the wish to construct a simulation machine capable [of offering] the subject perceptions which are really representations mistaken for perceptions. Cinema offers us a simulation of regressive movement which is characteristic of the dream—the transformation of thoughts by means of figuration."[24]

But we also need to consider the function of the screen itself—the wall of the cave—in the process that permits us to be unified with our perceptions.[25] To the prosthetic creations of humanity, such as the glasses, microscopes, and photographs Freud mentions, we should add the cinematic screen itself.[26] It is the ultimate prosthesis, the mother's breast that encompasses the viewer's very being. It not only permits "representations to be taken for perceptions"; it also makes us the field of those representations. In so doing, it breaks down our sense of alienation in the presence of the aesthetic object.

The Oral World of the Infant

Before examining the particulars of Lewin's theory of the dream screen, it will be helpful to present relevant psychoanalytical and physiological commentary from a number of sources. First the views of Sigmund Freud, Paul Federn, and Otto Isakower bear noting, inasmuch as they offer various hypotheses about the connection between the oral world of the infant and its psychic needs. Clinical observations and hypotheses about infant behavior offered by Truett Allison, Henry Van Twyver, Howard P. Roffwarg, and René Spitz provide significant information about the importance of oral behavior. Equally relevant are theories advanced by Jean Piaget, Julia Kristeva, and D. W. Winnicott in regard to the development of the infant. The following conclusions emerge from their observations and hypotheses: 1) Infants depend on oral activities to survive. 2) In addition to satisfying a physical need, oral activity connects the infant psychically with the world around it. 3) The sensations associated with the earliest oral activities can apparently be revived under certain conditions, most notably those of sleep.

Freud sees the first physical and psychic motivating force in the life of the infant as a desire for relief from the "internal stimulus" of hunger.[27] Its future wishes for satisfaction of similar needs result in a reviving of the memory it has associated with that relief. The infant wants the image in memory to be matched by an actual perception: "Thus, the aim of this first psychical activity was to produce a 'perceptual identity'—a repetition of the perception which was linked with the satisfaction of the need."[28] Held to the breast, the infant cannot "distinguish his ego from the external world as the source of the sensations flowing in upon him." When the breast does not appear when desired, the infant learns of the existence of something besides its ego—"an object, in the form of something which exists 'outside' and which is only forced to appear by a special action."[29]

The mental feeling the infant has when feeding arises from a union of its ego with the world and provides what Freud calls an "oceanic" feeling, rather, I would guess, like the feeling or state of being that Wordsworth imagines in the child before it is born into the sleep of life.[30] At such a point, as Freud explains in "Negation," the infant wishes to absorb the world to itself: "to introject into itself everything that is good and eject from itself everything that is bad."[31] The infant and the breast are one. But as adults, well beyond the primal unity of infancy that occurred during oral satisfaction, we are very much like Wordsworth's adults, cut off from the sense of oneness with our universe: "Our present ego-feeling is . . . only a shrunken residue of a much more inclusive—indeed,

an all-embracing—feeling which corresponded to a more in-
timate bond between the ego and the world about it."[32]

The sleep that follows the infant's feeding affords it a return
to the unity of its life in the womb. Freud describes such
sleep as "a reactivation of intrauterine existence, fulfilling as
it does the conditions of repose, warmth and exclusion of
stimulus. . . ."[33] The relaxation that accompanies this sleep
seems to him similar to that sleep which adults enjoy after
the pleasures of eating and of sexual activity. Children "go
to sleep after being satisfied (at the breast). Adults, too, fall
asleep easily *post coenam et coitum*. . . ."[34] In fact, Freud
views the activity of sucking as the most important act of an
infant's life, insofar as sucking satisfies its greatest early
needs while simultaneously initiating its sexual life.[35]

According to Paul Federn, dreaming releases the older
sleepers from whatever they sense as ego-feeling and permits
a return to the child's sense of ego. The ego itself contains
and retains "bodily ego-feeling." By the time we are adults,
our remembered sense of our childhood selves is clouded by
experience (more of Wordsworth's "shades of the prison-house").
But as we drift off to sleep, "the body-ego regresses to the
stage when the various parts of the body first came to be
included in the ego." One possible result as this regressive
process continues is "an actual loss of ego-boundaries."[36]
That is, as adults going to sleep we may regain a sense of
how—literally—it felt when the ego had not been separated
from the world of its oral gratifications and perceptions.

Federn's suggestion that sleep permits an adult to recapture
the infant's sense of unity with its world relates significantly
to various observations about the actual oral behavior of sleeping adults and infants. For example, Otto Isakower recorded
statements by his patients in psychoanalysis describing their
oral sensations when they were tired. These comments led
him to hypothesize the following: at the point at which one
begins to go to sleep, the sense that one's ego and the world

seem to be fading away is accompanied by intensified sensations in certain parts of the body. Specifically, "perceptions
are localized as sensations in a particular bodily region and
at the same time as processes in the external world. . . ."
The most striking sensations occur in "the oral zone or, more
exactly, the oral cavity."[37] He speculates that at this stage
of drifting off to sleep, "the structure of the body ego . . . is
comparable to that of the immediately post-natal ego. The
sensations in the oral cavity, at this stage of existence probably the most intense and also the most important for life,
are diffused over the whole skin, the outermost frontier of the
body, which, indeed, is scarcely yet recognized as such or
is perhaps almost felt to be part of the external world." In
effect, this "hypercathexis" (or supercharging of energy in-
ward in the bodily system) results in an extraordinary sensation: "I am all mouth." As such, the regression or reversion
of the bodily ego to an earlier state of sensation "revives an
archaic phase of development."[38]

He cites testimony from several patients as evidence that
individuals can experience and recall having had pronounced
sensations in their oral cavities.[39] One subject in particular
reported that "he felt as if he were lying on his back and
floating in the air and had a sense, accompanied by anxiety,
of some tiny object which became infinitely large. As it did
so, . . . he had a pleasant tickling sensation just behind his
upper and lower teeth, on his palate and the bottom of his
mouth. It was as if he were in the act of drinking something-
good. . . . The general feeling was 'like that in coitus'—only
he and the universe existed—'nothing but himself and something infinitely large'—he was 'inside.' "[40]

Reports on clinical observations of feeding infants connect
to the material above, for they suggest a correlation between
oral activities of the infant and its sleeping patterns. For
example, Truett Allison and Henry Van Twyver have written
on what they call "paradoxical" sleep in animals and children.

Using the electroencephalogram to measure brain waves of the sleeping beings and observing the eye movements, they noticed certain distinctive physical behavior in the subjects. The researchers report that in sleeping children, "facial movements often include sucking movements."[41]

Another team of scientists has observed a correlation between mouth activities and REM sleep that invites comparison to the other materials we have seen in which sensations in the mouths of adults appear in connection with the onset of sleep. Howard P. Roffwarg, Joseph N. Muzio, and William C. Dement describe the following motor activities accompanying REM sleep in infants: "Grimaces, whimpers, smiles, twitches of face and extremities are interspersed with gross shifts of position of limbs."[42] More specifically, "Just as a gradual diminution in muscle tone heralds a REM period, so do progressive increases in mouth movements (resembling sucking). This activity may be observed 5 to 10 minutes before a shift to REM sleep. . . . Hence, sucking activity seems to be connected mainly with the onset of REM sleep."[43] They are very careful to state that the presence (and exceedingly high percentage) of REM sleep in infants does not necessarily mean that the infants are dreaming. Determination of the point at which infants actually begin to dream is extremely problematic, and the levels of mentation and "dreaming" that occur in REM and NREM states, although fairly well differentiated, are not fixed precisely.

Another relevant aspect of oral behavior is its possible function as an instrument of perception, as René Spitz suggests. He finds it "significant" that for an infant who has a nipple in its mouth, "the *inside* of the mouth, *the oral cavity*, fulfills the conditions of partaking for perceptive purposes both of the inside and of the outside. . . . It is here that all perception will begin; in this role the oral cavity fulfills the function of a bridge from internal reception to external perception."[44]

Related to Spitz's argument is Isakower's interpretation of Freud's observation that "an infant responds to optical stimuli by opening his mouth and, rather later, by clutching at what he sees. This indicates that there is still a very close connection between perception and motor intention and also that perception is accompanied by tension within the body, i.e., within the ego."[45]

Jean Piaget has observed similar kinds of phenomena in infants confusing visual and oral functions. He argues that the action of "sucking plays as important a part in the organisation of the primitive sensory-motor schemas . . . as in the baby's affectivity."[46] The development of the important component of spatial order and succession depends in part on oral activity. This is one of the relationships that the child gradually assimilates and that "arise in primitive and rudimentary perception (e.g., in the exercise of the reflexes of sucking, touching, seeing patches of light, etc.). . . ."[47] Such a relationship "undoubtedly appears very early in the child's life, not merely when the baby's gaze or touch passes over a series of elements ranged in some fixed order (such as the rungs of his cot), but also when a series of habitual movements is guided by perception according to organized points of reference. For example, the sight of a door opening, a figure reappearing, and certain movements indicative of a forthcoming meal, form a series of perceptions organized in space and time, intimately related to the sucking habits."[48]

For Piaget, as for Freud, the state of the ego in the adult dreamer has reverted back to the level of an infant's: "The semi-consciousness of the dreamer is indeed comparable to the state of complete egocentrism characteristic of the baby's consciousness. In both cases there is a complete lack of differentiation between the ego and the external world. . . ."[49] And this withdrawal into a selfhood of perception and ego results in a crossover and confusion of motor activities. As an infant engages in the world, "he sometimes makes very significant mistakes. For instance, on seeing someone else's eyes close and open again, he will open and close his mouth, thus wrongly assimilating the visual schema of the model's eyes to the tactilo-kinaesthetic schemata of his own mouth. It is clear that the sleeper, having lost consciousness of his ego, is by that very circumstance, and apart from any question of repression, in the same situation as the baby. He also must translate (but inversely) his physical impressions into visual images, and he will be liable to make the same mistakes."[50]

Complementing the preceding observations is Julia Kristeva's description of the infant's acquisition of language as well as a sense of space. She accepts René Spitz's distinction between the "anaclitic" and "diatropic" states. The first term refers to the total dependence of the infant on its mother and the demands it makes of her; the second denotes the mother's supporting function as one of many possible activities in which she engages. Kristeva hypothesizes that the union of the anaclitic infant with the diatropic mother occurs in a *chora*. As Leon S. Roudiez explains, Kristeva draws the term, meaning "receptacle," from Plato's *Timaeus*. In his cosmogony it refers to the "space" and nature of the informing principle of the universe.[51] Plato speaks of two classes of substantive reality, intelligent archetypes and visible copies, to which he adds a third: "the receptacle, and in a manner the nurse, of all generation."[52] This "nurse" is "the universal nature which receives all bodies—that must be always called the same, for, inasmuch as she always receives all things, she never departs at all from her own nature and never, in any way or at any time, assumes a form like that of any of the things which enter into her; she is the natural recipient of all impressions, and is stirred and informed by them, and appears different from time to time by reason of them. But the forms which enter into and go out of her are likenesses of eternal realities modeled after their patterns in a wonderful and mysterious manner. . . ." This force, "the mother and receptacle of all created and visible and in any way sensible things . . . is an invisible and formless being which receives all things and in some mysterious way partakes of the intelligible. . . ."[53]

The infant's relationship to its mother after birth can be described as a kind of "semiotic *chora*."[54] In its vocalizations and cries (these actions themselves revivals of more primitive activities engaged in within the womb), the infant tries to survive by calling for food. The mother responds to these anaclises by offering herself. Notice the similarity of the terms used by Kristeva to describe the mother and the kind of language one might use to describe the viewing situation in a theater. The mother sustains the infant by "providing . . . an axis, a projection screen, a limit, a support for the infant's invocation. . . ." The union of infant and mother in the semiotic *chora* fixes a "space": "Orality, audition, vision: archaic modalities upon which the most precocious discretion emerges. The breast given and withdrawn; lamp light capturing the gaze; the intermittent sound of voices or music— these greet anaclisis, . . . hold it, and thus inhibit and absorb it in such a way that it is discharged and calmed through them. . . . Therefore, the breast, light, sound become a *there*; place, point, marker. . . . The mark of an archaic point, the initiation into 'space,' the 'chora.' . . . There is not yet an outside. . . ."[55]

At the end of the first three months, this relationship results in responsive laughter from the infant as it begins to differentiate itself linguistically. But, until that point, it is bound with the mother anaclitically: "Chronologically and logically long before the mirror stage . . . the semiotic posits itself as a laughter space. During the period of the indistinction between the '*same*' and the '*other*,' between the infant and mother, as well as between the 'subject' and 'object,' while no space has yet been designated (it will be designated with and after the mirror: the sign), the semiotic *chora* that fixes and absorbs the motility of the anaclitic facilitations discharges and produces laughter."[56] In other words, up to the age of three months, the infant is bound up and absorbed by the relationship with its mother. The mother who feeds, who silences the cries, and who encourages laughter, is like Plato's cosmic nurse—the unchanging receptacle which offers a space into which the infant enters. It is part of this being, as the being is of it; at this stage, "there is not yet an outside," since all is one.

Kristeva's conception of the *chora* reminds one of D. W. Winnicott's suggestions about the symbolic nature of the breast and "potential space." He argues that for the feeding infant, the breast is an illusion, something that the infant "creates" out of itself: "[T]he breast is created by the infant over and over again out of the infant's capacity to love or . . . out of need. A subjective phenomenon develops in the baby, what we call the mother's breast. The mother places the actual breast just there where the infant is ready to create, and at the right moment. From birth, therefore, the human being is concerned with the problem of the relationship between that which is objectively perceived and which is subjectively conceived of. . . . *The intermediate area to which I am referring is the area that is allowed to the infant between primary creativity and objective perception based on reality-testing.*"[57] The breast is thus a "paradoxical" object because it exists before it is created. His comments on the infant's involvement with the created breast should be considered in relation to Jacques Lacan's theory of the "mirror phase."[58] Both Winnicott and Lacan see the infant's development as involving an encounter with the imaginary.

When the mother gives the breast, she affords an "adaptation to the infant's needs" and "the *illusion* that there is an external reality that corresponds to the infant's own capacity to create. In other words, there is an overlap between what the mother supplies and what the child might conceive of. . . . The infant perceives the breast only in so far as a breast could be created just there and then. . . . Psychologically the infant takes from a breast that is part of the infant, and the mother gives milk to an infant that is part of herself."[59]

For Winnicott, "breast" can mean "the technique of mothering" as well as the physical part of the anatomy. In either case, the infant distinguishes its own self from the mother's self in connection with what Winnicott calls "potential space": "the hypothetical area that exists (but cannot exist) between the baby and the object (the mother or part of the mother) during the phase of the repudiation of the object as 'not-me,' that is, at the end of being merged in with the object."[60]

The Screen and the Mother's Breast

The various hypotheses and observations cited in the previous section suggest that the relationship between the infant and its mother, and the unity of the infant's ego with that of the mother and the world she provides for it, create a primal bond linking the two. Awake, the infant relies heavily on its oral activities to make its needs known, to connect physically with its world, and to perceive the confusing welter of experience. As it feeds and then falls asleep, the oral and psychic bond established with the mother makes possible a merging of its being with hers. The mother—the breast—in such a relationship becomes an extension of the infant.

The cinematic screen, the ultimate prosthesis in the history of human invention, serves as a surrogate, deriving from infancy, for the physiological and psychic union we enjoyed with the mother: the screen is both breast and infant, the mother and self. Our sense of reality as we watch a film arises from a revival of the dreamlike state of infancy when our ego was absorbed in the *chora* of the mother. This state occasioned by the dissolution of the ego results in a merger of viewer and object, making us "present" as a condition of the text itself. Given this hypothesis, we are, in fact, in two places at once: physically seated in the theater and psychically grounding the images that play over us.

My point of departure for the assertion that the screen becomes an extension of ourselves is a model derived from a theory first proposed by Bertram Lewin in 1946 on the basis of his experience with a female patient who was lamenting the fact that she had forgotten her dream: " 'I had my dream all ready for you; but while I was lying here, looking at it, it turned over away from me, rolled up, and rolled away from me—over and over like two tumblers.' " That is, the field on which the dream was inscribed "bent over backwards . . . and then like a carpet or canvas rolled up and off into the distance. . . ."

On the basis of this and other similar examples, from his own experience and those of fellow psychoanalysts, Lewin contends that this field can be conceived of as a "dream screen": "the surface on to which a dream appears to be projected. It is the blank background, present in the dream though not necessarily seen, and the visually perceived action in ordinary manifest dream contents takes place on it or before it."[61] His crucial assumption is that the background represents the breast, the last substance seen by the now satiated infant as it drops off to sleep: "When one falls asleep, the breast is taken into one's perceptual world: it flattens out or approaches flatness, and when one wakes up it disappears, reversing the events of its entrance." He calls the screen "sleep itself; it is not only the breast, but is as well that content of sleep or the dream which fulfils the wish to sleep. . . . The dream screen is the representative of the wish to sleep. . . . The blank dream screen is the copy of primary infantile sleep."[62] Again, "the baby's first background when it falls asleep" is the breast, which functions as a screen. The "dream picture is as if painted on or projected like a motion picture onto a screen. . . ."[63]

Helpful to Lewin are the findings of Otto Isakower, for these offer reports on physiological memories of adults, particularly as these involve traces of large objects, cloudlike structures that are seen or felt as looming prior to the onset of a dream. According to Isakower, the memories of such structures "are mental images of sucking at the mother's breast and of falling asleep there when satisfied. The large object which approaches probably represents the breast, with its promise of food. When satisfied, the infant loses interest in the breast, which appears smaller and smaller and finally vanishes away. The mother's breast is the sole representative of the objects in the external world; at this stage it is not the mother as a person but only her breast which is the object. The infant's mouth is full of something, 'but not of anything from outside.' . . ."[64]

Still this phenomenon is *not* tied strictly to feeding at the actual breast. Lewin cites various cases of nonbreast-fed individuals who offer what appear to be substitutes for the breast/screen—in some cases a round object. And, as Lewin works through his argument over a period of years, "breast" comes to mean more than a physical portion of the body. It "refers to perceptions in the infant: it is whatever the infant experiences at the lips or mouth. Bottle babies later learn what breasts are; the breast-fed sooner or later have supplementary bottle feedings; both presumably suck their fingers, perhaps their toes, their clothing, and so on. . . . [B]reast, bottle and finger are all viewed from the perspective of the greedy baby, and in terms of its satisfactions and frustrations."[65] In fact, the breast can be conceived of as a composite photograph comprising memory traces drawn from the life of the subject "blending different images of the breast."[66]

It is useful to distinguish between the physical breast and "breast" in the same way that psychoanalysts (including those as varied as Carl G. Jung and Jacques Lacan) differentiate between the penis and the phallus. The former term would denote a part of the anatomy; the latter would refer to a collective psychic perception of the signifying object. In any event, even one who might not have had actual contact with the breast during feeding still has a *sense* of the breast and will have displayed equivalent structures in describing dream experiences: "[T]he dream screen, or the dream as a whole, may be represented by solid articles like the finger, rubber, or glass that were experienced during or later than the sucking period, in connection with oral satisfaction."[67]

The most active response to Lewin's theory has been offered by René Spitz. Although basically supportive of the concept of the dream screen, Spitz challenges Lewin's claim for the exclusiveness of the breast as *the* site of the screen. According to Spitz, the infant does not look at the breast while nursing, but rather at the face of the person offering nourishment. He too cites Isakower's work, among others, to describe the tactile effects experienced and/or recovered in memory by the subject, but he does so in order to argue that the roughness of skin quality identified by Isakower can be seen to appear on the human face as well as on the breast. Thus, Spitz maintains that the Isakower phenomenon—the sense of an approaching mass with particular tactile qualities—"does not represent the approaching breast. . . . [I]t represents the visually perceived human face."[68] That is, the elements reported by Isakower such as "the cracks, the wrinkles, the roses, the spots," are not exclusive to the breast. Spitz cites Jonathan Swift's *Gulliver's Travels* to support his contention; the passage he adduces describing the faces of the Brobdingnagian women could have been replaced with one in which Gulliver offers a detailed view of a giant woman's breast to his readers.[69]

Still, Spitz's objection is more to the logistics than to the thrust of Lewin's argument, for his position is that "the infant, while nursing at the breast, is at the same time staring at the mother's face; thus breast and face are experienced as one and indivisible."[70] In satisfying its thirst, two sensory experiences that it cannot differentiate, feeling and seeing, are united for the infant in a "coenesthetic" experience (undifferentiated physical sensations—a totality of responses): "When the infant nurses and has sensations in the oral cavity while staring at the mother's face, he unites the tactile and the visual perceptions . . . of the total situation into one undifferentiated unity, a situation Gestalt, in which any one part of the experience comes to stand for the total experience."[71] Spitz envisions the following complex of interrelated phenomena: "The sequence which leads to the phenomenon of the dream screen in the adult [is] the following: the experience of tension reduction on the coenesthetic level, followed by the experience of the [oral] cavity sensation on the level of non-differentiation, and culminating in the percept of the breast on the level of diacritic visual perception. Therefore, the dream screen of the adult appears to be a representation of the most archaic human pleasure experience. It uses for this representation the archaic materials still available to the adult, i.e. coenesthetic sensations, and the later transition from these to the perception of the visual images in the dream screen."[72]

We have seen earlier that D. W. Winnicott advances the notion of the breast as a "paradoxical object," a signifier created out of the infant's need. The breast is an extension of the infant, which is itself a part of the mother. As the feeding relationship terminates, a "potential space" develops in which the infant begins to distinguish itself from the "not-me" with which it has been merged. Spitz also views the loss of the breast as an important stage in the child's differentiation of itself, and connects this loss with the impulse for the images which (presumably) will play on the dream screen.

According to photographic records taken by Spitz, when an infant who is nursing is deprived of the nipple, "the infant's eyes shift from the mother's face and, without focusing specifically on the breast, deviate more or less in its general direction. The breast is not fixated by the infant's eye, but its image is probably present in the peripheral parts of the retina, together with the face."[73] This pattern of behavior—loss of nipple followed by perception of breast and face—affects the infant's sense of identity and differentiation. In fact, Spitz sees it as a process engendering the "I" even as it explains, perhaps, the motive for the dream: "This sequence—cavity perception (of the nipple), unpleasure (upon the loss of the nipple), peripheral vision of breast plus face—plays a decisive role in that it expedites the infant's dawning awareness of the 'I' and 'non-I.' In this primal awareness 'I' is what one *feels inside*; 'non-I' is what one can *only see* after having lost what one felt inside. It would seem that it is from this loss, and from the wishful fantasy attached to what one can only see, that the dream screen described by Lewin is derived."[74]

Thus Winnicott and Spitz see the loss of the breast as beginning the process of ego differentiation in the infant. But Lewin offers a different assessment of the phenomenon with reference to the sleep and dream that follow the loss of the breast. At the moment of nutritive intake for the infant, as Lewin conceives it, "the baby does not distinguish between its body and the breast. . . . Ego boundaries are lost when there is a fusion at the breast. . . ." And this phenomenon *continues* after the feeding ends and the infant goes to sleep: "The dreamer, or sleeper, remains in unified contact with the breast and . . . this determines constant characteristics of the dream, such as the dream screen. . . . The sleeper has identified himself with the breast and has eaten and retained all the parts of himself which do not appear outlined or symbolized in the manifest dream content. . . . In short, the sleeper has lost his ego boundaries because when he went to sleep he became united with the breast."[75]

Accordingly, the dreamer's union with the breast is a synthesis of the subject and the field of the dream, the extension of the symbiotic fusion of self and other that occurs at the moment of feeding. In such a circumstance, the events of the dream will seem to be part of the dreamer and provide a linkage of subject and object, perceiver and perceived. We are what we dream, not only in a psychoanalytic sense, but in a perceptual sense as well.

Consider also what Lewin makes of the dream screen as it contributes to our sense of reality. The infant's experience at the breast is the most prominent form of simultaneous involvement with pleasure and reality: "Objective reality and pleasure coincide at the breast. Reality covers a limited area of consciousness, but the sense of this reality is preserved in memory traces, which can be evoked later in life. . . ."[76] The three worlds of experience as conceived by Lewin are "the oral world," the "sensorimotor world," and "the world of words and conceptions." In the first, "memory traces remain that can be inferred or discerned . . . in the hypnogogic state."[77] The infant at the breast in the oral stage knows no words, only states of being, a condition somewhat akin to that described by mystics explaining their sense of oneness with God. Lewin cites passages from St. Teresa and St. François de Sales to illustrate the parallel. The latter (as quoted by William James) writes: "The soul is like a little child still at the breast, whose mother, to caress him whilst he is still in her arms, makes her milk distill into his mouth without his even moving his lips."[78] That is, the most intense perception of ultimate reality for the mystic is here figured with reference to the earliest nutritive experience.

Lewin's dream screen, the breast or represention of the breast as ground and receiver of all dream images, occurs as a condition of all oneiric activity. Blank dreams without visual content are, in fact, dreams of the screen/breast/surrogate. My modification of Lewin's theory stresses the important aspect of ego fusion with the field of the dream, a field that is the union of the infant and the breast. As such, it effects a fusion of subject and object.

Our earliest dreams occur after and in connection with feeding. Whether or not at the breast, we play out our dream on a field drawn from our experience of the body or structures which act as substitutes for the union of breast and ego. The earliest dreams follow the moments of tension reduction; thus the earliest dreams occur after moments of pleasure. These experiences of pleasure are at the same time involved, I believe, with an intense sense of reality.

A major reason for our feeling of pleasure and sense of reality when viewing images on the cinematic screen must be that the experience triggers a revival of our earliest memories/dreams at the breast. Given the replication of the dreamlike state in the viewing process, our sense of ego differentiation is at first heightened: those characters up there on the screen are "not-me." But I believe the process is *reversed* by virtue of the atavistic experience. That is, the dreamlike film, the film as sensed and perceived as being like a dream, brings us back to a state such as Lewin describes, in which we are more susceptible to the loss of ego, and, hence, to identification with those characters who are "not-me."

Older readers of these words will recall that, prior to the growth of multiple theaters, virtually every movie house had curtains over the screen. The experience of film would begin with the parting of the curtains. In some cases, the film would have already begun, and so some of the images would play on the curtain before being caught on the white screen. In other cases, however, the curtains would part, and the blank screen would be seen alone, as we waited for the images to begin appearing. Perhaps the anticipation and excitement that occurred at this moment revived another experience from infancy—the parting of the mother's blouse or dress prior to offering her breast to the infant. Recall Kristeva's description of the "place" and its union of visual and auditory richness.

The screen into which we enter through psychic projection is, like the mother, Plato's *chora*, receiving us as we enter in, but remaining unchanged after we leave.

Film gives us the dreams we never had, the dreams we yet await. It makes us babies again, and reverses the process of ego differentiation by plunging us back in memory to that moment of identification with the source of nutrition. Film's overwhelming images invite a return to that state in which the ego dissolves.

The close-up, in fact, may be said to function in a most important way as a revival of our experience of the archetypal mass we recall only dimly—the breast, the face, the combination of these. Recall Spitz's point about the instantaneous perception of face and breast. The infant takes the part for the whole, the primal metonymy. So too, I believe, with the filmic image. The face in the close-up is, in essence, the mother's face, the breast, the primal unity of infancy.

The Forgetting of Dreams and Films

Even though we can experience a sense of oneness with the material we observe on the screen, we find that we forget parts and aspects of what we have viewed, a phenomenon that reminds us of our inability to hold our memory of what we have dreamed. I believe the very nature of the way we perceive films and dreams contributes to our inability to recall clearly and accurately.

Hugo Mauerhofer and Bruce F. Kawin comment informatively on the tendency of critics to mis-remember and/or recall differently the narrative and scenic aspects of a film.[79] George W. Linden suggests that this may result from our difficulty in turning visual experience into linguistic form. As with dreams, the sheer density of the film experience makes it difficult to recall what we have seen: "The critic remembers certain striking scenes or sequences, but it is very difficult, perhaps impossible, for him to translate the entire flow of sights and sounds into verbal equivalents. This may . . . explain why there are so many mistakes in film criticism and reporting."[80]

David R. Hawkins draws our attention to the problem of translating images into words as we mature. As children acquire language and begin "to think in word symbols," it may be harder for them to remember dreams: "The memories of young children of from two to five years of age are remarkably long, but they are visual and pictorial and without regard for the logic of space or time for the most part. Well-remembered scenes generally vanish with the acquisition of reading. Can it not be that the dream which is after all largely a pictorial or sensory experience is lost because we generally think in word terms and have lost most of our capacity for pictorial memory?"[81]

Harry Fiss also emphasizes the problem of language, specifically as a way of rejecting Freud's explanation of the forgetting of dreams. The latter argues that even though the dream state affords the dreamer a chance to create a wish-fulfilling narrative, the "resistance" to the satisfying of the wish by the "psychical censor" inhibits our attempts to remember all of the details.[82] In contrast, Fiss adopts Jean Piaget's theory that it may simply be our ignorance of the very "language" used in dream: "Since most dreams are forgotten in the normal course of events, it may be that most dreams are cast in a 'language' that makes it difficult to 'translate' them into the more conventional terminology of our waking lives. The argument does not necessarily support the Freudian view that dreams are meant to conceal. . . . [D]reams are so often obscure to adults because they are forms of thinking that are not readily 'assimilable' by waking consciousness, and not because of some presumed 'censor' transforming repressed infantile drives seeking 'discharge.' "[83]

Bruce F. Kawin suggests that the dominance of different functions by the left and right hemispheres of the brain may explain the phenomenon of forgetting dreams: " . . . the difficulty people have in recalling dreams may reflect their being asked to *describe*, i.e., in left-brain terms, an event whose terms and gestalt have been proceeding in an integrated and fundamentally nonverbal mode. This effort of translation is so difficult that it thoroughly engages the language centers . . . at the expense of that felt connection with the dreamworld of the right brain which alone could keep its imagery accessible."[84]

In accordance with his model of the dream screen, Bertram Lewin argues for the following position: "The act of forgetting dreams, their receding, is to be interpreted as a repetition of the withdrawal of the breast."[85] Each failure to recall the content of a dream signals the dreamer's dissociation from the breast, the site where the ego unites with its primal extended world. In addition, Lewin believes that the "blank" left in our memory when we cannot recall a dream is the now empty dream screen: ". . . properly considered this background too is made up of memory traces. It is composed of the very earliest ones laid down in infancy during nursing and dormescent experiences. Perhaps the background is a reminiscence of the 'primal dream' of the smallest infant, before the various sensations have been arranged and combined in significant and consistent formed perceptions."[86] When one remembers a dream, one is, in effect, prolonging sleep: ". . . to *remember* the dream is a quasi-prolongation of sleep and stands for sleep, while *forgetting* the dream repeats and stands for waking up and is a step in the weaning process."[87]

None of these theories considers an element that may be an important cause explaining the forgetting of elements in films and dreams. These erasures in our memories may be the secondary result of a primary failure on our part to regain the space that we inhabit during the cinematic and oneiric experience.

Several writers have addressed the issue of space in film and dreams. For example, Susanne Langer observes: "One of the aesthetic peculiarities of dream, which the moving picture takes over, is the nature of its space. Dream events are spatial, often intensely concerned with space—intervals, endless roads, bottomless canyons, things too high, too near, too far—but they are not oriented in any total space. The same is true of the moving picture and distinguishes it—despite its visual character—from plastic art; *its space comes and goes*. It is always a secondary illusion."[88]

Robert Curry comments on the difference in the spatial worlds of film and dream: "The space of a film world is made vividly, even authentically present to us—we live in it imaginatively, as we say—but we can *inhabit* our dream worlds." Moreover, "The space of a dream world is not merely visual space: it can be fallen through—it is a space into which the dreamer can enter as agent and not just as a spectator."[89]

F. E. Sparshott discusses the "ambiguous and dreamlike character of film space." Speaking in phenomenological terms, he argues: "[I]n film our sense of space is somehow bracketed or held in suspense: we are aware of our implied position and accept it, but are not existentially committed to it. We do not situate ourselves where we see ourselves to be."[90] Such an "alienated space" is similar to that in dreams: "In my dreams, too, I see from where I am not, move helplessly in a space whose very nature is inconstant, and may see beside me the being whose perceptions I share."[91]

Possibly one reason we forget narrative and other details of dream and film arises from the effects of the regressive nature of the oneiric and viewing experience on spatial perception. Asleep, or seated before the screen, we become very much like the children described in the experimental models created by Jean Piaget and Bärbel Inhelder to determine the ages at which we acquire various kinds of spatial mastery.

The numerous experimental designs have been explained at length in *The Child's Conception of Space*. The most significant experiment for our purposes involved a pasteboard model of three mountains, individual scale models of these, photographs of the model, and a wooden faceless doll. Various tests were administered to children up to the age of twelve. First they were given the scale models of the mountains and asked to arrange them on a table in a way which reconstructed the view that would result if they were being observed from several specified positions around the table. In another test, the children had to determine which of the photographs matched the assumed viewpoint of the doll as it was positioned around the table. The final test required the children to begin with a picture and tell the researcher where the doll should be placed in order to photograph it.

Their results indicate that "the child [four to seven years of age] distinguishes hardly or not at all between his own viewpoint and that of the other observers (represented by the doll in different positions). . . . [The pictures] all show the mountains from a single point of view, that of the child himself."[92] By the time the child has reached the age of nine to ten years, it has achieved the ability to understand and master perspective, or projective relations.

Piaget and Inhelder compare the immature child who cannot imagine any other perspective besides its own to a baby who has not yet fully grasped the concept of the constancy of shape. The task of figuring out how another would see something forces the child "to deduce or imagine in anticipation some virtual perception not actually experienced but referred to another observer." A young baby is unable to distinguish the feeding end of its bottle from the base: "Perception is not 'decentrated' towards virtual rotations of the object but remains centred on it as it appears just at the moment. In a similar way, the four-to seven-year-old child who gazes at the group of mountains, unable to conceive of any perspective but his own, reveals a type of spatial imagination which is likewise not yet decentrated as regards changes of position, but remains centred on a position (or previously experienced positions) corresponding with his present viewpoint."[93]

As the child matures, it learns "that the left-right, before-behind relations . . . between the mountains vary according to the position of the observer." With the development of spatial sophistication, the child becomes capable of "relating the object to his own viewpoint, as one of which he is fully conscious. . . . [T]o become conscious of one's own viewpoint involves distinguishing it from other viewpoints, and by the same token, co-ordinating it with them." Ultimately, the development of perspective involves an activity that is "not perceptual but conceptual." In fact, "to extend space beyond the confines of the perceptual field is the task of imagination."[94]

Compare the immature child to ourselves as spectators and dreamers. The child cannot yet *imagine* any perspectives other than its own: "Indeed, he cannot imagine any perspective but that of the passing moment, since with a change of position he repeats his performance in terms of the new position!"[95] Film and dreams force us to regress back to a level of childish perception inasmuch as we are constantly assaulted with "scenes" that we must appropriate initially as belonging solely to *our* perspective.

The characters in the film may be likened to an army of Piaget's faceless, wooden dolls. At times we are supposed to be able to imagine what they might see. Occasionally, cinematic coding can provide us cues to what they are looking at, as in the common shot/reverse shot/shot pattern of cutting, when we are invited to appropriate the respective gazes of speakers, a phenomenon relevant to recent discussions of the "suture."[96] But, at other times, the scene before us is simply "there," not connected to the viewpoint of any one character.

I have argued that both the oneiric and cinematic dream screens are extensions of ourselves. We "see" events on a field in a way that involves us in the dual action of perceiving and "being." At the time of viewing, we are bound in and with our perceptions, seemingly present in the space in which the events unfold. But we were never there. And because we are not truly functioning in a real space as we dream and watch films, we lack the kind of sensory cues and stabilizing elements that might help our memory of having been "there"— such things as genuine experience with proximity, distance, tactile experiences, etc. Accordingly, it is harder to remember particular events and details because they are not anchored in a real space which we ourselves inhabited.

Lewin's comment on the "curved space" of the dream screen is relevant here: "Flatness, physics and geography tell us, is a local illusion, a quality of limited areas. The ordinary screen in adult dreams is flat; but it is also enormous, and the sharp boundaries it sometimes shows are as illusory as the horizon that surrounds us in daily terrestrial life. In my global thinking about the breast and the dream screen, I realized that curved space, of which we read so much in modern science, may itself be a very early experience in the life of an individual, forgotten under the impact of later Euclidean perceptions. For, from the global perspective, the dream screen is seen to be both flat *and* curved; it is a flat segment of an enormously curved body, the original breast, and the same surface may be represented now as a plane, now as a segment of curved space."[97] Is it possible that the regressive nature of the dream, and, related to this, of the film, creates or reactivates a condition in which we are for the moment "perceiving" in a manner similar to that which precedes our acquisition of Euclidean perspective?

In any event, our attempts to remember force us to exercise

not only memory but the imagination. The kind of activity I speak of here is related to, but should not be equated with, Freud's notion of "secondary revision," by which the conscious mind tries to order and interpret the dream events.[98] As we attempt to reconstruct the events of the dream or film, we are first of all engaged in positioning ourselves back in the "space" of each. To enter into such a space, we must, like Piaget's children, exercise our imagination to project into a world not present to our perspective and a world that we experienced initially in a regressive manner, from a purely egocentric perspective. In other words, recollection can be seen in part as a *creative* activity. In this interpretation, we are not so much "distorting" or "mis-remembering" as we are attempting to re-create a perceptual experience in a lost space. Under such circumstances, it is not surprising that events and details are altered.

Part Two

WATCHING
THE DREAM
SCREEN

A TAXONOMY
OF DREAMS

THE FOCUS of the discussion now shifts from a theoretical investigation of the dream screen to a practical
application of the concept. In this section of the study, we
look at dreams that are generally identified as belonging to
specific characters. The dream may be introduced and defined
through the use of such devices as voice-overs, fades and
dissolves, superimpositions, or shots of a sleeper followed by
a dream. In whatever form the filmmaker chooses to present
the dream, we understand it as a psychic projection of a mind
made visible on the screen.

At the moment that the dream appears, we enter into a
new phenomenological relationship with the cinematic screen
and with the dreaming mind represented there. Prior to the
appearance of the dream, we watch the narrative events on
a screen with which we are unified, our experiences as infants
with our own dream screen having helped create a sense of
oneness with the cinematic screen. The gap between ourselves
as perceivers and the world we observe outside us is temporarily closed. When a dream appears on the cinematic
screen (a prosthetic extension of ourselves) the consciousness
of the viewer merges with the projected consciousness of the
dreamer whose thoughts and images are manifested on a
screen that we have provided for the character.

The extent of our involvement with the mind of the dreamer

depends on the narrative content and on the technical elements used to render the dream. At times, filmmakers succeed in reaching us primarily through the narrative situation itself; at other times, we are particularly influenced by technical devices used to approximate or imitate sensations we experience in our own dreams. In some cases, both the narrative content and technical elements work cooperatively to involve us in the dream.

I do not want to imply that we automatically respond more fully to dreams than to the non-oneiric sections of a film; nor do I suggest that we necessarily feel more involvement because a character is known to be dreaming. Some cinematic dreams are so opaque or bizarre or offensive that certain viewers are distanced rather than drawn to the oneiric content. And, obviously, the technical devices used in filmic dreams such as superimpositions, slow motion, and distortion appear elsewhere in films to help depict events that are not dreams.

Nonetheless, when we are particularly involved in the dream, the cinematic/dream screen becomes a vehicle affording us greater contact with a character's mental life than is ordinarily the case. To this screen we bring memories of how we experience the rapid jumps, incoherent connections, and ambiguities of our own dreams. These serve as constitutive psychic coordinates helping us to follow through the dreamer's experience. In some ways this process is analogous to that described by Immanuel Kant who says that the very nature and structure of our minds provide us the coordinates of time and space through which we order perceptual experience.[1]

In this sense, our involvement in the filmic dream seems to be part of a collective dream experience. Carl G. Jung has suggested that certain elements and symbols in the narrative content of dreams are archetypal images which are part of the collective psychic experience of the human race.[2] A similar comment seems appropriate here to describe the manner in which viewers participate in and respond to the strange and disruptive content of the filmic dream.

The taxonomy of dreams which follows should facilitate our examination of the practical applications of the dream screen. Four of the six categories explore cause-effect relationships: dreams resulting from mind/body isomorphism; dreams of traumatic events; anxiety dreams; and dreams of desire. Two other categories involve special cases: the dream state, which is used to evoke a general oneiric condition; and the proleptic dream, which serves to foreshadow later events. Readers who think of films not mentioned here ought to be able to assign them to one of the categories.

Mind/Body Isomorphism

Common to dreams in this category is a form of mind/body isomorphism; we understand the dream to be a response to a physiological stimulus. Two general divisions occur in this category. In the first, the dream depicts the state of mind of someone who is drunk or drugged; that is, the dream is primarily a result of something a character consumes. This is the kind of cause-effect relationship that Freud was rejecting when he argued that dream is caused primarily by psychic rather than somatic phenomena. In the second, the dream conveys the mental activity of someone responding to a more severe form of physical trauma or stimulus.

Edwin S. Porter's *Dream of a Rarebit Fiend* (1906) portrays humorously the evils of overeating and drinking and employs a number of imaginative techniques to suggest the dreaming state. We first see the hero (the fiend of the title) gorging himself in a restaurant; then he goes out on the street. In his drunkenness he cannot walk steadily or see clearly: streets seem to merge and lampposts to rock wildly before the eyes of the drunken man, thanks to superimpositions and trick photography. After he has reached his home and climbed into bed, his boots move around the floor under their own power. Tiny demons appear to be probing his head with pitchforks. Then his bed begins to shake, ascends through the ceiling, and sails over New York City. Porter uses a horizontal split screen to depict this flight; the dreamer sails in the top band while observing a panorama of the city in the lower band. Eventually the bed catches on a weathervane, he falls, and the dream ends. The film was designed to produce laughter and delight. Yet the ludicrous quality of the situation prevents us from identifying very closely with the character, even though we appreciate the clever techniques used to render his dizziness and drunken sleep.

In contrast, because we are interested in the character of the hotel porter played by Emil Jannings in F. W. Murnau's *The Last Laugh* (1924), we empathize much more with the hero. He too has fallen into an inebriated dream state, in this case after celebrating at a wedding. He dreams that he has returned to the hotel and that he is a powerfully strong man who can lift a heavy trunk as if it were a balloon. If he really had so much power, he would never have been dismissed from his post, as he was earlier in the day. The revolving door now has gigantic proportions and spins at a dizzying pace. As the porter carries the trunk into the lobby, Murnau shoots the sequence with a subjective camera that moves us through an out-of-focus array of faces belonging to the staff and customers who all applaud his strength. Murnau's special effects convey accurately the drunken impression of the world in the pathetic man's mind.[3] The technical aspects of the sequence support the content and involve us as fellow dreamers who feel concern for the porter as a human being and who know the disorienting effects of too much liquor on ensuing sleep.

The second kind of mind/body isomorphism appears in films that show the dreams or dreamlike hallucinations of characters who have experienced some kind of physiological trauma. For example, in Mervyn LeRoy's *Thirty Seconds over Tokyo* (1944), Ted Lawson (Van Johnson) has been shot down during an air raid. To save his life, doctors have to amputate his leg. During the operation, the anesthetized hero dreams he is looking out of a window into a snowy landscape and watching a tree being chopped down. The tree falls, and he awakes to discover the loss of his leg.

Another example of physical trauma occurs in Roman Polanski's *Rosemary's Baby* (1968) in which a character translates a real assault on the body into a mental image. Rosemary (Mia Farrow) does not know that her husband Guy (John Cassavetes) has made a pact with the devil who wishes to impregnate a mortal. Working in league with Roman and Minnie Castevet (Sidney Blackmer and Ruth Gordon), Guy feeds Rosemary a drugged chocolate mousse made by Minnie, but her ensuing dream is not simply a result of something she eats. Once asleep, she has a fantastic dream which pictures her emergence from the bed onto water, a journey on a yacht, and a meeting with a throng of demons. Most prominent is her scaly demon lover who appears at one point in a gigantic close-up.[4]

Rosemary understands the visual and physical experience as a dream while we realize that it is the result of physical trauma.[5] Some force has manifested itself to her in and *as* the dream, rather in a way that reminds us of what occurs in Greek epics when characters are visited by "dreams." In the earlier literary works, the dream is an actual being; so, too, here, the devil comes to her in the *form* of a dream, but he has actually been present while she was dreaming.[6] After awaking, she has a dim sense of having had an unusual dream. Guy tells her that he had intercourse with her while she was asleep.

Two musical films that explain dreams as the result of physical trauma are Victor Fleming's *The Wizard of Oz* (1939) and Bob Fosse's *All That Jazz* (1979). The creators of *The Wizard of Oz* decided to use Technicolor as a way of indicating that Dorothy (Judy Garland) has entered a dream state after being injured during the tornado in Kansas. Before that occurs, the narrative is in sepia; it returns to sepia at the conclusion of the dream. One thinks of Wordsworth's description of his poems; he says he attempted "to throw over them a certain coloring of the imagination, whereby ordinary things should be presented to the mind in an unusual way." Here the coloring of Dorothy's imaginative experience during her dream suggests the special reality that she enters during the oneiric experience. People from her ordinary existence like Miss Gulch (Margaret Hamilton) and Zeke (Bert Lahr) now appear transformed (but not completely altered in regard to character) as the Witch and the Cowardly Lion.

All That Jazz presents the story of director Joe Gideon (Roy Scheider), who suffers from a progressive heart disease. As the film draws to its conclusion, the hero lies in a hospital and has a fantasy/dream populated by entertainers and characters from his past; they have returned to be part of a last tribute to his life. This dream sequence, the final production number of the film, presents an excessive and unrelenting barrage of images and sounds suggesting the extent of the bodily pressures on his comatose mind. Under these circumstances he is unable to order or "direct" all the creatures of his imagination and memory in a fully coherent manner. As happens in *Meshes of the Afternoon* (discussed below), the termination of the dream literally marks the end of the dreamer's life. The garish and flamboyant content of his last production number clashes jarringly with the grimly realistic shots depicting what happens to his body after death, in particular, the placement of his corpse into a body bag.

Ken Russell's *Altered States* (1980) is also relevant here. Eddie Jessup (William Hurt) searches for a state of consciousness that will connect him to archetypal essences from human prehistory as well as to the equivalent of the Jungian collective unconscious. To bring them forth, he takes hallucinogenic drugs and places himself into an immersion tank. Combined with his powerful will to achieve contact with the archetypes, these actions lead him into extraordinary dream states. As he continues his activities, though, he is overwhelmed by his contact with the past and is drawn back in space and time to different bodily states. The montage and color used by Russell to convey the sheer density of the visual and tactile perceptions that Jessup experiences in his psychedelic dreams are impressive. They reveal the same impulse one sees in Stan Brakhage's *Dog-Star Man* (discussed below), in which the filmmaker uses the medium to attempt to render the ineluctable—that which defies verbal equivalents and returns us to the world of sensory impressions felt in dreams. In such "altered states" of consciousness, the dream becomes a reality for the hero and for the audience.

Dreams of Traumatic Events

Two recent films which show characters dreaming of traumatic events involve drowning incidents. In *The Story of Adele H.* (1975), François Truffaut presents a recurring nightmare in which the heroine (Isabelle Adjani) dreams she is drowning; we have learned earlier in the film that her sister died in this manner. On two occasions we see a rapid series of superimposed images of water and her face inundating the image of her in bed. Given the somewhat languid pace of the film generally, these insertions of the drowning dream accompanied by the strident intensity of Maurice Jaubert's music disturb us and throw us psychologically off balance. Such a practice here manages to duplicate the experience we have in dreams in which we are taken unawares by the unexpected. Truffaut wants to make us feel Adele's terror as he involves us in the seething mental life of his crazed heroine. These sharp oneiric punctuations within the film provide unsettling jabs at our consciousness.

In Robert Redford's *Ordinary People* (1980), Conrad (Timothy Hutton) dreams of the boating accident in which his brother Buck was killed. Redford paces our sight of the dream carefully. Very early in the film we see Conrad awaking from what clearly has been a nightmare. But it is only later that we again see Conrad in bed, this time tossing uneasily in his sleep. Then the dream follows, picturing the waves that overwhelm the boat as Conrad and Buck try to survive. Redford's narrative strategy of delaying our view of the dream offers a formal parallel to the process of repression at work in Conrad. Only in the emotional climax of the film can he confront his actual feelings about Buck. Both Adele and Conrad offer examples of the kind of dreamers whom Freud discusses in *Beyond the Pleasure Principle*—those who dream of traumatic events from their pasts as a way of trying to master their fears and horror.[7]

Anxiety Dreams

The primary causes of anxiety dreams are characters' fears and uncertainties. The seven films discussed in this section offer representative examples of such dreams. I begin with G. W. Pabst's *Secrets of a Soul* (1926), which has the distinction of being the first narrative film created to demonstrate Freudian psychoanalytic theory and method.[8] The film concerns a chemist (Werner Krauss), his mental breakdown and cure through psychoanalytic treatment.

One morning as he is about to shave some hairs off the back of his wife's neck, cries of "murder" occur from a neighboring apartment: a man has cut his wife's throat. This incident troubles Martin and is, we learn, confused in his

2. Martin's psychiatrist attempts to help him.

unconscious with feelings of jealousy toward Eric, his wife's cousin who is about to return from India for a visit. That evening, we see Martin having a disturbing dream. When he awakens, rather like a child who has experienced what dream researchers call *pavor nocturnus* (night terror), he cannot remember any of the disturbing content. The next day, Martin develops a knife phobia and, unable to function, sees a psychoanalyst who helps him to recall the dream and to understand how jealousy caused his phobia. The key to his cure lies in reviving a memory of an event from childhood in which he was excluded from playing with his wife and Eric.

The dream itself presents Martin's unconscious fears about his impotence and violent impulses toward his wife. It begins by showing Martin, clad only in pajamas, as he walks out onto his terrace. The distortion achieved by alteration of the size of the sets makes him appear very small in relation to

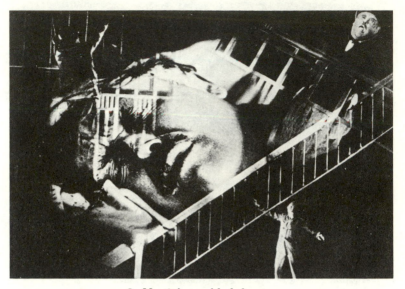

3. Martin's troubled dream.

his surroundings, appropriately enough since the film depicts him as an infantile and ineffectual being. He shoots a gun, actually a toy rifle; he falls from a height (an action rendered effectively in a shot that functions like a downward zoom); and he climbs stairs but does not reach the top of the tower to which they lead. Throughout, he watches helplessly as various events happen beyond his control: trains seem to rush at him; he stands trial for murder; and, after observing Eric and his wife pull a baby out of water, he imagines himself stabbing his wife. Pabst uses superimpositions and distortions of the images masterfully to suggest the confusion in Martin's dreaming mind and employs the mise-en-scène to underscore the childlike nature of the dreamer.

On a narrative level, we can appreciate Martin's plight and

sympathize with his desperation. On a visual level, as we participate in the dream, we are caught up by the techniques Pabst uses to present his character's nightmare. The task facing the filmmaker is twofold: to make us "see" what Martin hallucinates in his nightmare, but, equally important, to let us "feel" his response to what he sees. Pabst succeeds in reviving our memory of experiencing similar sensations in dreams.

The scene in which Martin struggles to stand up on books so that he can look out a window grating at Eric, his wife, and their "baby" (a doll being drawn out of water), may be interpreted as a repetition of Martin's earlier witnessing of a primal scene. But more interesting for our purposes is the method that Pabst uses to render this section of the dream. He crosscuts between close-ups of the screaming Martin and long shots of the happy couple, smiling and waving at him from the boat. The cutting intensifies the contrast between the enclosed space in which Martin finds himself, emphasized by the grating through which he looks, and the sense of open freedom associated with Eric and the wife. Pabst clearly seems to be using the rhythm of his cutting to create psychological tension in us by involving us in Martin's frustration as he looks at the couple.[9]

Pabst employs technical devices in a number of other scenes to replicate Martin's feelings. For example, the rapid lowering of the camera in a manner that anticipates the effect of using a zoom lens imitates the sensation we had as children in the "falling dream." We seem to accompany Martin as he plummets to the ground, having been shot down by his cousin Eric. The shots of the gigantic figures, which dwarf him at the "trial," and the huge close-ups of people laughing at him make us share Martin's sense of helplessness in this dream world of giants.

In addition, the sense of trying to reach a destination and failing to be able to move is mirrored in Martin's two climbs up the tower which has risen magically from the ground. Obviously, the tower serves as a phallic symbol; and stair-climbing, according to Freudian interpretation, would reflect Martin's desire for sexual intercourse. But I suspect we respond first to the shared sense of impotence we feel as dreamers who never can move where we want to, and only later do we understand the events on a symbolic level.

Dream research has demonstrated that the sense one has of being unable to move in a dream, an experience common to all of us, is connected to the actual physiological conditions of REM sleep in which motor control is severely limited. In the dreaming stage of sleep, we really do experience a kind of physical paralysis. This scene, in which Martin looks up at the faces in the tower he cannot climb and has to continue watching the female faces inserted in the bells and the subsequent series of male faces laughing at him from above, offers an equivalent for the dreamlike state in which we are unable to move away from threatening or unpleasant forces. Here, Pabst involves us in Martin's physical impotency by locking us into a character's point-of-view shot.

We feel a similar sense of confusion when Jack Clayton inserts a brief dream in *The Innocents* (1961) to convey the anxiety of Miss Giddens (Deborah Kerr), the heroine of his adaptation of Henry James's *The Turn of the Screw*. Having met Miles and Flora, the children who are her charges at Bly, and having been drawn increasingly into the fairy-tale world of their charming fictions as well as into the demonic abyss associated with Peter Quint and Miss Jessel (who are ghosts), Miss Giddens has a nightmare. It combines images and aspects of her life at Bly in a series of confused images. For example, Flora's music box provides the sound for a grotesque dance of shadows. In addition, the children deck their tortoise with flowers, almost as if it were a sacrificial beast. The governess's fears about the sexual knowledge the children may have acquired from Quint and Jessel appear in her dreamed perception of Miles and Flora walking dutifully with the ghosts. Like the dream sequence in *Secrets of a Soul*, this suggests the welter of images flooding the mind of the dreamer. Since at this point in the film's development we too are uncertain as to what is happening, the ambiguous dream draws us into sympathetic union with the equally baffled governess.

A special kind of anxiety emerges in the dream of Buffalo Bill (Paul Newman) in Robert Altman's *Buffalo Bill and the Indians or Sitting Bull's History Lesson* (1976). Buffalo Bill appears to awaken from a sleep induced by liquor (according to the script), but the dream is quite different from those seen in *The Dream of a Rarebit Fiend* or *The Last Laugh*. Rather than portraying physical actions, Buffalo Bill's dream reveals his attempt to cope with his unconscious sense of inadequacy as a man and as a legend.

The dream occurs in a context that has stressed the importance of dreams. Earlier, Sitting Bull has joined the Wild West show troupe because he dreamed that the president would come to visit him; and, indeed, Grover Cleveland arrives unexpectedly for a performance of the show in which the members of the troupe reenact an attack on Indians who have captured a settler's cabin. But Cleveland refuses to do anything about the Indians' needs. The cynical Ned Buntline (Burt Lancaster) contrasts Sitting Bull with Buffalo Bill. Only in dreams can the Indians find solace; but at least they dream. As Buntline sees it, though, Buffalo Bill has no dreams at all, the only dream he knows being the Wild West show.

In a scene shortly after Buffalo Bill tells Buntline he can no longer be associated with the show, we see Buffalo Bill awaken from sleep and hear him exclaim: "I don't dream!" But he is, in fact, dreaming, as he rants and asserts his superiority. The monologue reminds us of the experience we can have in dreams when, anxious or afraid, we talk incessantly to silent or disbelieving auditors. His audience for this oneiric performance is Sitting Bull, who stands impassively as Buffalo Bill speaks of his own youth, his reputation, and, most tellingly, his sense of superiority: "In one hundred years . . . in other people's shows . . . I'm still *Buffalo Bill . . . star*! You're still . . . *The Injun*!" He tells Sitting Bull that the latter's act with the dancing horse helps prepare the audience for himself: "*It makes me true*! 'Cause truth is whatever gets the loudest applause!"[10]

Throughout this patter, Altman varies the framing and camera angles in a way to emphasize the stolid, dignified reserve of Sitting Bull in contrast to the posing and uncertain movements of Buffalo Bill. The Indian's lack of response is supported by the shooting technique which stresses the desperation of the cowboy's bravado. He continually encounters an indifferent audience everywhere in the room, since, as Robert T. Self has suggested, Altman constantly moves Sitting Bull *between* cuts in a way that contributes to the sense of numerous Sitting Bulls, all oblivious to the speaker.[11] The restrained use of technique here demonstrates that cutting and mise-en-scène can help support the oneiric content of a scene, independent of the more traditional devices used to convey a dreamlike sense—such as the superimpositions or distorted images Altman uses one year later for the dream of Pinky (Sissy Spacek) in *Three Women* (1977).

The other films in this category reveal anxiety through dreams depicting the sense of doubleness that often characterizes oneiric experiences. Some dreamers say that they have seen themselves in dreams; others find that rarely, if ever, are they aware of watching themselves as actual participants, as if on a screen. Nonetheless, although we may be feeling rather than witnessing our physical presence, we still sense that somehow we are two places at once.

George W. Linden speaks informatively of this phenomenon: "Perhaps one of the first things one notices about dreams is their bi-sociative character, which is expressed in the ex-

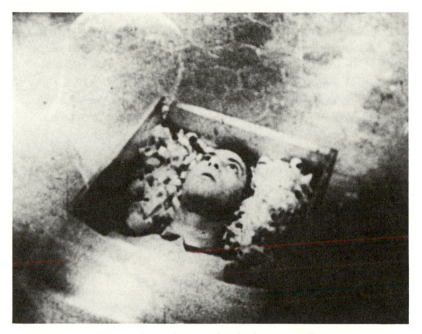

4. David Gray observes his body in a coffin.

perience of the individual as a sense of psychic bi-presence.
One is both in his dream and not in his dream at the same
time. This ambiguity is further expressed in the relation of
possession, that is, it is both one's own dream and not his
own dream."[12]

The first notable example appears in Carl Dreyer's *Vampyr*
(1931). The gray world of this dreamlike film is unsettling to
begin with. A young man, David Gray, enters a mysterious
town and finds himself combatting a vampire and its cohorts
who are destroying the young women of a family. The film's
strangeness is made even more intense midway into the narrative when the anxious hero falls in a field. As he lies
unconscious, that part of him which is the dreaming David
Gray emerges out of the prone figure as a superimposition,

leaves it, and goes to a building where he enters a room that contains a coffin in which he discovers his own body. Dreyer cuts from this shot to one from within the coffin and uses a subjective camera to link us to Gray's point of view as he looks up at figures preparing to remove him. We sense what he feels as he is carried from the room and placed on a carriage which conducts him to the cemetery. As the dream comes to its conclusion, the hero awakes in the grass and watches the casket being drawn forth by horses on the road.[13]

The splitting of the dreamer from the sleeper pertains to my suggestion about the dream screen. In dream sequences that begin with the dreamer as a dissociated superimposition, generally the dreamer ceases to be photographed as a superimposition once out of camera range of the sleeper. The continuation of the dream, after the cessation of the superimposition, can be understood to occur on the sleeper's dream screen, a structure that we as viewers provide for the dreamer in the form of the cinematic dream screen to which we are bound in the theater.

It is difficult not to see a similarity between the dream in Dreyer's film and the opening dream sequence of Ingmar Bergman's *Wild Strawberries* (1957). This film depicts the events and dreams during a day lived by an elderly physician, Isak Borg (Victor Sjöström), who is receiving an honorary degree. The first dream of the hero is introduced with a voice-over; he simply tells us he had a dream and then we see him in bed for a moment before his dream begins. In his dream, he confronts an empty, terrifying world, made more so by the stark overexposed photography and the quick cuts used to present the streets and walls of the town. In one shot Borg is alone. A moment later, he sees a form standing at the end of the previously empty street; when he touches it, it falls on the ground, its face exuding fluid. Toward the end of this dream, Borg observes a casket that has fallen off a hearse. He looks at the casket and discovers himself; the "dead" Borg in the casket tries to pull the "living" dreamer inside, and the nightmare ends.

The idea of splitting a single character in order to suggest the anxious individual's concern with death is as effective here as it was in Dreyer's film. Bergman uses voice-over rather than superimposition to begin the dream but communicates the same powerful sense of strangeness. He also offers reverse shots from the presumed point of view of the casket's inhabitant. Thus we watch Borg struggling against the Borg who attempts to drag him down into death; but we also look up from the casket into the face of the terrified Borg who resists death.

This condition of being an observer and participant appears again in one of Borg's dreams about Sara (Bibi Andersson), the girl he loved as a youth but did not marry. He dreams she is explaining his faults to him, particularly his coldness. To force him to confront his lack of feeling, she holds a mirror to his face and we watch Borg seeing himself in the reflection. In effect, then, we understand that Borg as dreamer is watching himself looking at himself in a mirror. Again, another part of this dream sequence includes an examination dream in which Borg fails to identify a substance under a microscope. Bergman uses a point-of-view shot that shows Borg looking in the microscope and seeing only his own eye as it looks back at him.

We know how dreams reveal another side of us *to* us and, as dreamers, have sensed this curious feeling of dissociation before. The shots of the casket, mirror, and microscope on the cinematic dream screen that we share with Borg thus replicate the phenomenon we have sensed, even if we have not actually experienced it in dreams: the dual presence of ourselves as observers and participants. The nature of the screen itself, as I suggested earlier, defines such a situation of doubleness since it is constituted in part by the dreamer.[14]

Equally disturbing is a work many consider the most important contribution to the development of the American avant-garde film, Maya Deren's *Meshes of the Afternoon* (1943). This remarkable film draws us into the nightmare world of a woman (acted by Deren) who is watching herself experience a number of strange events within a dream. Deren has said that she wanted "to put on film the feeling which a human being experiences about the incident rather than to record the incident."[15] The feelings presented here include anxiety, dissociation, and a form of psychic vertigo.

As the film begins, we watch the heroine walking on a street. She observes a man in a black suit turn a corner, picks up an hibiscus from the street, enters her bungalow where a knife protrudes from a loaf of bread, and sits in a chair where she goes to sleep. In the dream sequence, Deren makes brilliant use of the subjective 16-mm camera to convey the lack of firm positioning the woman has in reality. At times we move jerkily up stairs. Occasionally, her editing lifts the viewer from one scene to another by cutting on movement. Thus in one shot we see a foot lifted and about to move in a given space; in the next shot, we watch the foot complete its motion as it descends in a different space.

Deren repeats with variations a scene in which the woman tries to pursue a hooded figure in a black habitlike robe. The figure seems to have grown out of her sight of the man in the black suit, but, in the dream, it turns into a frightening and elusive force which has a mirror in place of its face. Early in the dream we see the woman on the street trying to catch up with the hooded figure. At various points throughout the dream, the sequence recurs and usually includes shots of the woman's feet intercut with shots of the retreating figure. The cutting of the chases conveys expertly the sense we have in dreams of attempting to catch up with someone who is trying to elude us. In these repetitions, Deren shoots from the upstairs of the bungalow, so that we see the woman looking down at herself in pursuit of the figure.

Such shots of the woman as she watches herself point to the dreamer's sense of dissociation. This state of mind becomes important for the working out of the various situations that occur in the film. As it progresses, first one and then another woman appear to complement the woman of the dream. In one particularly disconcerting shot, all three are seated at the dining room table on which rests the loaf of bread with the knife. The multiple selves of the heroine appear to represent her lack or confusion of identity; thus the dream is a particularly effective vehicle to render her state of mind.

At another point, as she looks at herself in the bedroom, the hibiscus, which is on the bed, disappears and is replaced with the knife. The knife and hibiscus are linked to a key, and all appear to be used as symbols of her own confused sense of sexual identity and desire. The apparent object of her passion is a man whom we see in the bedroom with her. But what begins as the overture to love-making quickly ends as she wields the knife in his direction, an action that results in a radical shift in scene from the room to a beach. In the shocking climax of the film, this man discovers the woman seated on the chair she occupied when she went to sleep. We see that her throat has been slit.

More recently, R. W. Fassbinder's *Despair* (1977) displays a dream sequence that conveys the dreamer's anxiety and confusion in an even more complicated manner. Adapted by Tom Stoppard and Fassbinder from Vladimir Nabokov's novel, the film concerns Hermann Hermann (Dirk Bogarde), a schizoid personality suffering from the delusion that he has found his perfect double, Felix (Klaus Löwitsch), an itinerant worker.[16] Hermann may be a creation of Nabokov, but in this film he joins a number of other characters in German literature and film who have encountered their doppelgängers. Even though the supposed double looks nothing at all like Hermann, he is destined to be murdered by Hermann who plans on assuming the dead man's place, escaping from his present life as a candy manufacturer, and living off the insurance money that will be awarded to the widow of the "dead" Hermann.

Early in the film Hermann attends a silent movie in which he observes the following sequence. Identical twins find themselves in a house: one is a gangster, the other a policeman who has come in to capture his "bad" brother. The latter shoots the "good" brother and attempts to escape by passing himself off as the policeman. The other officers learn of the trick and shoot the imposter.

Later we see a dream of Hermann's that incorporates material from the film. In the dream, he is seated in a chair in the house seen earlier in the silent film. Fassbinder uses crosscutting to show Hermann greeting his double who has entered (actually himself, Bogarde, at this point of the dream). He then walks to the chair where his "twin" is seated. But when Hermann touches the head of the double, we observe the slightly pasty face of the apparently dead Felix (Löwitsch) roll to one side. We then see the anxious Hermann awaken in his bed. The rhythm of the cutting has been flowing smoothly between Hermann and Hermann. This sudden jolt with a rapid cut to Felix effectively involves us in the confusion of Hermann's dreaming mind. The sequence could occur only in a film, with its ability to master spatio-temporal limitations.

Hermann has dreamed of his twin selves, stimulated by a silent film involving twins. In that film, the twins appear simultaneously on the screen by virtue of the cinematic trick of the line down the middle of the screen; two scenes with the same actor are photographed separately and then matted together. Hermann's illusion in non-oneiric experience (he has a genuine double whose life he can assume) combines with his experience at a film to form a dream which he projects on his own private dream screen.

There are numerous Hermanns populating or figuring in the dream: Hermann the dreamer; Hermann who sees himself in the dream; and "Hermann" (actually Felix) who appears as the guest in the the dream. It is this last Hermann who turns into someone else, at least to our eyes, in that abrupt cut when Hermann turns his head. Our eyes, that is, see *Felix*, not Hermann, at the conclusion of the sequence. The situation is complicated since here Fassbinder's hero "sees" something on *his* dream screen that we do not see on the same screen we offer to him: *he* sees himself dead, and is shaken; *we* see Felix.

Perceptual ambiguities have formed the basis of two recent films, Joseph Losey's *Mr. Klein* (1976) and Luis Buñuel's *That Obscure Object of Desire* (1977). But the situation presented in Fassbinder's film seems to me to be the richest, certainly in scenes such as the dream sequence when the basic confusion in Hermann's perceiving mind (whether awake or asleep) about his other identity is presented so effectively.

An observation of Freud's seems relevant at this point. He argues that dreams are populated by figures who are themselves merely extensions of the dreamer: "Dreams are completely egotistic. Whenever my own ego does not appear in the content of the dream, but only some extraneous person, I may safely assume that my own person lies concealed, by identification, behind this other person; I can insert my ego into the context. On other occasions, when my own ego *does* appear in the dream, the situation in which it occurs may teach me that some other person lies concealed, by identification, behind my ego."[17] If we entertain this argument in relation to the cinematic dream screen and to *Despair*, we see that, in a curious way, the character mistakenly thought to be a double for Hermann (Felix) is, in the dream at least, *genuinely* an extension of Hermann. Thus Fassbinder has, consciously or not, immersed us in a dream sequence that in its complexity manages to approach the almost indefinable nature of our own dreams. Character and viewer are involved in a joint perception of something (Hermann as Felix) in which the character's perception is both "right" and "wrong." One thinks of Freud's comment that there is nothing like the word "no" in dreams; instead, dreams "show a particular preference for combining contraries into a unity or for representing them as one and the same thing."[18] So, too, on Hermann's dream screen, where the hero and the viewers experience the doubleness of self, in which what we both see is in some ways true and false at the same time. Fassbinder has created a condition we know from our dreams when "yes" is sometimes really "no."

Dreams of Desire

This category of dreams includes those that exist primarily to depict desire. The very nature of the medium which allows a filmmaker to realize the impossible is admirably suited to picture what a character dreams. Jean-Paul Sartre's observation on the imagination and desire is relevant: "The desire constitutes the object for the most part; it determines itself as desire to the extent to which it projects the unreal object before it."[19] The more intensely realized the imaginary object, the more it signals the extent of the subject's desire. Dreams of desire are the closest cinematic equivalents to what Freud describes as wish-fulfillment dreams.

Various kinds of desire appear in filmic dreams. One example of a dream caused by politically motivated desire occurs in S. M. Eisenstein's *The General Line (Old and New)* (1929). Martha, a poor peasant who is trying to convince her fellow villagers of the virtues of collective life, has just succeeded in rescuing the cash that had been put away to buy a bull. She falls asleep leaning on the cashbox, and a superimposition of a giant bull fills the top half of the screen. The dream continues with visions of the various forms of economic success that the community will come to enjoy. Eisenstein has chosen to portray oneirically what is denotatively and literally a dream—her desire for a means to enhance the community. And the visionary quality of her aspirations, signaled here with the gigantic bull in the sky, effectively captures her hopes.

Dreams can also reflect aesthetic or creative desires. Marshall Deutelbaum has drawn my attention to two films about creative characters. In *And the Villain Still Pursued Her; or The Author's Dream* (director unknown; Vitagraph, 1906), a hack writer falls asleep over his melodramatic story and enters into the narrative he has just been creating—one filled with chases, a damsel in distress whom he loves, and precipitous chasms over which the characters must leap. In *The Sculptor's Nightmare* (director unknown; American Mutascope and Biograph, 1908), a sculptor who has been assigned to make busts of the political candidates dreams that the piles of clay in his studio actually form themselves into busts of contenders such as William Howard Taft, William Jennings Bryan, Theodore Roosevelt, as well as the GOP Elephant.[20]

In Charles Vidor's *Hans Christian Andersen* (1952), the hero (Danny Kaye) has created a ballet, "The Little Mermaid," for Zizi-Jeanmaire whom he loves. Before the performance, he is accidentally locked into a closet where, eventually, he falls asleep. His dream takes the form of the ballet he (and the audience) had been waiting to see performed. Thus his expectations and ours coincide in the performance he dreams on the screen we offer him.

The most common kind of desire presented in the dream sequence is erotic. One precursor of this use of the medium is Georges Méliès's *The Clock Maker's Dream* (1903). In this film a clockmaker falls asleep, and the large clocks on which he has been working turn into richly attired women who form a *tableau vivant*. Méliès brings about the transformation by replacing the shot of the clocks and sleeping man with a shot of the women in exactly the same places. The dreamer would rather be surrounded by beautiful women than by clocks.

5. Charlie's dream of desire—the "Oceana Roll."

No such transformation occurs in Charlie Chaplin's *The Gold Rush* (1925), where a dream is used to depict the hero's desire for Georgia, a dance hall girl. We see the Tramp in his lonely cabin waiting for Georgia and the other girls who are supposed to join him for a lavish New Year's Eve dinner. As the evening wanes, and no girls appear, he drifts off to sleep and dreams that they have arrived and are enjoying his hospitality. The climax of their visit comes when he entertains them with the wonderful "Oceana Roll" dance of the bread rolls and spoons. But he awakens to an empty room, the candles almost melted down. The scene in which the Tramp realizes he has been dreaming is one of the most poignant in Chaplin's films.

Note that Chaplin chooses to do very little with the devices

he might have used to render the dream. During the Oceana
Roll, in fact, the camera is in a fixed position. Thus our
response to the dream does not involve us on a technical
level as much as on a narrative one.

Often the dream sequence in musical comedies serves the
specific function of revealing the characters' erotic desires or
the confusion these cause. For example, in Fred Zinnemann's
film of *Oklahoma!* (1954), in a sequence retained from the
Broadway production created by Richard Rodgers and Oscar
Hammerstein II, Laurie (Shirley Jones) has a dream in which
we see her love of Curley (Gordon MacRae) and fear of Judd
(Rod Steiger) presented in the form of a ballet ("Out of My
Dreams," danced by Bambi Lynn and James Mitchell).

Several of the dream sequences in Vincente Minnelli's
musicals also become vehicles for showing a character's desires. Minnelli says his aim in *Yolanda and the Thief* (1945)
was "a simple attempt to show the interplay between the
dream and reality. Every dream is an arrangement of some
real aspects. Ideals, aspirations, and desires consciously or
subconsciously color the thoughts, actions, and relationships
with other people. Only in the dream does all this become
real, do we get to the truth at all."[21]

In *Yolanda and the Thief*, which Minnelli claims is the
first film to present a Surrealist ballet, Fred Astaire plays
Johnny, a confidence man attempting to swindle the heroine,
Lucille Bremer. He falls in love with the intended victim,
and the dream ballet ("Will You Marry Me?") depicts his
ambivalent feelings and confusion. Somewhat atypically for
dream sequences in musicals, it ends as a nightmare with
Johnny wrapped up in his bed sheets (in the dream, the bride's
veil).

The ballet in *An American in Paris* (1951) reflects the
uncertainties in the mind of its artist-hero Jerry (Gene Kelly)
about the woman he truly loves, Lise (Leslie Caron). Generally
regarded as the most spectacular of all dream sequences in

musical films, its mises-en-scène include various reproductions of Paris as rendered by representative famous artists such as Henri de Toulouse-Lautrec, Pierre Auguste Renoir and Raoul Dufy. As such, they provide appropriate settings for showing the longing and perplexity in the mind of the artist in whose dream they occur.

Other musicals that offer inventive dream sequences include Minnelli's *The Pirate*, with Gene Kelly and Judy Garland (1948), and Jean Negulesco's *Daddy Long Legs*, with Fred Astaire and Leslie Caron (1955). The first presents Manuela (Garland) dreaming of the romanticized pirate Macoco (Kelly, apparently). The second uses the dream sequence to explore the aging hero's love for the younger heroine and his fears about the possibility of the relationship's success.

Mitchell Leisen's *Lady in the Dark* (1944) is unusual in that it uses dream sequences to portray various states of mind of the heroine, Liza Elliott (Ginger Rogers), in a specifically psychoanalytic context. These work in connection with the actual therapy that she is undergoing in the course of the film.

Speaking directly of musical production numbers in general, rather than of dream sequences in particular, Patricia Mellencamp follows Christian Metz's suggestion and argues that at the moment when such numbers begin, a "gap" is opened in the narrative. As a result, the narrative is revealed as an illusion: "The spectator is awakened to the 'here and now' of performance and to the awareness that the events of the 'once upon a time' of the fictive narrative are not 'real.' . . . Spectacles can be considered as excessively pleasurable moments in musicals, awakening the spectator to the fact of filmic illusion."[22]

I wonder if, in fact, the opposite is true in dream sequences in musicals. These seem different from announced and naturalistically "appropriate" moments of spectacle in show-business films like the "Gotta Dance" number in *Singin' in the Rain* (Stanley Donen and Gene Kelly, 1952), or the spontaneous and unnaturalistic moments when characters burst into song and dance in a nontheatrical setting, such as "It Only Happens When I Dance with You" in *Easter Parade* (Charles Walters, 1948). Rather than necessarily opening a gap, such dream sequences actually gain a kind of ontological validity as the property of a particular dreaming consciousness who would probably "dream" in the form that the production number takes. That is, the dream sequence closes or seals the potentially disruptive aspects of its production values and codes by locating the source of them in an individual mind.

Parker Tyler addresses the same issue with a different argument. Speaking of the dream ballet in *Yolanda and the Thief*, he suggests: "Whereas the hero of the . . . movie could hardly be expected to have such dreams, Mr. Astaire himself might have had them. The choreographic fantasy comprises an obstacle dream, and though the hero's path is directed towards a fair young lady, conceivably Mr. Astaire's path, subconsciously, might be directed towards the classic heights of legitimate ballet. . . ."[23]

In *An American in Paris* the dream is one that its artist-hero might have. When, in a film like *Yolanda and the Thief*, the character's profession seems logically to preclude having such a dream, the very persona that the entertainer, "Fred Astaire," has developed over the years as a dancer who appears in musical films can accommodate or naturalize the dream sequence for us. I am puzzled by Tyler's assumption that Astaire would *personally* dream in the framework of classical ballet since his films for well over ten years before *Yolanda and the Thief* had been solidly in the tradition of American musical comedy—for example, *Top Hat* (1935), *Swing Time* (1936), and *Shall We Dance?* (1937). In addition, critics generally agree that over the years both Astaire and Kelly have created a particularized style and manner of dance which audiences automatically acknowledge (the suave, lithe sophistication of Astaire as opposed to the more energetic naturalness of Kelly).[24] It is possible, in fact, that in such dream sequences with well-known performers like Astaire and Kelly, as viewers we experience truly privileged moments of identification with them as artists, actors, and "dreamers."[25]

The last two dreams to be considered in relation to the general motif of desire share a common theme, a son's love for his mother. In Luis Buñuel's *Los Olvidados* (1950), Pedro, a young and impoverished boy living in the slums of Mexico City, dreams that he receives food and love from his mother; earlier she has denied him both. We watch his superimposed form rise from his sleeping body and observe his mother who, in slow motion, has stepped onto his bed and handed him a hunk of raw meat. But his pleasure is short-lived. An arm extends up menacingly from beneath the bed, and its owner, Pedro's friend Jaibo, competes with Pedro for the mother's affection. The boys wrestle and Pedro awakes from his violent nightmare.

The sequence is disturbing, not only because of the obvious Oedipal content, but also because the grotesque hunk of meat so effectively presents a symbolic image of the characters' desire. As Carlos Rebolledo notes: "In *Los Olvidados*, hunger is the permanent driving force for all the characters. Pedro's dream is a concrete symbol of this primal urge, mixed though it might be with all the other drives and desires—particularly sex. In Buñuel, desire is a totality. All desires are one—the desire to survive, to reproduce, to create."[26]

A very different relationship between mother and son is portrayed in David Lynch's *The Elephant Man* (1980). In this film the love of John Merrick (John Hurt) for his mother is a force that helps sustain him in a vicious world. There are no sexual overtones in the love of the misshapen man, only desire for the comfort and warmth he associates with his mother. After being rescued by Dr. Frederick Treves (Anthony

Hopkins), Merrick becomes the permanent ward of a hospital. He manages to survive the kidnapping by his former jailer/impresario Bytes (Freddie Jones) and returns to London, where he spends his last days tended by the hospital staff and supported by the actress Mrs. Kendall (Anne Bancroft). Aware that he is dying, Merrick decides to end his life by sleeping in a normal position, an act that will cause his death because of his physiological handicaps. He looks at a sketch on the wall of a normal little boy lying in a bed and then slowly removes all the pillows from his own bed. After glancing at the pictures of Mrs. Kendall and his mother on the nightstand, he settles down to his final sleep. Earlier he has shown his mother's picture to visitors and friends. We have seen it in detail as a giant close-up at the beginning of the film and again as he entertains in his room.

After he lies down, the camera lingers on him in a close-up; then it pans to his right past the pictures of Mrs. Kendall and his mother to the blowing curtains of his window. Once outside the window, the camera's motion increases as it travels through stars and clouds, finally arriving at a close-up of his mother's face that fills the screen. We hear a woman's voice promising, "Nothing will die," and the screen becomes increasingly white as we move into her eyes. Then the screen goes dark and the film ends. The image of the mother's face should make us recall what Lewin says about the dream screen and its function for the dreamer. Perhaps Merrick's last oneiric vision is a repetition of the first dream he had ever had, one in which his dream screen was totally absorbed by the image of his mother's face.[27]

Dream States

Some filmmakers use the medium to depict a dreamlike condition rather than a specific dream of a particular character. At such times, they employ film as a way of replicating the activities associated with the oneiric experience. This is evident in such works as *Un Chien Andalou* (1928), *L'Etoile de mer* (1928), and *Dog-Star Man* (1961-1964).

Luis Buñuel's and Salvador Dali's *Un Chien Andalou* is not a dream per se. In it, the creators exemplify the aims of the Surrealist movement with which they are associated. André Breton had defined Surrealism in 1924 as "pure psychic automatism, by which it is intended to express, verbally . . . or by other means, the real functioning of thought. The dictation of thought in the absence of all control exercised by reason and outside all aesthetic or moral implications. . . . Surrealism rests in the belief in the superior quality of certain forms of association neglected heretofore; in the omnipotence of the dream and in the disinterested play of thought."[28] Breton would later praise both *Un Chien Andalou* and *L'Age d'or* (1930) since they *"bring about the state where the distinction between the subjective and the objective loses its necessity and value."*[29]

Buñuel describes the aim of the film in similar terms: "In the working out of the plot, every idea of a rational, aesthetic or other preoccupation with technical matters was rejected as irrelevant." They were not attempting to film a dream, but rather to exploit the essential nature of the medium: "The plot is the result of a CONSCIOUS *psychic automatism*, and, to that extent, it does not attempt to recount a dream, although it profits by a mechanism analogous to that of dreams."[30] In a later lecture, Buñuel explores the ideas of Jacques B. Brunius on the relation of films and dreaming. His fellow Surrealist had noted "that the night which bit by bit invades the cinema is equivalent to closing the eyes. Then begins, on the screen and within the man, the excursion into the night of the unconscious; the images, as in dreams, appear and disappear through 'dissolves' and fade-outs; time and space become flexible. . . . The cinema seems to have been invented to express the subconscious life. . . ."[31]

Un Chien Andalou presents the same leaps in time and through space one knows from dreams. Beginning with the early shots of the slitting of the eyeball, Buñuel and Dali lead us into a world that denies traditional vision, and, even more, the expectations that accompany it.[32] The apparent logical clues in the titles ("Once Upon a Time," "Eight Years Later," etc.) only defeat our attempts to impose order on the irrational events: the bicycle accident, the attempted rape, the death of the androgyne, the priests hauling the grand pianos, and so forth. External logical demands have no place here, for the principle of construction is one of association, including the visual and symbolic affinities of objects and elements from different contexts (the doorbell and the cocktail shaker, the crowd around the androgyne and the ants around the stigma). We experience the work as if it were our own dream, one from which we cannot escape or awake. Only after repeated viewings do we begin to see some connections in the events and images (despite Buñuel's warning that there is no symbolism in the film).[33]

One of the most interesting films presenting a dream state is Man Ray's *L'Etoile de mer*, which focuses primarily on the erotic. The film is based on a poem written by the Surrealist Robert Desnos. The poem, reproduced in the intertitles, is a highly elliptical Surrealist work on woman and beauty, punctuated at points with apparently illogical comments that depart from the work's theme (for example: "Il faut battre les morts quand ils sont froids"). Like *Un Chien Andalou*, Ray's film is not a dream as such, but, rather, uses the movements of the dreaming state to unfold the scenario, particularly in regard to the erotic content.

A man and woman meet on a street, enter an apartment and proceed up the stairs to a bedroom where the woman sits on a bed and removes her clothes as the man watches her. Later the man encounters a different woman, who gives him a starfish in a bottle. He studies it, and in a prism shot, Ray

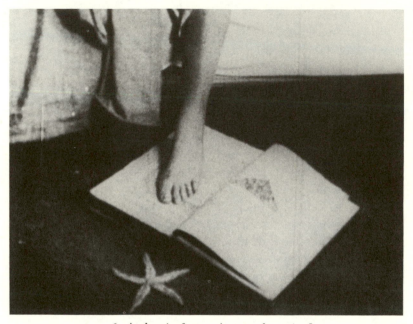

6. A shot in focus: Are we dreaming?

combines a number of images of different starfish. At two other points the camera returns to the bedroom and catches the first woman in various forms of undress. Eventually the man and woman meet again on the street, and she walks off with another man (Desnos).

Ray shoots the first erotic sequence and much of the film through a lens that blurs the image. Presumably his aim here was to mollify the censors, for the semi-opacity of the lens, which was coated with gelatin, obscures our view of the precise physical details of the woman, the erotic object of the poem and film. When Ray returns for the first time to the bedroom, we see a blurred shot of the woman who sits on and then lies in the bed. Then she makes a move to rise, and we see her foot swing away from the bed and move to the floor where it rests on a book. In a moment, Ray, shooting now in focus, displays the foot resting on the book, next to which is a starfish. Near the end of the filmed poem, a brief shot of the woman, nude, is followed by the title, "vous ne rêvez pas." By obscuring the view of the object of the desire through the use of the coated lens and by cutting to her foot, Ray reminds us of the way our own dreaming minds sometimes hide erotic goals from inner vision. The most pornographic space in our dreams is often the one we cannot perceive. The film can be seen in this light as both a comment on and an example of our status as voyeurs. The medium itelf is used to duplicate the way we sometimes find ourselves experiencing erotic stimuli in dreams. And when we actually see the woman nude, the poem tells us that we are not dreaming.

Earlier Desnos had championed the use of the cinema as a way of conveying eroticism and had linked this to its dream-like nature: "One of the most admirable things about cinema . . . is its eroticism. . . . An inborn poetry circulates through these luminous beams, ready to be cut out into aureolae. More supernatural than tongues of fire at Whitsuntide these ethereal mouths speak across frontiers, to any mind initiated in the dream."[34]

The treatment of women as erotic objects in film generally has become a highly charged critical issue. A key document in the controversy is Laura Mulvey's "Visual Pleasure and Narrative Cinema," in which, following Sigmund Freud's theory of the fetish and Jacques Lacan's description of the scopic drive, she argues that woman functions as an erotic object in two ways—for the characters in the narrative and for the viewers of the screen. In the opinion of Mulvey and others, various cinematic codes of representation for the female have contributed to help fix her as a fetish for the gaze of voyeuristic males who see her both as a castrated being (and hence a threatening reminder of their own vulnerability) and as a symbol of their dominance.[35]

Other commentators also explore how the conditions of the medium and the viewing situation contribute a sexual dimension to the experience. For example, Stanley Cavell suggests that "the ontological conditions of the motion picture reveal it as inherently pornographic."[36] Christian Metz speaks of the inherent voyeurism of the viewing situation: "Cinematic voyeurism, *unauthorised* scopophilia, is from the outset more strongly established than that of the theatre in direct line from the primal scene. Certain precise features of the institution contribute to this affinity: the obscurity surrounding the onlooker, the aperture of the screen with its inevitable keyhole effect."[37]

Even more pertinent is Metz's observation that techniques of shooting are themselves constitutive elements that contribute an erotic dimension to the viewer's experience: "The framing and its displacements . . . are in themselves forms of 'suspense.' . . . They have an inner affinity with the mechanisms of desire, of its postponements, its new impetus. . . . The way the cinema with its wandering framings (wandering like the look, like the caress) finds the means to reveal space has something to do with a kind of permanent undressing, a generalised strip-tease. . . ."[38] Even though evidence supports the charges that filmmakers have in fact used the camera in a way that binds women in various roles and iconographic determinations, the potential application of the technology is not limited exclusively to picturing and entrapping women as the object of the male gaze. That is, those very activities of the camera that Metz identifies may be conducted with reference to any erotic content. Our examination of Kenneth Anger's *Fireworks* in the section on retroactively recovered dreams will afford an opportunity to see the applicability of Metz's remarks to a film that is concerned exclusively with homosexual rather than with heterosexual eroticism.

Stan Brakhage's *Dog-Star Man* depicts a psychic state in a dreamlike manner as it presents a mythopoetic epic about vision. The film's "episodes" do not exist to render a narrative. Rather, Prelude and Parts I-IV explore the nature of light, film, human sentience, and the bond between the human and natural worlds. As Brakhage has said over the years, his aim is to make us *see*. Seeing means feeling the snow on the mountain that the "hero" (Brakhage) climbs; squinting at the blinding light; and sensing the parallels between the sun and moon and the human breast. Particularly in the first part, we share the dreamlike ascent of Brakhage as he climbs the mountain with his dog and cuts down the tree even as we are lost in the confusion of images which flash on our eyes and overwhelm our perceptions. In this silent masterpiece, we return to the state described earlier by David R. Hawkins— the infant's world prior to the time when it acquires language. Present in this dreamlike universe, we witness explosions of imagery that return us to a preverbal state in which impressions of nature, human beings and sensations mix coenesthetically as they impinge on our consciousness.

One is reminded by this film of Maurice Merleau-Ponty's comments on the potential of film. He sees "phenomenological or existential philosophy" as "largely an expression of surprise at this inherence of the self in the world and in others, a description of this paradox and permeation, and an attempt to make us *see* the bond between subject and world, between subject and others, rather than to *explain* it as the classical philosophers did by resorting to absolute spirit. Well, the movies are particularly suited to make manifest the union of mind and body, mind and world, and the expression of one in the other."[39]

Brakhage's comments on his aims recall Wordsworth's description of the perceptual oneness enjoyed by the infant with its world before it is overwhelmed by the "prison-house": "Imagine a world alive with incomprehensible objects and shimmering with an endless variety of movement and innumerable gradations of color. Imagine a world before the 'be-

ginning was the word.' " Such a world is lost as the child
develops: "Once vision may have been given—that which
seems inherent in the infant's eye, an eye which reflects the
loss of innocence more eloquently than any other human
feature, an eye which soon learns to classify sights, an eye
which mirrors the movement of the individual toward death
by its increasing inability to see. But one can never go back,
not even in imagination."

Still, Brakhage believes the artist can use the camera in
an attempt to return to the kind of true vision by which the
infant knows its world. He does not promote a "traditional"
camera eye which he associates with Renaissance perspective
and composition as well as with the standard use of color.
Rather, by altering the conditions of the filmmaking process,
he tries to achieve a return to primal vision. Therefore he
changes the speed of the projector during filming, spits on
the lens, or scratches the film. Such actions bring the imagery
closer to the kind of perceptions one knows in dreams: "Suppose the Vision of the saint and artist to be an increased
ability to see—vision. Allow so-called hallucination to enter
the realm of perception, allowing that mankind always finds
derogatory terminology for that which doesn't appear to be
readily usable, accept dream visions, day-dreams or night-
dreams, as you would so-called real scenes. . . . There is no
need for the mind's eye to be deadened after infancy. . . ."

Brakhage says that as he began editing Prelude he was
influenced by Freud's discussions of dreams: "I wanted
PRELUDE to be a created dream for the work that follows
rather than Surrealism which takes its inspiration from dream.
I stayed close to practical usage of dream material . . . for
a while before editing. . . . Once I had wanted very much
to make a film called FREUDFILM which would illustrate
the process of dream development, and would show how a
dream evolves out of the parts we don't remember into those
we do. In PRELUDE I wanted to make a film which would

swing on those transformations of unacceptable to acceptable images."[40]

Siegfried Kracauer, a theorist committed to a realist aesthetic, offers a general statement on film and dream that seems particularly applicable to Brakhage's achievement here. Kracauer sees films being most similar to dreams "when they overwhelm us with the crude and unnegotiated presence of natural objects—as if the camera had just now extracted them from the womb of physical existence and as if the umbilical cord between image and actuality had not yet been severed. There is something in the abrupt immediacy and shocking veracity of such pictures that justifies their identification as dream images."[41] The psychic state Brakhage shares with us is one of wonder at the world that the camera has discovered beneath the surfaces of reality.

Proleptic Dreams

The last category includes dreams foreshadowing material that will occur later in the narrative. Two examples might be mentioned.[42]

One of the many elements retained in the translation of Margaret Mitchell's novel *Gone with the Wind* to the screen (Victor Fleming, 1939) is the sequence in which Scarlett O'Hara (Vivien Leigh) dreams she is lost in the fog searching for someone to protect her. We see her experience the dream once in the film, although she says it recurs often: she is running desperately in the fog by a wrought-iron fence. The repetition of this sequence is not a dream. It occurs after the death of Melanie (Olivia De Havilland). Distraught, Scarlett leaves the Wilkes house and attempts to go home. But as she runs through the fog-laden street, she realizes that she is now "in" the recurring dream and that the person she was searching for must have been Rhett (Clark Gable).

A somewhat different form of proleptic dream appears in Claude Chabrol's *Violette* (1978). We see the heroine (Isabelle Huppert) asleep; a man's face appears in a rapid series of repeated superimpositions. We have not encountered him previously in the narrative and are puzzled by the image. In fact, Violette has been having a dream about a person she has never met, but when she does meet the man whose image so obsesses her, she becomes his slave. She steals, and she even murders her father (the mother survives) in order to get money for him. In this film, the dream does not predict an event, but rather, the person who will be the cause of a number of incidents. The confusion we feel on the first appearance of the dream is extremely useful to Chabrol. Rather like our position watching the dream in *The Innocents*, we are unsure what to make of the image before us, a condition that occurs often in our own dreams.

This taxonomy of representative oneiric experiences in films has been designed to draw attention to the various kinds of dreams and the conventions and technical practices used to present them. Many narrative situations and applications of technical devices may evoke responses from us because of our own experience as dreamers. At certain privileged moments, we offer our own cinematic/dream screen to characters who are as confused or terrified or euphoric as we have been ourselves. The linkage between the characters and ourselves is more intense at such times because the dream screen serves as a meeting place for shared oneiric experiences.

Section 2

MANIFEST DREAM
SCREENS

W E TURN now to a detailed study of films in which a character's dream screen actually appears on the cinematic screen we are watching: Buster Keaton's *Sherlock, Jr.* (1924); Alfred Hitchcock's *Spellbound* (1945); Federico Fellini's *The Temptations of Dr. Antonio* (1961); and Ingmar Bergman's *Persona* (1966). The presence of the dream screen in these films permits us to be involved even more intensely with the consciousnesses of the dreamers than we are with those discussed in the previous section. When the dream screen manifests itself on the screen, we find ourselves linked to to a character who is watching the same screen. But, unlike similar situations in which we watch a character who is looking at projected films on screens in theaters, such as in *Uncle Josh at the Moving Picture Show* or *Les Carabiniers*, the physical screen now displays the images that are on the characters' minds. The dream screen of the characters is engrafted onto the cinematic dream screen we bring as viewers and dreamers to the experience of film.

The Dream Screens of Sherlock, Jr.

Keaton is not the first filmmaker to incorporate part of the medium as an element into the narrative text. We have already referred to Edwin S. Porter's *Uncle Josh at the Moving Picture*

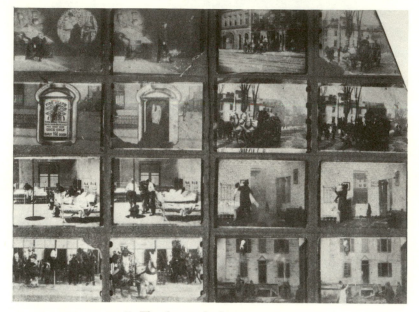

7. The fireman's dream screen.

Show and could also mention other films from the early silent period: Georges Méliès's *The Magic Lantern* (1903) and D. W. Griffith's *Those Awful Hats* (1907).[1] Keaton's self-conscious use of the screen is the most striking example of this practice in silent film because of its complexity. Uncle Josh is merely an observer at the moving picture show, but Keaton's hero, Buster, is the projectionist. Porter's character tears down the screen, but Buster enters it, through the agency of his dream.

The most important precursor of *Sherlock, Jr.* is Porter's *Life of an American Fireman* (1906). As far as I have been able to determine, this film offers us the first use of an insert that functions as a dream screen. Bruce F. Kawin's suggestion that the film reveals an early use of what he calls "mindscreen" is certainly relevant here.[2] But the film initiates an even more important practice.

It opens with a fireman, seated in a chair, asleep at the fire station. He dreams uneasily of his wife and child who he fears are in danger. Their images appear in a large circular insert cut into the screen on his left; we see the wife putting the child to bed. Porter shows the dream in the form of a filmed insert, thus imposing one image (the "seen") onto another, the field of the screen in general. This dream is interrupted by a dissolve to a shot of a hand reaching for a fire alarm, and then the film depicts the activities connected with rescuing the wife and child from their burning home. As the fireman's uneasy dream suggested, his wife and child were in danger.

It is significant that Porter seems to reveal his recognition of the relationship between film and dream as early as this in the development of the medium. I know of no other film-maker who had chosen by this time to figure the connection in this manner. Notice that the dream balloon is positioned in such a way in the frame to suggest that it "belongs" to the dreaming fireman. Porter does not cut away from a face to a scene as Griffith does a few years later to suggest that an image is the mental product of the person we have seen prior to the cut. Rather, to signal that the image is on the mind of the figure from whom it emanates, he presents it as if it were literally on a screen of the dreamer's psyche.

Sherlock, Jr. begins with the appearance of Keaton, who wears a false moustache as he sits in the audience of an empty movie theater reading a book on how to be a detective. Although he would like to be the world's greatest sleuth, he works as a projectionist and janitor in the movie house. He loves a girl (Kathryn MacGuire) who looks very much like Mary Pickford. He would like to impress her with a large box of candy that costs 4 dollars but can only afford to buy a smaller one that costs 1 dollar. To disguise its cheapness, he changes the "1" to a "4."

His rival for the affections of the girl, the Sheik (Ward Crane), enters her home and steals her father's watch, which he pawns in order to buy a genuine large box of candy that costs 3 dollars. He arrives with this and interrupts a visit of Buster and the girl; Buster has just proposed. The Sheik takes her into the parlor and draws the curtains, excluding our hero who tries unsuccessfully to get her attention.

Shortly after this, her father discovers the theft of the watch, and the Sheik slips the incriminating pawn ticket into Buster's pocket. As an amateur detective, Buster supervises a brief investigation, but without success. The Sheik then insists that the detective himself be frisked. When he is revealed to have the pawn ticket for the watch, the father orders him out of the house in disgrace, and the girl returns his engagement ring.

Buster follows the Sheik from the house to a railroad yard but learns nothing; in fact, he only succeeds in getting himself soaked with water from the tower. Dejected, he returns to the theater and begins showing *Hearts and Pearls; or, the Lounge Lizard's Lost Love*, a film about the theft of a string of pearls. He falls asleep, and out of the figure of the sleeping Buster emerges another Buster, in the form of a superimposition. I am not aware who first used a superimposition of the dreamer leaving the sleeper's body to signal the beginning of a dream. But I feel fairly secure in suggesting that Keaton is the first filmmaker to include the dreamer's *hat* in the process, for here Buster grabs for his familiar hat and takes a superimposed form of it from the wall.

Buster ceases to be a superimposition after leaving the projection booth. He goes downstairs and joins the audience to watch the action on the screen in the theater: a father, obviously the head of a wealthy household, puts a string of pearls into a small safe; a young man and woman are having what appears to be a lovers' quarrel. At various times the screen characters turn their backs to the audience; after momentary dissolves, they turn again, reincarnated as characters from the world of Buster. The girl's father and the girl are

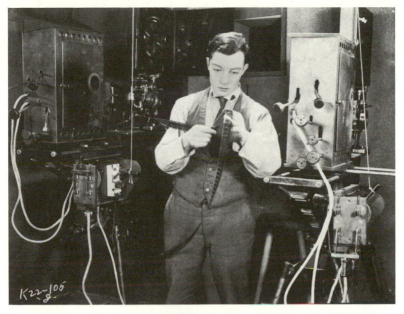

8. Buster, awake, examines the film he will project (and dream).

9. Buster about to begin his attempt to enter the screen.

now the characters in the projected film, and the Sheik is the young lover. Buster draws closer to the screen and tries to enter it. But the Sheik throws him out bodily. (At this point Keaton cuts back to the sleeping Buster who registers the imagined assault with a twitch.)

Undeterred, Buster again tries to enter the screen. This time he steps from the stage into a garden scene and sits down on a bench. But the inanimate setting is as unaccom-modating as the Sheik to this invader from the audience. The world he is trying to enter now becomes the site of a series of transformations. In one of the most brilliant montage se-quences in silent film, Keaton positions Buster in such a way that he holds the same pose from the end of each shot to the beginning of the next. Thus, when he sits on the bench and it disappears, he appears in the next shot sitting in the position he had in the former one, only now his position is awkward. This situation occurs throughout the montage sequence; Bust-er's position is never appropriate for the new setting into which he has been plunged. The garden becomes a busy street; then Buster finds himself on a mountain, then in a jungle with lions circling about him, now a desert where he dodges a train. He sits on a mound of sand, but this turns into a rock in the middle of the ocean; he dives from it but lands headfirst in a snowbank. Once extricated from that, he leans against a tree, but that disappears as he tumbles back into the original garden scene.

At this point the screen he has entered darkens. The cam-era appears to dolly in toward the stage and enter the screen completely; the proscenium arch and outline of the screen disappear; and the film within a film begins again. Now all the characters from Buster's world appear; the girl's mother is a servant, and her father's handyman a butler and ac-complice to the villainous Sheik. We witness a theft as the Sheik and butler steal the pearls we saw earlier. The father calls for Sherlock, Jr., "the world's greatest detective"—

10. The dream turns into a nightmare.

Buster, naturally, who has been transformed into a suave and debonair sleuth. Although he is initially unsuccessful in detecting the criminal, he does manage to avoid being poisoned by a drink and being blown up by a bomb hidden in a billiard ball.

The next day he and his assistant Gillett (in reality his boss at the theater) try to learn more. He tracks the Sheik to his hide-out and then escapes by assuming a clever disguise (achieved by jumping into a dress and hoop left outside the thieves' den). More incredible is another escape in which he appears to jump through Gillett (disguised as a tie saleswoman). A wild chase on a driverless motorcycle concludes with Sherlock's rescuing the girl, who has been kidnapped by the Sheik and is about to be raped by the butler. Although Sherlock gets the pearls and blows up the thieves' car, his own car ends up floating in the river. He tries unsuccessfully to make a sail out of the roof, but he and the girl begin to sink into the water. Buster wakes up in the projection booth. The girl, having discovered the real thief of her father's watch, comes into the booth to apologize. Buster watches the screen (now restored to its original characters) and draws hints from the hero on how to kiss his girl. After a dissolve in the film within the film to indicate the passage of time, the screen lovers appear with twin babies, and Buster can only scratch his head in puzzlement. The film ends.

The screen in Buster's theater figures significantly as a common meeting ground for both Buster and us in the audience in a way that anticipates a much more complex variant of a shared screen in Bergman's *Persona*. Here we and the sleeping hero seem to be watching the same screen. It is the last thing he was concentrating on before he got comfortable on his stool in the projection booth and drifted off to sleep. But, once asleep, the screen that he watches is really his dream screen, the surrogate for the original dream screen of infancy. Buster the projectionist has oneirically projected himself into this screen by means of his dream. As I suggested earlier, the field of the dream embodies the dreamer in that the screen becomes an extension of the dreamer. The union with the dream screen of infancy affords the dreamer a sense of oneness with the external world. This effect is repeated in our perception of film, as it is here with Buster's involvement with the screen. Thus, observe the complexities of this cinematic situation. First, we watch a screen on which *Sherlock, Jr.* is projected; this experience revives in us our sense of oneness with our primal dream screen. Second, we also see a screen that exists in the space of the film, *Sherlock, Jr.*, the one onto which *Hearts and Pearls* is projected. Third, eventually we observe a cinematic dream screen that belongs to Buster, the one that has become the field of his projected wishful dream to be the world's greatest detective. When the screen in Buster's theater goes dark and the proscenium and sides of the inner screen disappear, the screen in the room where we watch the film, the screen in Buster's theater and his dream screen merge; all fuse in a structure to which we are psychically bound by virtue of our experience as dreamers.

As the dream begins, there is not yet a complete bonding of Buster as dreaming perceiver and perceived, of subject and aesthetic object, a condition suggested by the superimposition. Hence the dream screen resists Buster: a character throws him out; he cannot position himself in the dream world. But as the dream continues, after the montage sequence, the camera moves in and overwhelms the screen, signaling the complete identification of Buster with his dreamed world.

Once entrenched in the dream world, bound in and to the screen, Buster becomes what he has always wanted to be, the world's greatest detective. Thus the dream affords him the fulfillment of a wish that we know guides his waking behavior and provides an example of the gratification of wishes Freud ascribes to dreams. Even more interesting, Buster incorporates the characters and events of the day as well as the problem on his mind (the theft and his disgrace) into the dream as identifiable parts of what Freud calls the "day's residue." But these enter indirectly, in the form of condensation and displacement, rather than directly. For example, during the day before he had his dream, Buster walked on top of a train car; when he lowered himself from the water tower, he was doused. In the dream, he follows the Sheik to the top of a building and is trapped on the roof. But now he simply grabs the top of an upright railroad crossing gate, swings down and drops handily into the villain's car. Thus, Keaton (not self-consciously Freudian as far as I know) offers a fine example of the way that events of the day (a prior unsuccessful attempt to escape from a high place connected with transportation) can be transformed by the dream-work and the wish to succeed.

Again, in reality, Buster missed seeing the trick by which the Sheik slips the pawn ticket into the innocent man's pocket; in the dream, Sherlock looks in a mirror and observes the Sheik and butler planting a lethal billiard ball on the gaming table and thus manages to evade their plot. Yet another example of a transformation of the day's residue pertains to the theft. Instead of being wrongly accused of stealing a watch, as Buster was, Sherlock does indeed steal one that belongs to one of the gangsters who has, he recognizes, just stolen Sherlock's watch. The false moustache Buster wore in the theater is worn by the theater manager in the dream as he serves as Sherlock's assistant.

In addition, the transformations (both Sherlock and Gillett are disguised as women), the associations of ideas (stolen watches, stolen pearls), and the tricks (Sherlock opens a vault door and walks out onto a busy street) recall for us the kinds of connections Freud makes in *Jokes and Their Relation to the Unconscious* between wit and condensation and displacement.[3]

The film's complexity extends to even more challenging possibilities. Freud attributes the ultimate source of a dream to an infantile wish. It is not clear how wanting to be a detective could be considered a necessarily infantile wish. But I am impressed by the curious infantile quality of Buster himself as a character (an aspect that by no means is a constant feature of the Keaton persona). In one sense he is like a little boy who wants to be a detective when he grows up. His lack of sophistication and of physical stature as compared to the Sheik highlight his immaturity. And, to expand on a point suggested briefly by Marsha Kinder, there seems to be something in the nature of an Oedipal rivalry set up between the childish Buster and the more mature-looking Sheik.[4]

This rivalry is most evident when the Sheik arrives with his box of chocolates. The jealous Buster is relegated to the front parlor while the rival takes his sweetheart into the back parlor to show her the larger box of chocolates that he bought for her. I think it is reasonable to suggest that the candy functions as a symbolic displacement for sexual power. And the sexual implications are emphasized when the Sheik pulls the curtain between the two parlors so that Buster cannot observe what he and the girl are doing. The angry Buster pulls open the curtains (after all, the girl has just agreed to marry Buster!) and sees the Sheik touching her.

The nature of the situation invites speculation on it as a symbolic equivalent of the primal scene.[5] The childish Buster knows "something" must be going on in the room curtained off from his eyes. His rival has a bigger box of chocolates and has taken the object of Buster's love away into another place, into a scene which can only be imagined. Thus he tries to "see" what is going on by ripping open the curtains. The Sheik sends him back to the front parlor.

Buster then decides to make his rival ridiculous by tricking him into tripping on a banana skin. He beckons the Sheik out of the inner parlor, hoping that he will slip on the skin placed strategically on the floor. But this ploy involving the phallic banana fails, and Buster himself skids on the peel, hoist, as it were, on his own petard.

Even at the end of the film when the girl has apologized, Buster still seems quite childish as he watches the screen's figures for cues on how to kiss. He appears completely baffled by the appearance of the babies. Where *did* they come from?

In the dream, Buster as Sherlock seems much more in command of his masculine powers. Not only the world's greatest detective, he also controls objects linked symbolically to the male. For example, he is a master of the cue in the billiard game. He pockets the deadly billiard ball and uses it handily to attack the gangsters later in the chase. He cleverly avoids being struck by the ax, which the butler has positioned to fall on him as he sits in a chair in the billiard room. Significantly, one should remember that the first claimant of the title "world's greatest detective" might (appropriately enough) be Oedipus. In his dream, Buster overcomes the older, more mature rival, rescues the girl from the rape of the butler, and wins her for himself.

The interpenetration of Buster's dream and the internal film draws attention to their similar ontological status in the larger film, *Sherlock, Jr.* That is, a dream, which is *like* a film, here becomes a film seen on the viewers' screens. Christian Metz's remark that as viewers of a narrative film, we "will have dreamt a little bit of the film," seems particularly applicable here to Buster as perceiver.[6] The film he projects as part of his job is transformed by his *psychic* projection of characters and events from his own experience and memory in the course of the dream. The film he watches and enters is *literally* his dream.

As I have suggested, he dreams his way into the screen; that appears to be the only way one can integrate one's reality and status as perceiver with the object perceived. Such an action involves a particular act of the imagination, an act that permits one to go out of one's self. This dreamer watches his dream. But he is in fact watching it as a projection of his own psychic action. It is what he "wants"—the fulfillment of a desire—somehow made tangible. Desire brings him to the screen; unified with it, as surrogate for the breast and as extension of himself, he dreams the world he wants.

Buster's dream suggests a model for our own experience as viewers. Not only do we dream part of the film, as Metz suggests, but we are bound into it by our own desires and natures. We want the screen, the way the infant desires the breast. As viewers, we wish to be part of the screen. Like the infant, we think/feel, "it shall be inside me"—the sentiment Freud attributes to the feeding infant.[7] As he explains in "Negation," a positive judgment is, in effect, the sign of a decision that something is good as *part* of one. A negative judgment, on the other hand, reflects an antipathy to having something as part of one; it is a rejection proceeding first from an oral basis: "I do not want to eat this."

What awakens Buster from his dream is a threat of death. He wants to repress such a possibility. For Freud, "To negate something in a judgement is, at bottom, to say: 'This is something which I should prefer to repress.' "[8] In other words, Buster wakes up when he wants to break contact with the dream screen, when he no longer wishes to partake of the images and narrative that have afforded him the gratification for his desire. We might speculate here that an element contributing to our own rejection of material on the cinematic screen is linked, psychically, to our experiences as dreamers. When we turn away from the content of a dream and attempt to wake ourselves up from unpleasant or frightening content, we are, in effect, breaking the bond that has been formed between ourselves and the surrogate for the breast. When we are displeased or terrified by the images on the screen, we also desire to turn away; we no longer want to "see" what is there. But the ultimate basis of our rejection may lie in the oral experiences of infancy: "This shall not be part of me," we are saying.

Sherlock, Jr. offers us a fascinating example of the dream screen in use by a filmmaker. The hero's interaction with the screen is in many ways a model of our own experience with the screen. To enter wholly into the events and to enjoy complete identification with the characters requires the kind of imaginative activity that attends the state of dreaming. The hero's dream is a film, made part of him narratively and psychically. He wakes up when the dream/film ceases to please. In effect, he rejects the breast and the oneiric world when it no longer satisfies his desire.

The Interpretation of J.B.'s Dream in Spellbound

Alfred Hitchcock has described *Spellbound* as "just another manhunt story wrapped up in pseudo-psychoanalysis."[9] Some of the critics seem to agree. For example, Eric Rohmer and Claude Chabrol note the confessional aspects of psychoanalysis (a relevant aspect of their interpretation of the "Catholic" Hitchcock) and conclude: "The scenario . . . was designed to show the protective and maternal role of woman considered as guardian angel. The plot is certainly a model of logic, but its didactic nature is too obvious."[10] William F. Van Wirt observes that the film actually undercuts the psychoanalytic content: "*Spellbound* is a subtle put-down of psychoanalysis in that it insists on proving scientifically what can be guessed with common sense all along."[11] More, the film appears to be a "a dead-end on Freudian theory, a pretext for Hitchcock's own compositional psychoanalysis."[12]

Raymond Durgnat thinks the film is more complex. It is true that some parts are obvious: "Murchison is the evil father-figure, angry at being supplanted, and Constance's analyst . . . is the kindly father-figure, willing to yield the mother-figure to the son." Still, the various visual connections that Hitchcock develops in the film are impressive: "That sort of associative visual thinking certainly isn't pseudo-psychoanalysis, and would be looked upon as pretty sophisticated as part of a critical interpretation of a film."[13] Royal S. Brown offers a Jungian rather than Freudian reading of the film, seeing Constance as the central figure in a complex psychodrama: "In the course of her adventures as a Freudian sleuth, [she] passes through all the stages outlined by Jung and his disciples for the so-called 'process of individuation.' "[14] *Spellbound* is, in his view, "consciously Freudian and unconsciously Jungian."[15]

The particularly fine psychoanalytic interpretations of the film by Van Wirt and Brown have not addressed what I believe is an important dimension of the narrative: the occurrence of the dream screen at a crucial point in the working out of the psychoanalytic cure of the hero. It is remarkable that Lewin first proposed the theory of the dream screen in 1946; thus he must have been formulating it at around the time the film appeared. My discussion will address the structure of the film, and then concentrate on the significance of the dream screen.

As many have observed, *Spellbound* and the novel on which it is based, *The House of Dr. Edwardes*, use the same narrative premise as *The Cabinet of Dr. Caligari*: a madman is in charge of an asylum. In *Spellbound*, Dr. Murchison (Leo G. Carroll) directs Green Manors, a psychiatric hospital in Vermont. Having had a nervous collapse himself, he is being forced to relinquish his command. His successor, "Anthony Edwardes" (Gregory Peck), arrives at Green Manors, but the new director also seems to be mentally ill; he displays erratic behavior and responds strangely to parallel lines and to the color white. He is soon revealed to be an imposter, John Ballyntine, or J.B. The real Dr. Edwardes is missing. Constance Petersen (Ingrid Bergman), a psychiatrist at Green Manors, has fallen in love with J.B.; after discovering that he is an amnesiac who believes he is responsible for Edwardes's death, she sets out to help him regain his memory.

First she follows him to New York City where he has fled after being exposed as a fraud. Then she takes him to the home of her mentor, Dr. Brulov (Michael Chekhov). The morning after their arrival, J.B. relates a dream he has had just before awakening. The dream itself defies effective prose description. Designed by Salvador Dali, it occurs in a Surrealist sequence in which we see huge eyes painted on a

11. The world of J.B.'s dream.

curtain, a scantily clad girl working in a gambling house, giant scissors cutting drapes, a masked man who quarrels with J.B.'s card partner and later drops a wheel, a bearded man who turns up again in the dream as he falls off the top of a roof, and giant wings that seem to be pursuing J.B. Those who have not seen the film might try imagining what Dali's "The Persistence of Memory" would look like if it were presented as a film.

As a result of their joint analysis of J.B.'s dream, Constance and J.B. go to the Gabriel Valley ski resort where he realizes that his amnesia and sense of guilt over Edwardes's death are rooted partly in a childhood trauma (he accidentally killed his brother). The revelation about the earlier accident and its connection to his present amnesia occurs when Constance and J.B. go skiing. As they descend the slope, the downward motion revives in J.B.'s memory the accident that caused his brother's death: he was sliding down a stone balustrade outside an apartment and, upon reaching the bottom of the structure, pushed his brother onto an iron spike fence, thus impaling him. Hitchcock presents this memory in a rapid and chilling montage sequence that permits us to see the trauma that has been buried in J.B.'s memory. Even though innocent of any crime, he is arrested for Edwardes's murder and imprisoned.

Constance, believing that J.B. is innocent, returns to Green Manors. A chance remark by Dr. Murchison alerts her to the fact that he must be the murderer; he had earlier claimed never to have seen Edwardes, but now mentions that he indeed knew him. Troubled by this remark, Constance visits Murchison's room under the pretext of enlisting his aid in interpreting J.B.'s dream. The two discuss the meaning of the eyes (the guards at Green Manor), "21," and the quarrel. Constance reveals that she knows Murchison was the figure fighting with Edwardes at the "21" Club, a scene witnessed by J.B. The fall of the man from the roof was actually Edwardes's collapse when Murchison shot him. Her explanation of the "wheel" occurs as Murchison reaches in his desk for the object signified, the revolver he used to kill Edwardes. Although he threatens to shoot Constance, she defies him and leaves the room. Realizing he is caught, Murchison turns the revolver on himself and commits suicide. Thus Constance has literally played the part of detective on two levels: as psychoanalyst, she unearths the true nature of her patient and lover, J.B.; as investigator, she exposes the real personality of Murchison.

The psychoanalytic ethos underlying the narrative is plainly (and naively) Freudian. For example, Constance defends her

actions to Brulov by exclaiming: "You yourself taught me
what Freud says . . . that a man cannot do anything in amnesia
that his real character wouldn't have done."[16] Again, in dealing with Mr. Garmes, a patient in the hospital who thinks he
killed his father, Constance tells him: "People often feel guilty
over something they never did. It usually goes back to their
childhood. A child often wishes something terrible would
happen to someone. And if something does happen to that
person the child believes he has caused it. And he grows up
with a guilt complex—over a sin that was only a child's bad
dream."[17]

A much more overt use of ideas adapted from *The Interpretation of Dreams* occurs in connection with the dream
sequence. To counter J.B.'s skepticism about psychoanalysis
("That Freud stuff is a lot of hooey"), Brulov says: "I explain
to you about dreams so you don't think it is hooey. The secrets
of who you are and what has made you run away from yourself—
all these secrets are buried in your brain." The amnesiac
tries to avoid the secrets: "Now here is where dreams come
in. . . . They tell you what you are trying to hide. But they
tell it to you all mixed up like pieces of a puzzle that don't
fit. The problem of the analyst is to examine this puzzle and
put the pieces together in the right place—and find out what
the devil you are trying to say to yourself."[18] Brulov might
as well be using Freud's analogy of the dream as a rebus
here, referring as he does to the dream as "puzzle." And
when J.B. mentions an attractive, scantily clad girl in his
dream, Brulov knows J.B. must have had Constance in mind:
"This is plain, ordinary wishful dreaming."[19]

The actual analysis of the dream occurs in two parts: first,
in Brulov's home and then later at Green Manors when Constance discusses it with Murchison. In the first attempt to
figure out the puzzle, she and Brulov determine that Constance is the girl, and that the bearded man must be Dr.
Edwardes, who took J.B. skiing for therapy. It seems there

12. Brulov and Constance try to assist J.B.

was an accident at Gabriel (an association with the giant wings) Valley (the slopes). J.B.'s violent reaction to the sled tracks outside the window just after he relates the dream provides a clue to his strange behavior throughout the narrative to parallel lines and to white; the tracks he so fears are connected with the marks of skis. But much of the dream remains obscure. As we have seen, other elements in it become clear only later as Constance and Murchison examine it.

I believe our examination of the circumstances preceding the dream will reveal that Hitchcock has used what Lewin would call a blank dream screen to signal the beginning of J.B.'s dreaming sleep. We do not see the dream "in progress"; in fact, we do not really know that J.B. had a dream at all until after its occurrence. But, as we reflect on the way Hitchcock presents J.B.'s loss of contact with reality, we see the relevance and applicability of Lewin's theory.

The events that lead to J.B.'s entrance into the dreaming world occur in an extremely tense scene. J.B. wakes up in the room he shares (discreetly) with Constance and goes into the bathroom. He tries to shave but is unable to because the bathroom is filled with white objects, which only exacerbate his repressed associations with snow and Edwardes's death. Razor in hand, he goes back to the bedroom where Constance is sleeping beneath a chenille coverlet that has the upsetting linear pattern on it. Dazed, J.B. walks downstairs still carrying the razor, a fact emphasized by Hitchcock's framing with low-angle shots. At the bottom of the stairs he meets Brulov who, claiming he has been unable to sleep, offers J.B. some milk, which he accepts.

Hitchcock shoots the conversation from behind J.B. When Brulov returns from the kitchen with the glass of milk, a subjective point-of-view shot is used to present the approach of the glass to J.B.'s mouth. As he "drinks" from the glass, the milk floods the space of the screen and we see the famous "white-out"—a white screen made whiter still with milk offered by Brulov. This "white-out" can be seen as the dream screen on which J.B.'s dream will be projected, and then recovered in the narrative by us. Lewin describes the dream screen as "the surface on to which a dream appears to be projected. It is the blank background . . . and the visually perceived action in ordinary manifest dream contents takes place on it or before it."[20] The screen "is sleep itself; it is not only the breast but is as well that content of sleep or the dream which fulfils the wish to sleep. . . . The blank dream screen is the copy of primary infantile sleep."[21]

The effective cause of the white image, J.B.'s dream screen, is the milk which *literally* puts him to sleep, since it contains a bromide. It is offered by Brulov, a surrogate parent. And the glass itself which contains the milk is part of the structure of elements functioning as the breast. Lewin's comments are particularly relevant here: "The 'breast' refers to perceptions in the infant: it is whatever the infant experiences at the lips or mouth. . . . [T]he dream screen . . . sometimes appears as a glass. . . ."[22]

Notice that the "white-out" figures in a complex image designed to reproduce what Spitz would call a coenesthetic experience. The white is supposed to signify the milk as it is ingested, thus combining taste, vision, and smell. J.B. drinks a substance that, from our perspective behind the subjective camera, overwhelms him and what he/we can see. In effect, then, the union of drinker and milk appears to be a bonding of subject and object; they are one, and, as a result, involve *us* in the imitation of the coenesthetic experience.

It is interesting to observe how Hitchcock's mise-en-scène and the dialogue appear to blend appropriately with the issue of nurturing. After the "white-out," Hitchcock dissolves to a shot of Constance waking up the next morning. She goes downstairs and discovers Brulov slumped in a chair. We are relieved to learn that he has not been killed by the crazed J.B. but is only sleeping. When her mentor awakens, he and Constance observe J.B. who is sleeping on a couch in the living room.

The manner in which Hitchcock shoots the three characters is significant. We have two shots of the sleeping J.B., one primarily from Constance's angle, and another in which Hitchcock carefully frames Brulov and Constance standing over the couch. The shot establishes them as attentive "parents" watching over their troubled, sleeping "child."

This last shot supports a number of references to parenting that occur elsewhere in the dialogue. For example, Murchison says earlier that he plans to stay around Green Manors: "I shall hover around for a while—like an old mother hen—at least until Dr. Edwardes is firmly on the nest."[23] Dr. Fleurot, jealous of the attention Constance pays to J.B., says: "I detected the outcroppings of a mother instinct toward Dr. Edwardes."[24] As Brulov and Constance interpret J.B.'s dream, Brulov cautions her: "You are not his mama. You are an analyst. Leave him alone. He will come out of this himself."[25] And Brulov offers to serve J.B. as a father: "Don't fight me. I am going to help you. . . . I am going to be your father figure."[26]

The counterpart to the "white-out" appears at the end of the film when we see the revolver which Murchison points at himself. Hitchcock actually built a large model of a gun and hand so that the image would appear to be greatly enlarged. In fact, at the point of Murchison's suicide, Hitchcock wanted the screen to turn red for a moment in this otherwise black-and-white film. None of the prints I have seen, including that at the Library of Congress, contains this momentary burst of color or "red-out." Even considering just the milk and gun shots alone, though, one sees a well-balanced antithesis in regard to the issue of nurturing. The "good" father figure, Brulov, offers the milk which will lead to J.B.'s sleep and dream—a major key to unravelling the mystery. The ultimate revelations buried in the dream, once interpreted, reveal that Murchison, the "mother hen" is actually a "bad" father.

It is true that by offering J.B. the drugged milk, Brulov succeeds in unmanning him in a sense; that is, the doctor wants to knock him out in order to retrieve the threatening razor. But there is no suggestion of an Oedipal struggle between the two men. Brulov seems to be beyond sexual desire; all he wants is a good cup of coffee. As far as he is concerned, "Any husband of Constance is a husband of mine."[27]

The Good Breast and the Bad Breast in The Temptations of Dr. Antonio

Recently Federico Fellini has described his conception of cinema in terms that bear significantly on our analysis of the dream screen in his *The Temptations of Dr. Antonio*: "I think the cinema is a woman by virtue of its ritualistic nature. The uterus which is the theatre, the fetal darkness, the apparitions—all create a projected relationship, we project ourselves onto it, we become involved in a series of vicarious transpositions, and we make the screen assume the character of what we expect of it, just as we do with women, upon whom we impose ourselves. Woman being a series of projections invented by man. In history, she became our dream image."[28] In this short film, his contribution to the Carlo Ponti production of *Boccaccio 70* (1961), Fellini pictures this relationship in a comic fashion by examining an individual, Dr. Mazzuolo (Peppino de Filippo), who attempts to repress his desire for woman and for cinema.

The film begins with a child who represents Cupid identifying Dr. Mazzuolo as an enemy to love. Cupid thwarts his opponent by sending him into an hallucinatory dream state designed to punish the doctor for his prudish and repressive attitudes toward love. In this state, Mazzuolo finds himself interacting with Anita Ekberg, whose picture has been plastered on a huge billboard outside his apartment.

As the film begins, we hear a childish voice identifying himself as the god of love; he says, "Only one man is against me." Then we meet his enemy, Dr. Mazzuolo, on his apparently daily rounds of prudishness. First, he flashes his car's spotlight on automobiles parked in a lovers lane. Next he interrupts the performance of scantily clad chorus girls in a theater and pulls the curtain across the stage.

Then Cupid provides a flashback (with a grainy film clip that looks like a home movie) of an outdoor luncheon given the previous summer. When a woman wearing a revealing gown sits at a table near the doctor and other dignitaries, he walks over and covers her shoulders and bosom with a napkin, slaps her, and then drives her away. His campaign for female purity continues as he rips down pinup magazines from a newsstand.

Following this, we find him presenting awards and offering

moral encouragement to Boy Scouts. He begins to tell them about an incident in his youth when he resisted temptations of the flesh but is interrupted by construction vehicles and workmen who are erecting an immense billboard. The men assemble it in stages, and, when completed, it reveals an enormous picture of Anita Ekberg lying seductively and holding a glass of milk near her bosom as she encourages viewers to "drink more milk." The billboard has about the same dimensions as a CinemaScope screen. One of Ekberg's most recent appearances in film had been in Fellini's widescreen *La Dolce Vita* (1959).

The doctor is outraged by the presence of what seems to him a lascivious poster. Claiming he is defending the family, he attempts to have the billboard removed, first by imploring the workmen and then some bureaucrats. He tells the latter that the billboard gives "offense to the most sacred activity of nursing." He tries unsuccessfully to enlist the Church in his campaign. In desperation he hurls ink bottles at the billboard. The only response to his complaints is a makeshift operation; workmen slap papers over the billboard and cover Ekberg's figure and face.

Mazzuolo appears to be getting increasingly distraught. For example, one morning when he is shaving he thinks he sees the reflection in the mirror of a black-gloved hand holding a glass of milk. Later, one evening when he is entertaining friends at a small gathering, he imagines he sees Ekberg lying on his desk. After the guests leave, he sits wearily and tells himself that he is bothered by overwork. Stepping to the window, he sees that the rain which had begun during his party is washing away the paper covering Ekberg, thus effecting a kind of striptease. She seems to be making faces at him. He calls his sister and maid to the window, but they see only the original picture.

Grabbing his umbrella, he goes out to explore and finds himself in conversation with Ekberg. Although he demands that she leave, his order meets with laughter. After observing a four-foot-high milk glass on the ground, he discovers that Ekberg has left the poster. The gauzy hem of her gown covers Mazzuolo and he moves helplessly around her legs. She asks, "Why are you afraid of me, Antonio?" and rolls on the grass as Mazzuolo cowers behind his umbrella.

Moving away from the now empty billboard, they walk through the streets of Rome. Ekberg claims she wants to have a talk with him and touch him. Then she picks him up and holds him at her breast, an image which, as John Stubbs suggests, is reminiscent of Gulliver in the land of the Brobdingnagians.[29] As she threatens to eat him, Fellini pictures her face and mouth with enormous close-ups. Mazzuolo screams and moves like an enraged infant after she has put him on her breast. After she sings a lullaby he appears to relax somewhat and moves his hands on her breast, sighing, "Mama, Mamma, I loved you so."

After she puts him down, she assumes normal human proportions and asks him for a kiss. Mazzuolo is clearly attracted to her but resists. He says: "I would like to think there's something still good in you. I might be able to lift you out of this iniquity. You're too beautiful to be entirely bad." Succumbing to his repressed feelings, he takes a strand of her flowing blond hair in his mouth and asks her to stay with him. Immediately repulsed by his action, he reverts to his earlier hostile behavior. In response, she threatens to take off her clothes.

To protect the purity of the audience, he tries to hide this sight from the viewers and uses articles of her clothing to block the camera. He even takes off some of his own clothes for this purpose. Suddenly, he too is transformed; instead of appearing in his underwear, he now stands in armor with a lance. His image complements the painting we have seen in his apartment of St. George attacking the dragon. He throws

13. The greatest test of will.

the weapon at her and the next shot shows the lance hitting Ekberg's chest on the picture displayed on the billboard.

Mazzuolo then appears in daylight sitting on the top edge of the billboard in his underwear. Sometime during the night he must have climbed up on the sign as he dreamed. As puzzled onlookers gape, the police come and take him away in an ambulance. As he lies on the stretcher, the crazed Mazzuolo whispers, "Anita." Riding on top of the ambulance is Cupid who giggles triumphantly and sticks out a playful tongue at the audience. Clearly, Cupid has engineered Mazzuolo into a dream state in a way that blurs the distinction between reality and illusion for the now hopelessly befuddled man.

It is true that we do not actually see Mazzuolo fall asleep though he appears tired after the party. And his address to the audience might seem to break the texture of the dream mode in an unfortunate manner. In addition, it might be more appropriate to include the film in the retroactive mode, for like *Fireworks* and *City of Women*, special examples belonging to that category, the events in *Dr. Antonio* are of a sufficiently fantastic nature that we think, "This must be a dream," *before* the actual revelation occurs that "it was only a dream." But there is a distinction worth noting that justifies discussing it here rather than later. The fantastic events in *Dr. Antonio*, such as the hallucinations and Ekberg's coming to life, are *immediately* recognized by us as the products of his mind. In contrast, as we shall see, we watch the beginning scenes of *Fireworks* and *City of Women* with some degree of belief in the actuality of the events, however strange they might appear to be.

The main reason for including the film in its present location, though, has to do with my hypothesis about the dream screen. The rigid Mazzuolo refuses to admit that desire has value for its own sake. Ekberg and the sexuality she represents are anathema to him. Nonetheless, he is drawn to her image and what it signifies. Fellini presents this complex attraction by involving Mazzuolo with a "screen"—the billboard on which Ekberg lies as if she had been photographed for a still from a widescreen film. In his dream, he interacts with the figure on the billboard which becomes his dream screen, the field on which his oneiric desires are projected.

He believes he should champion rigid moral values, but one of the greatest, the importance of the pure mother and her milk, seems to him to have been corrupted by using a sex symbol to advertise. He is afraid of the combination of sex and milk pictured on the poster because it suggests that they exist together in human affairs. There is more to male-female relationships than merely creating and nurturing, but not for Mazzuolo—at least consciously. Fellini has depicted the paradoxical longings in the doctor most effectively by confronting him with an image that includes the only two dimensions of female sexuality Mazzuolo can imagine: woman as mother or as whore.

In his dream, the repressed sexual desire for woman emerges. Even though he continues to uphold his values and attempts to send her away, he displays his longing for her at the breast and again when he caresses her hair. His physical attack on her with the lance seems to be a disguised way of representing his desire to penetrate the image sexually.

It may be appropriate to consider here what Melanie Klein describes as the infant's relation to the mother's good breast and bad breast. She argues that after the infant's early attachment to the nurturing breast, a source of pleasure, there follows a stage of destructive behavior, a form of oral sadism, which is also pleasurable.[30] The infant forms what she calls "object relations" with the breast: "The infant projects his love impulses and attributes them to the gratifying (good) breast, just as he projects his destructive impulses outwards and attributes them to the frustrating (bad) breast. Simultaneously, by introjection, a good breast and a bad breast are established inside. Thus the picture of the object, external and internalized, is distorted in the infant's mind by his phantasies, which are bound up with the projection of his impulses on to the object. The good breast—external and internal—becomes the prototype of all helpful and gratifying objects, the bad breast the prototype of all external and internal persecutory objects."[31]

Mazzuolo is not an infant, although he acts like one at Ekberg's breast. But he is not an adult either, in the sense of having entered into a stage where he can deal with all the elements that constitute sexual maturity. Ekberg seems to recognize this as she taunts and chases him.

From our standpoint, it is fascinating to observe Fellini choosing to depict Mazzuolo's repressive sexual desires in connection with the screen (the billboard); with film (the sexpot star); with sadistic behavior toward the breast (the lance lands in the spot where the figure's heart would be); and with aggressive actions toward the entire body of the woman (the lance as phallic symbol).

This distorted being has never established a satisfactory relationship with women. His attack on the screen seems to be his way of fighting the unconscious desire which has begun to work its way out in his dreams: he wants to see a voluptuous woman take off her clothes. Consciously he can accept the glass of milk and the lettering, "Drink more milk," which can be viewed as suggesting the good breast. But he cannot admit to the attraction that the woman who offers the milk holds for him and thus projects his anger and frustration against the poster, which now functions as the bad breast for him. Awake, he attempts to injure the picture with ink while he castigates it; the same physical and oral aggression occurs in the dream, but now he can speak to the image and drive a lance through its heart.

The film presents the story of a frustrated man who has never matured. In contrast to Fellini, for whom "cinema is a woman," the "woman" in "cinema" is unacceptable to Mazzuolo. He wants to hide the billboard (the screen) from public view. But the screen and its contents which he would repress are, so the narrative shows, the images that lie buried in his mind and that he is forced to confront in the dream caused by Cupid. His treatment of the screen, which I have argued is a surrogate for the mother's breast, is reminiscent of Klein's description of the behavior of infants toward the mother's breast. An infant can enjoy a degree of pleasure from attacking the breast that first sustained (mother's milk) and now repulses it (denial of milk). Mazzuolo attacks the screen, the site of his dream screen and also a surrogate for the breast, with equally divided behavior.

Like Buster, in *Sherlock, Jr.*, the doctor dreams his way into the screen; like J.B. in *Spellbound*, his dream screen is represented initially by a surrogate, the billboard in the form of a screen. But unlike both, the encounter with his unconscious desires has driven him mad.[32]

The Surface of Reality: Screen as Mirror in Persona

In *Sherlock, Jr.*, the physical screen in Buster's theater becomes the field of his dream; his interaction with the screen offers us a model of our own experience as viewers. In *Spellbound*, Hitchcock employs a technique, the "white-out," to provide an imitation of J.B.'s experience as he ingests milk from the father/mother figure and is overwhelmed by sleep. The shooting style of the sequence involves us partly in his coenesthetic experience, since we are also swept over by the white screen. Retroactively, then, we realize that the rendering of the shot has made us parties to his blank dream screen. In *The Temptations of Dr. Antonio*, a billboard becomes the dream screen for the crazed hero. In all these films, the characters' dream screens are linked to the cinematic dream screen that we provide as watchers of the physical screen in the theater.

In *Persona*, something different occurs. The screen constitutes a complex physical and psychic structure permitting a unique kind of interaction between viewers, characters, and artist. Bergman addresses us as beings implicated in *his* dream, the film, and hence breaks down the ultimate physical and psychic barrier between us and his narrative; the work now becomes partly *our* dream as well.

Bergman considers all his films dreams and says they mirror the disturbing modern world: "The reality we experience today is in fact as absurd, as horrible, and as obtrusive as our dreams. We are as defenseless before it as we are in our dreams. And one is strongly aware, I think, that there are no boundaries between dream and reality today."[33] This film, in particular, draws us into Bergman's dark vision of reality.

Many critics have discussed the self-reflexivity of *Persona* and noted that it is a film about filmmaking. Although self-reflexivity in some artists can simply be self-regarding or needlessly pretentious, Bergman integrates references to the medium and to his craft brilliantly into the narrative of Alma (Bibi Andersson) and Elisabet (Liv Ullmann). The interpenetration of their psyches and mutual absorption of each other's Jungian "shadows" defy ordinary means of representation; these can only be manifested in film, where the very nature of the medium is used to imitate the interaction of their shadows. That is, the only way Bergman could have told his story was in film. It is not simply that as an *auteur*, he "writes in film," to use Jacques Rivette's phrase. Rather, he "projects" his film onto the dream screen we share with him.

The film has nothing like a traditional, linear plot. Rather, its structure is similar to that of a poem in which we observe shifting relationships: unity giving way to tension; patterns emerging and dissolving; images appearing and transforming. Rather than talk of plot, we must consider the *shape* of the film. The overall design of *Persona* might be compared to a welter of cells seen under a microscope. As we observe, a form emerges before our eye, constantly seething, turning in on itself, fusing and splitting. Eventually, this mass breaks into pieces, and the process begins again.

The film opens with a rapid montage of images referring to various aspects of reality: the nature of the apparatus, such as carbon arcs and film leader; Bergman's own *oeuvre*, such as the silent film sequence he used in *Prison* in which a "devil" chases a man, and allusive shots of a spider (*Through a Glass Darkly*); the natural world, such as the snow and landscapes; and the world of human beings, such as the hands of a child, and, eventually, the corpses in the morgue, including a little boy's. These images begin the poem. Bergman says of these shots of bodies in the morgue: "It's just my poetry. . . . I felt like that little boy. I was lying there [in the hospital], half dead, and suddenly I started to think of two faces, two intermingled faces, and that was the beginning, the place where it started."[34] Elsewhere Bergman avers his aim was to create poetry: "I had it in my head to make a poem, not in words but in images, about the situation in which *Persona* had originated."[35] Bergman's comment that he wished to use images rather than words for his poem reminds one of Pier Paolo Pasolini's argument in "The Cinema of Poetry" that "an image is more dreamlike than a word. Your dreams are cinematographic dreams. They are not literary dreams."[36]

Marsha Kinder has offered a stunning interpretation of this opening sequence as an analogue for the passage of the dreamer through the various stages of sleep. Thus, the progression from the first stage (shots of the cinematic apparatus) would represent the condition of the dreamer before the actual onset of sleep. As the prologue continues, the images represent equivalents of mentation occurring as the dreamer moves closer into the rapid eye movement phase of sleep. In stage 1, NREM sleep, the dreamer, Bergman, is still partly awake; consequently, his thoughts would be directed at the outside world, represented by the medium. The illusion of the cartoon suits the entrance into stage 2, as the dreamer moves into a deeper sleep. The richer, more symbolic imagery of the next part of the prologue seems appropriate for stage 3; this presents allusions to his films and to mythology. The final stage of NREM sleep preceding the actual burst of eye movements is linked with the morgue. The opening section has led us "from the external medium to the interior of Bergman's brain."[37]

At this point we encounter the corpses and a little boy. The latter lies on a slab, covered by a sheet, and appears dead. The little boy who was dead, the shadow figure Bergman imagines as his own persona in the film, awakens from his

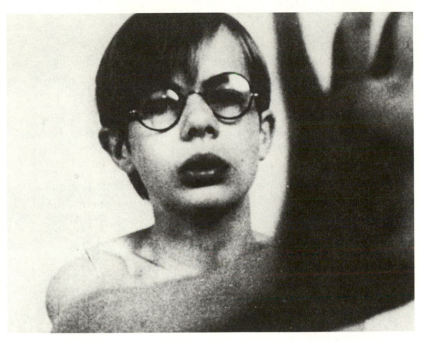

14. The little boy reaches out to the dream screen and to us.

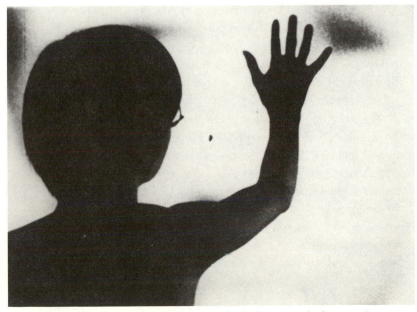

15. We and our mirror image, the little boy, watch the merging faces.

deathlike sleep in the morgue, disturbed by the ringing of a phone. He tries to return to sleep, but gives up, then picks up a book (the one, it is often noted, he was reading in *The Silence*). But he turns away from it; something has drawn his attention. He looks at us and reaches out in our direction with his hand toward the screen we share in common. He seems to be trying to touch us, the beings on the other side of the screen. A reverse shot reveals that he is watching huge faces projected on the wall. These faces merge into one another. He stares at them and moves his hand around the contours of the shifting faces which gradually come into clearer focus. We discover that he has been reaching for the faces on the screen he can see in the morgue, a screen that has, as it were, been wrested from us during the reverse shot. Now, positioned behind him in the morgue, we watch the screen with the faces, the cinematic dream screen that belonged to us prior to the appearance of the faces.

It is as if the boy's glance and movement toward us initially connect us as mirror images. Now, as he watches, we also (the beings implied by his first glance) duplicate his perceptual activity. As Susan Sontag has observed, "The surface he touches suggests a movie screen, but also a portrait and a mirror."[38] We are each other's mirror images—both involved literally and metaphorically in grasping or, to use Sontag's word, caressing the images on the screen.

The hand on the wall/screen/breast unites the boy with the dreaming ego of the viewer. We are linked, as we and our mirror image watch the merging faces. These come to us as a shifting composite image, establishing paradigmatically the theme of doubling and transformation that controls the film. Bergman asks us to identify with him and with his attempt to grasp the images. With him, we are hoping for contact with the face and the breast, the primal metonymic structure which is embodied in the screen. In other words, our viewing cannot be passive; we must struggle along with the artist to reach into the space of the receptacle.

In accordance with her suggestion about the stages of sleep, Kinder considers the credit sequence with its barrage of flashing titles and interspersed images "a strong analogue for the first onset of rapid eye movements that introduce the primary images that the narrative REM dream will develop."[39] Thierry Kuntzel, considering the credits in *The Most Dangerous Game*, offers a comment applicable to *Persona*: "The film is not spread out flat; it is only apparently successive. It has its own internal dynamics, its own forces of generation, compression and relaxation. The credits [sequence] . . . is the matrix of all the subsequent narrative representations and sequences."[40]

The narrative itself then begins with a blank screen—another wall such as the one we saw in the morgue. A doorway appears to be etched onto this blank screen, and Alma, a nurse, enters through it. She has been assigned the task of tending Elisabet Vogler, an actress who has withdrawn into total silence. Initially diffident about the job, Alma becomes more assured. The women go to the summer home of Elisabet's psychiatrist where they interact well. Alma talks about her life and plans for a family; she also describes an orgy she participated in with a young woman and two boys. Elisabet still does not talk; she only listens.

One night Alma appears to have a dream in which she is visited by Elisabet. The latter enters her room, embraces her, and brushes her hair. The event seems so real to Alma that she asks Elisabet the next day if it happened, but Elisabet shakes her head, denying she had come into the room.

Their happy relationship is disturbed when Alma reads an unsealed letter Elisabet has written in which she describes her nurse in a patronizing, mildly contemptuous manner. To revenge her injured pride, Alma purposely leaves a piece of glass where Elisabet will step on it. When we hear her cry of pain, the film ruptures, and the narrative breaks down; the hole in the film figures the gap in their relationship. Gradually the film appears to readjust, slowly returning to an image in focus of Elisabet.

From this point, tension builds steadily between them. Alma tries unsuccessfully to goad her companion into speech. Instead, physical violence ensues, leaving Alma with a bloody nose. When she threatens Elisabet with a pot of boiling water, she does elicit the word "Don't!" from her, but that is all. Earlier, after her recitation of the orgy when the two sit drinking at the kitchen table, Alma thinks she hears Elisabet talk, but it is not clear if, in fact, she has spoken.

Now the film becomes even less naturalistic, and we seem to be entering a world in which we are unsure of whose mind we inhabit, if any. Bruce F. Kawin's discussion of the mind-screen suggests that our very inability to identify where we "are" in the diegesis reinforces our sense of being caught in a dreamlike world.[41] We lose any points of reference that might anchor us in reality and give us a perspective through which to view the action.

In contrast to the increasingly diffused rendering of the general narrative, Bergman presents an extremely detailed examination of a particular photographic reality when Elisabet finds a picture of a group of obviously doomed victims of the Nazis. She pays special attention to the figure of a little boy. Through a montage sequence of thirteen shots, Bergman probes the photograph, beginning and ending the sequence with visual attention to the boy. The scene fixed in the photo-graphic record offers another example of horror such as Elis-abet had watched earlier in the film when she observed the self-immolation of a Vietnamese monk. In the television re-port of this event, we watch the monk move and fall. Now, Bergman's active cutting within the space of the photograph creates a sense of movement within the static image.

Moreover, his camera scans the surface and space of the

16. Bergman attempts to penetrate the photographic image of the doomed victim.

photographic reality in much the same way that earlier we and the boy surveyed the merging figures on the screen. That is, Bergman seems to be grasping with his camera and employing montage in a way that offers an equivalent of what his surrogate, the little boy, did earlier as he, too, tried to penetrate the photographic images before him on the screen.

Significantly, the little boy in the photograph is the second child we have seen with an outstretched hand, the first being the little boy who had died, Bergman himself in the prologue. The little boy in the photograph appears to look out at Elisabet and stare at us as well. She has torn up a photograph of her son, a child whom she did not want to have and whom she now avoids. Bergman has also torn into a photograph: the image of Alma which he destroys after Elisabet cuts her foot on the piece of glass left there by Alma to injure her.

There are a number of victims in the film, all touched in one way or another by violence: the children, the monk, Alma as image and Alma as object of Elisabet's attack. It may be that Bergman is projecting a conception of the artistic process in these images of violence. The work of art resists, must be thrown away, reworked; sometimes it simply destroys itself, uncontrollable. Bergman seeks visual equivalents, objective correlatives for the complex relationships existing between artist, aesthetic creation, and perceiver. These equivalents inhere in the narrative of Alma and Elisabet. They do not overwhelm the story of the women in a way that makes of it a mere vehicle for a complex allegory about art. Rather, the issues figured in their relationship—love, domination, betrayal—are presented as one and the same as those that trouble the artist and audience. The intractable forces that define and inhibit unity in human relationships are the subject of the artist. But, like the events in a dream, they elude attempts at organization. As we try to make sense of the events in a dream and to build in the kind of logical connections which Freud includes under the operations of the secondary revision, inevitably we distort and adjust them to a conception that is not "there" in the narrative and psychic space of the relationships presented in the dream.

Alma's dream of Mr. Vogler offers an example of this frustrating state of things. Alma appears to hear Elisabet's name being called, rises from her bed, and goes out where she meets Elisabet's husband. He is wearing dark glasses. Is he blind? He thinks this woman is his wife and makes love to her, asking if she is satisfied. Elisabet appears and watches their lovemaking with an inscrutable expression. Perhaps she is again enjoying being a voyeur, as she did when she listened to Alma's confession of the orgy earlier in the film. Alma cannot stand the duplicity and cries, "I am not Elisabet."

Sexual satisfaction comes to her as a result of playing a role, but she rejects the assumed mask.

Elisabet denied one kind of role-playing already when she stopped acting parts on the stage. The psychiatrist realizes why Elisabet withdrew from her part as Electra and tells her: "I do understand, you know. The hopeless dream of *being*. Not doing, just being. Aware and watchful every second. And at the same time the abyss between what you are for others and what you are for yourself. The feeling of dizziness and the continual burning need to be unmasked. At last to be seen through, reduced, perhaps extinguished. Every tone of voice a lie, an act of treason. Every gesture false. Every smile a grimace. The role of wife, the role of friend, the roles of mother and mistress, which is worst?"[42]

The theme of role-playing becomes the central message of Alma's repeated monologues as she castigates Elisabet. The two sit across from one another at a table. Bergman shoots the first recitation of the monologue with his camera pointed in Elisabet's direction; during the second version, he shifts and points the camera in Alma's direction. The monologue begins with a reference to Elisabet's child. The picture which she tore in half earlier lies on the table between them, the two parts positioned closely to give the illusion of the complete image. Alma attacks Elisabet brutally by explaining how Elisabet decided to have a child and then had misgivings about bearing it; the actress is disgusted by her son and his love for her.

As others have noted, Alma's accusations about Elisabet's inadequacies and hypocrisy can be seen in relation to her own sense of guilt. As a result of the orgy in which she participated, she became pregnant and had had an abortion. In attacking the actress for having a son she did not want, Alma seems to be projecting her own feelings of guilt and shame by casting onto Elisabet what Carl G. Jung calls the shadow. The shadow, as he explains it, is a "moral problem."

17. Alma and Elisabet framed as one being.

18. Alma's dream of Elisabet's visit. Whose hand strokes Alma's hair?

That part of the shadow that a subject cannot absorb into the conscious personality is attributed unconsciously to others by means of projection. When such unconscious projections occur, "the effect . . . is to isolate the subject from his environment, since instead of a real relation to it there is now only an illusory one. Projections change the world into a replica of one's own unknown face. In the last analysis, . . . they lead to an autoerotic or autistic condition in which one dreams a world whose reality remains forever unattainable."[43] The consciousnesses of these troubled women appear to have merged; Alma's invective is directed as much at herself as it is at Elisabet. And to signal this merger of psyches, Bergman puts their faces together, combining them in a way which incorporates the halves of each face that were in shadow during the monologues.

This shot provides the imagistic climax of the mergers that began in the prologue and that have continued throughout the film.[44] Recall the formations. First, we see the women cleaning mushrooms in a shot that seems to be a flattening out of a mirror image: each wears the same kind of hat, and each appears similarly in relation to shadows, given Bergman's choice of shooting angles and lighting. Second, the scene in which they smoke cigarettes presents them as merged bodily; Bergman frames them in such a way that Elisabet's arm appears to belong to Alma. Third, when Elisabet comes into Alma's room during the dream and strokes her hair, the women's hands seem interchangeable.

Now, as the second monologue reaches its climax, the shot of Alma is altered. The right side of her face is lighted, the left in shadow. Bergman completes the dark side by adding the left side of Elisabet's face. Bergman returns briefly to a shot of Alma's face alone as she proclaims her individuality by exclaiming, "No   I'm not like you. You are Elisabet Vogler. I am Sister Alma." Then the sutured photograph appears again. Thus, the scene begins with the pieces of the ripped

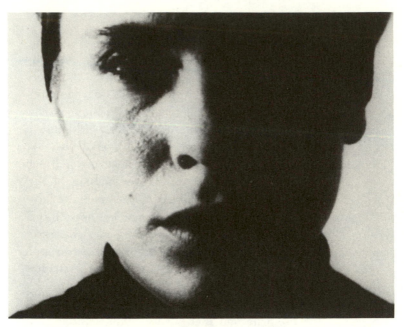

19. Alma.

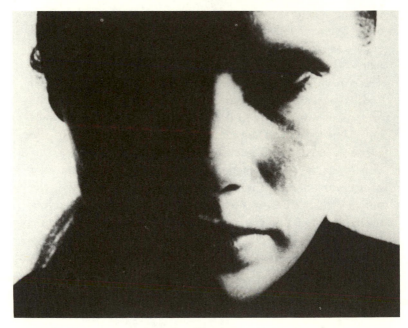

20. Elisabet.

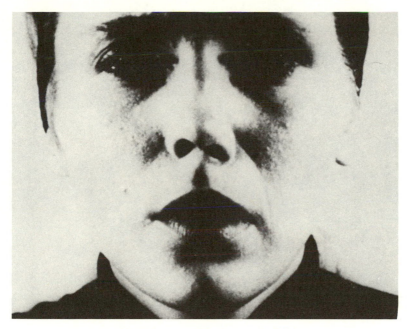

21. Alma, or Elisabet, or both?

photograph of Elisabet's boy put side by side and ends with an image formed by combining parts of photographed images of each woman.

Two more shots showing their faces together occur in the film. First, in what appears to be a dream (whose, is unclear), we again see Elisabet's hospital room. The hair-brushing scene from the earlier dream recurs, in a way quite similar to the first version. The last such merging occurs as Alma prepares to leave the summer house. But now we do not see each woman's form distinctly as we had previously. Instead, Alma looks into a mirror and brushes back her hair; Elisabet's superimposed image appears over Alma's. The complex image is visually out of synchronization; we see it as we would a 3-D movie without the special polarized glasses.

22. A failure in condensation revealed in the contest between two visual images.

The image of the merged faces first presented in the prologue has thus entered syntagmatically into the poem Bergman set out to make in *Persona*. The interpenetrating faces appear like a recurrent image, visually echoing the original even as they modify it. Significantly, the last occurrence of the image, a superimposition of Elisabet's form on Alma's, bespeaks Bergman's and our inability within the dream we share to effect a union *of* and *with* the women. From a psychoanalytic point of view, there has been a failure of condensation.

Freud explains condensation as he discusses the operation of the dream-work. Essentially, an example of condensation in our dreams would be a "dream-image . . . composed of visual features belonging in reality partly to . . . one person and partly to the other." He says "the dream figure may bear the name of one of the persons related to [its composite image]."[45] Recall Mr. Vogler's call for Elisabet, Alma's enactment of Elisabet's role, and then her denial of that role. The very fact that there is "the possibility of creating composite structures" lends the dream "a fantastic appearance." Things that have never existed become the objects of actual perception, like the Galtonian photographs Freud mentions often in *The Interpretation of Dreams*. The composite figure in a dream is like a centaur; it takes elements from different beings and combines them in the dream thoughts. But if the elements that the dream-work attempts to merge resist the action, the result will not be as fully defined and individualized as the completely condensed image: "If the objects which are to be condensed into a single unity are much too incongruous," he tells us, "the dream-work is often content with creating a composite structure with a comparatively distinct nucleus. . . ." In such a case, "the process of unification into a single image may be said to have failed. The two representations are superimposed and produce something in the nature of a contest between the two visual images."[46]

This is precisely the point to which the narrative of *Persona* leads us. The final superimposition, with its clear contest between the superimposed, desynchronized images, offers a variation of the image which appeared in the split faces at the end of Alma's monologue. Unsuccessfully condensed, superimposed, they come to us not as the projection of any individual psyche in the film but as "projections" of Bergman and of us as perceivers sharing his dream.

Our relation as spectators to *Persona* offers the best illustration I can think of to exemplify what Keith Cohen (who does not mention the film) describes as the "creating subject": "The movie spectator *is supplied*, syntagmatically, with a filmic image, a substitute for his own mental image, though the spectator *supplies*, paradigmatically, a mental construct that associates images along various axes. The spectator is

like a dreamer or a voyeur in that self-consciousness is reduced to a minimum and he easily projects some part of his
mind, be it conscious or unconscious, onto the objects referred to by the filmic image. But unlike the dreamer, the
spectator is not simply the passive observer: he retains the
needed power to surmount the passing flux of images by
applying his reflexive mind to their organization."[47]

The characters cannot find a way to accommodate one
another; so too, the film seems to say, human beings cannot
hope to achieve union with one another. Everyone exists as
an isolated entity; any kind of interaction that helps one
achieve momentary linkage with another can occur only by
playing a role, by deceiving, by putting on a mask, the word
denoted by persona. Alma's cries that she is not Elisabet are
attempts to maintain her integrity; they are similar to Elisabet's decision to stop talking. Our attempts to interact expose
us as actors, literally putting on a face, like Prufrock, to meet
the other faces.

The film's presentation of the superimposed image, then,
suggests that within the dream, which is this film, Bergman
as artist/dreamer feels he cannot, must not, unite the images.
To do so would be to distort the reality which he sadly accepts.
Clearly, art appears here as a mirror not of what ought to be,
but of what is: human isolation. The artist asks us to acknowledge a painful reality by using Alma and Elisabet as
models of the human condition, cut off, frightened by the
roles they play.

Bergman shares his characters' confusion and despair. The
creative consciousness, like that belonging to the dreamer
attempting to recall and make sense of the dream, will distort,
will fail to capture the real essence of the dream. The shifting
faces in the prologue, which signal a failure of condensation
on the one hand, point, on the other, to our inability to see
clearly. Life is diffuse. Its kaleidoscopic images will not fix
themselves in orderly patterns and remain neatly arranged

while we watch. Instead, the images will shift, escape our gaze as they do in dreams, tease us into interpretations that miss the meaning.

Just as the boy's gaze at the beginning of the film fails to fix the faces merging into one another, so too is *our* gaze incapable of stopping the unceasing interpenetration of images comprising life. As the boy looked at the screen in the prologue, the shot put him in the position of reaching out to us, groping at the dream screen we share. But behind the screen/mirror, he sees the merging faces of Alma and Elisabet superimposed over us; that is, we are part of the indeterminate reality that Bergman as the boy observes. And we see him, on the other side of the screen, like ourselves engaged in the futile gesture of trying to bring order. We are both linked at the mother's breast, the screen, caught in a dream in which we want to return to a sense of oneness with the external world.

Compare the boy's gesture toward the screen with Elisabet's as she takes photographs, midway through the film. She rises from below the frameline and snaps a picture, looking directly at Bergman's camera. Then she moves toward the back of the screen, and, standing with Alma, takes another picture, again, looking in our direction. As separate viewers watching the film, we each form the apex of a perceptual triangle that has as its base the field of the screen. The act of taking photographs makes Elisabet the apex of a triangle that has as its base the reverse field of the shot: the screen and what lies beyond, the audience. It is as if we were involved in a complex structure involving two interpenetrating cones that have the screen as their base of interaction.[48]

Perhaps her actions taking photographs should be compared to Bergman's attempts to reach at us on the dream screen. But the boy who reaches for the images of the women is not only Bergman; he also represents and mirrors us in the way I mentioned earlier. Even though he (we) can make

23. Elisabet takes our picture.

contact with the surface of the screen, he cannot possess the images; they merge into one another like the unsuccessful condensation of two figures in a dream—his dream, Bergman's, ours, projected on the wall of a morgue.

The self-reflexive nature of *Persona* is in some ways its message. We watch, and must be content with, images projected onto surfaces. Film's images defy our easy interpretations. Yet we want them to "mean" something. Recall Alma's relationship to Elisabet. She has seen the actress in movies, known her first as an image on the screen. True, now that she is present to her, she can be touched, as in the mushroom scene when they share physical gestures of affection. Except for her laughter, though, Elisabet refuses to speak. Her cry of "Don't!" when Alma threatens to throw the water at her is almost like film itself cautioning viewers to remember the distance between image and reality. We might consider the letter in which Elisabet reveals her patronizing views of Alma functioning in part like the delayed intertitles of a silent film. At the house, Alma encounters an unspeaking image in the same way we watch actors in silent film. Now, as Alma sits reading Elisabet's letter in the car, it is as if she were seeing the explanatory titles that reveal what the image has been "saying."

Alma thinks she and Elisabet look alike: "I think I could turn myself into you. . . . I mean inside. . . . And you wouldn't have any difficulty . . . turning into me. You could do it just like that. Of course, your soul would stick out a bit everywhere, it's too big to be inside me."[49] On one level, this speech presents a common kind of desire: the viewer's fantasy to be like an actor, larger than life. But, by extension, it demonstrates the human condition. One cannot hope for more than contact with surfaces. To go beyond this by attempting spiritual contact is to risk danger. Alma has not been able to *be* Elisabet; instead, there is only an unsatisfactory merging of the two personalities, effected by the projection of her shadow onto the actress. Bergman's poem concludes by reasserting our terrible and frightening isolation.

Section 3

THE RETROACTIVE
MODE

DREAMS in the films discussed thus far evoke certain kinds of responses in us, given their relation to the cinematic dream screen on which we behold them. The content of the dreams and the cinematic techniques used to render them can stimulate our recall of feelings and sensations we have had in our own dreams. In many cases we establish a particularly close bond with the dreaming character whose dream is played out on the cinematic dream screen we provide. When the dream screen of a character actually appears, as in the films discussed in Section 2, we are put in an even more complex position in relation to the film, for our dream screen becomes a point of intersection between ourselves and the world of the characters. In some cases we watch the same screen, as in *Sherlock, Jr.*, *The Temptations of Dr. Antonio*, and *Spellbound*. In *Persona*, the most complex example of a manifest dream screen, the fusion of our dream screen and the characters' creates a situation in which the boundaries established by the screen seem to slip away; the screen we share becomes a kind of psychic two-way mirror in which we look into ourselves.

The films to which we now turn offer another kind of presentational mode. We learn only retroactively that the material which appeared on the screen has been a dream. Films employing this mode can be grouped into two categories: in the first, part of a film is seen to have been a dream; in the second, the entire film. The phenomenological implications and effects of this occurrence are worth exploring. We find that our cinematic dream screen has in a sense been appropriated without our knowledge. In contrast to our experience of watching films in which cues immediately alert us to the fact that we are providing a dream screen for characters, we discover that our screen has already become the site for another's dream screen. While we have been lulled into offering a dream screen, we have also for the time lost the ownership of our vision.

Films that demonstrate the use of what I call the retroactive mode situate us as viewers on the other side of the screen. That is, we watch the characters' dream screens in a way that does not maintain the psychical and physical distance between us and the characters; instead, we are plunged unknowingly into another's consciousness. In some instances, once the revelation about the retroactive nature of the dream occurs, we may be forced to rethink our position in relation to the characters and to the values that have been set forth in the narrative. In certain cases, this condition allows the filmmaker to make ironic and satiric statements about the characters and about ourselves.

The Other Side of the Screen

Films in the first category include those in which a part of the work is discovered retroactively to have been a dream: Georges Méliès's *The Dreams of an Opium Fiend* (1908), which seems to offer the first display of the practice; a narrative about murder, D. W. Griffith's *The Avenging Conscience* (1914); and a film that ends with a dream, John Boorman's *Deliverance* (1974). Four other films in this category provide hints that we are watching dreams, even before the dreamers recognize this: Federico Fellini's *8 1/2* (1963) and *City of*

Women (1980), Alain Resnais's *Providence* (1977), and Kenneth Anger's *Fireworks* (1947). Finally, Peter Weir's *The Last Wave* (1979) uses the retroactive mode as it presents proleptic dreams.

First, however, two films deserve mention, even though neither contains what I would consider strictly a dream: Robert Wiene's *The Cabinet of Dr. Caligari* (1919) and Robert Enrico's *An Occurrence at Owl Creek Bridge* (1961). In both we observe what we only later discover to be a fantasy of the main character. Once we learn that what we have watched did not happen in reality, the effect on us is virtually the same as that which might occur were we to learn that we had witnessed a dream. In these films, our cinematic dream screen is appropriated by what Bruce F. Kawin would call the mindscreen of a character.

In *The Cabinet of Dr. Caligari*, a young man, Francis (Friedrich Feder) tells his older companion about a strange series of events in which he was involved. An evil doctor, Caligari (Werner Krauss) brings a somnambulist, Cesare (Conrad Veidt), to his town in Germany and creates mayhem, for Cesare murders various people, including one of Francis's friends. Luckily Francis's fiancée Jane (Lil Dagover) is saved from the somnambulist. After Francis and others discover that Caligari is a madman who fashions himself after an earlier director of somnambulists, they put the doctor in a straitjacket.

But this report of the bizarre events, which appear to happen against distorted Expressionist sets and irregular painted backdrops, turns out to be the fantasy of Francis, the narrator. *He* is the madman who, with Jane and Cesare, is kept at an asylum run by the kindly looking Werner Krauss. The director appears, Francis erupts, and his behavior alerts the doctor to his problem. Now that he realizes that Francis thinks him to be Caligari, he will be able to cure him.

Originally, the work was to have consisted only of the

internal narrative: Caligari was really to have been put in a straitjacket. But, at the suggestion of Fritz Lang, the frame story was added, thus making the main narrative purely a product of Francis's diseased imagination. The history of how the film came to acquire the frame story and the implications of this for German cinema have been explored at length, most notably by Siegfried Kracauer.[1]

Since we accept the internal narrative as real while watching it, we are shocked and disconcerted to discover that we have been immersed in the consciousness of a madman. The identification we felt during the narrative is thus shown to have been misguided; we were linked to someone who lives entirely in the world of fantasy. As a result, we sense a curious disorientation upon learning the truth about Francis and, in a way, try to cancel our experience of the past sixty minutes. But we cannot—a major reason, I believe, for the unsettling aftereffects of the film.[2]

Robert Enrico's *An Occurrence at Owl Creek Bridge* produces the opposite effect. Here we feel considerable dismay about the main character's fortunes, rather than horror, when we discover that we have been observing a fantasy. A Confederate soldier (Roger Jacquet) is about to be hanged by Union officers. As he stands on a bridge, at the moment of execution, the rope around his neck breaks, and he escapes by swimming away. Once out of the water, he proceeds on foot, trying to make his way home to his wife and the refuge he believes awaits him. Home at last, he is within reach of his wife when Enrico cuts back to the scene of execution. The soldier's "escape" was only a fantasy—a wish that flashed through his mind while he awaited the signal for his death.

In this case, since we are bound to his point of view by the nature of the narrative, his death is particularly jarring: someone we have come to know, if only briefly, has ceased to exist. Even though his escape is a fantasy, our response involves the same emotions—regret, surprise—that would have been elicited had the event been portrayed in a dream. That is, our identification with the character and with his desire would be unchanged.

As far as I have been able to determine, the first film that contains a dream belonging to the retroactive mode seems to have been made by Méliès. According to John Frazer, *The Dreams of an Opium Fiend* opens by showing us a man in an opium den who receives "a particularly potent pipeful." He goes home where his wife serves him dinner, an event followed by "phantasmagoric" happenings. These include the appearance of a woman who sits on part of a crescent moon. The face in the moon is drinking beer. When the man attempts to grab the woman who has been sitting in the moon, she changes into "a grotesque. The man strikes this creature and suddenly finds himself in the dope den again attacking the Chinese attendant."[3] Thus the events at home were simply part of a drug-induced dream, the existence of which we learn about retroactively. As with the examples of dreams from the Méliès period discussed earlier, I think it is impossible to make any claim of complexity for the effects produced here by the manifestation of the dream.

A much more elaborate example of the paradigm occurs in D. W. Griffith's *The Avenging Conscience* in which the retroactivity of a large part of the film invites serious consideration. In this film we discover that virtually the last two-thirds of the narrative have been a dream. Incorporating elements from several works of Edgar Allan Poe ("The Cask of Amontillado," "The Tell-Tale Heart," and "Annabel Lee,") the story concerns a young man (Henry B. Walthall) who has been raised by his uncle (Spottiswoode Aitken). The narrative complication involves the young man's love for Annabel Lee (Blanche Sweet). The uncle finds her an unacceptable match for his nephew and forces them to separate. After a sad parting from her at an afternoon tea, the discouraged nephew observes two violent natural scenes: a spider captures a fly; then the

spider is caught and devoured by a troop of ants. The nephew
returns home and sits down in a chair, apparently to rest and
to reflect on his plight. But we learn later that after the nephew
sits down, he is not simply resting but actually sleeping and
dreaming. Thus all the events which follow after that action
until he awakens are part of an elaborate dream, actually a
nightmare.

As soon as the nephew sits down, Griffith quite consciously
begins to confuse our sense of the difference between appearance and reality by offering us a shot of Annabel preparing for bed and one of her walking to the window. These
are followed by the title: "Realizations that his uncle, on
whom he depends, stands between him and happiness." More
shots of Annabel in her room follow a shot that returns us to
the nephew, thus suggesting that the two spatio-temporal
realms maintain their existence as "realities" in the narrative.
But this is a trick by the director to make us think either that
he is crosscutting between the nephew and the girl or that
the shots of Annabel represent the young man's thoughts of
her.

Griffith uses intertitles in the first part of the non-oneiric
narrative that also seem designed to fool us, even as they
prepare for a number of elements in the ensuing dream. For
example, at the party, we see a man brush against the hero;
they eye each other, and a title announces him to be "A
gentleman whom we shall meet again." Similarly, before returning home from the party, the nephew bumps into a la-
borer, "The Italian—an impression that plays its part later."
From a Freudian perspective, these men constitute part of
the day's residue that is incorporated by the dream-work as
it constructs the nightmare. From a narrative perspective,
though, the intertitles function as any number of similar intertitles might in a melodrama—to anticipate later events.
Griffith knew nothing about Freud, but he was very much
aware of how to whet interest and generate suspense in his

audience. Thus these titles which foreshadow later events contribute to our sense that what happens in the narrative is real.

The nephew rises from his chair, bent on devising a plot to murder his uncle. He forges a note that draws the uncle out of town on a useless errand; no one in town sees the uncle's return to the house. When he enters, he encounters the nephew who is trying to determine the best way to kill him. The presence of "The Italian" outside precludes the use of a gun. Eventually the nephew strangles his uncle and walls him up in the fireplace. "The Italian" has witnessed the murder through the window, though, and blackmails the nephew into giving him part of his inheritance.

The troubled conscience of the youth leads to his exposure, for although he was able to hide the body successfully, he cannot escape from his guilt. This manifests itself in visions of his uncle, effected in superimpositions. On one occasion, the superimposed ghost emerges from the fireplace. On another, we see the nephew trying to sleep; he seems to be having a dream in which his uncle's ghost enters through the window and approaches him in bed. On a first viewing of the film, we suppose that he is having a nightmare in which the ghost he imagined when awake now appears as an oneiric hallucination. This "dreamed" ghost intensifies our sense of the reality of the *rest* of the ensuing events attending the murder. That is, this "dream" comes to us in the same cinematic way as the ghost, through superimposition. Both visions belong appropriately to someone who is losing his mind. But the dream of his uncle throws the murder into relief as something that "really" happened. It is as if we were encountering an anxiety dream with all the appropriate cues: character shown sleeping, superimposed figure approaching, and so forth.

A friend of the uncle and the stranger encountered at the party become suspicious of the nephew; Annabel worries that he may have done something horrible. The nephew's stay in a sanitarium fails to alleviate the effects of the avenging conscience. When he returns home, the stranger, actually a detective, visits him and succeeds in breaking the young man down completely. As he cracks, he sees visions of satyrs, demonic creatures, and a skeleton that binds him. Griffith conveys a sense of the youth's terror by thrusting the camera at him in a way that anticipates the later use of the zoom lens. At this climactic point, the nephew struggles with the superimposed ghost of the uncle, while to the right of this struggle on the screen, a superimposition of the earlier murder appears.

He escapes from the detective, and attempts unsuccessfully to hang himself. Meanwhile, Annabel throws herself off a cliff in despair. Suddenly the nephew wakes up from his nightmare, shaken considerably by the frightening dream. He embraces his uncle who has come into the room, and they reconcile their differences. Annabel enters fortuitously during their reunion, and the uncle agrees to bless their marriage. The film ends by showing that the nephew has become a successful author, and by presenting him and Annabel seated in a forest, posed in an allegorical *tableau vivant* of the sort that Griffith would use again in *The Birth of a Nation*.

From a Freudian point of view, the nephew's murderous dream does indeed satisfy a wish, not necessarily an infantile one (although the Oedipal implications of the relationship are not to be discounted). More interesting, perhaps, is the way the avenging conscience punishes the young man for his criminal thoughts. Such a conclusion to his dream (Annabel dead, the young man caught) is quite in accordance with a position Freud advanced later in regard to punishment dreams in "Revision of the Theory of Dreams."[4]

More to our purpose here, though, is the phenomenology of the dream experience. We are as pleased as the nephew to discover "it was only a dream." Now we are not implicated in the crime, and the sense of sympathy that figured in our uneasy sense of identification with him turns out to be more acceptable; the revelation has the effect of absolving us of our complicity in his murderous impulses—not that we approve of the murder, but that the very nature of the narrative involves us with the mental life of the nephew by making him our primary object of identification.

Nonetheless, before learning that the murder and subsequent events are only a dream, and, as such, belong to the nephew and *his* dream screen, we assume that what happens in the narrative is simply a series of melodramatic events. We take the second appearance of the ghost as part of the nightmare the nephew has while sleeping. By drawing us into a larger oneiric structure without our knowledge, Griffith has produced a complex aesthetic situation. As viewers, we have been *more* involved, not less, than we believed we were when we thought the events had really occurred. That is, our response to the material in the diegesis as we first observe it is not "right," for we misapprehend the true nature of what we see. We believe we are looking at events from our side of the screen, but, in fact, we are seeing them from the psychic point of view of the nephew. In a sense, Griffith's trick turns our relation to the dream screen inside out, for we discover we were not where we were. Instead, we have inhabited another mind.

In the experience of dreams discussed earlier, we know through various cues that a character is dreaming. In a situation such as that which presents itself in Griffith's film, *we* are as surprised as the dreamer to learn that "it was only a dream." We have shared his ignorance and lack of awareness, even as we thought we were superior to him in the course of events. More, retroactively we discover that the screen has somehow been wrested from our possession. Rather than being phenomenologically in the position of sharing it with a character, we and our screen have been overwhelmed by another person's consciousness.[5]

Speaking of another work presenting a retroactively dis-covered dream in which it appears that the hero has committed a murder, Fritz Lang's *The Woman in the Window* (1944), Leo Braudy observes: "Although we may be fascinated by the character who accidentally commits a murder, we do not necessarily identify with him. But when we discover that his murdering was a dream, we become more identified with him through our own half-perceived, dreamlike impulses to vio-lence." Equally useful is Braudy's assertion that "the closed film actually raises the fear of never waking up. . . . Lang's [hero] waking from his dream is the audience waking from the film. . . ."[6]

John Boorman uses a dream in the retroactive mode at the end of *Deliverance* to renew the fear we have felt earlier. Ed (Jon Voight) has returned home after a disastrous canoe trip in the wilderness of Georgia. Instead of the rugged idyl that he and his companions had hoped for, they have experienced horrors: rape and murder. Now Ed sits silently with his wife and child at home, and we hear a faint reprise of "Duelling Banjos." Boorman dissolves from this shot to one outdoors, and we assume that the scene has, in fact, shifted back to the river. A lifeless-appearing hand rises from below the water and remains partially extended in the air. Has a body been found which will implicate Ed and his companions? Then we hear Ed shout "NO!" and cut back to him as he awakes from a nightmare. His wife attempts to comfort him, and the film ends.

The sequence suggests that Ed may be having the first of what will turn out to be a series of recurrent nightmares; his horror will continue as long as there is a possibility that the police may discover the actual facts surrounding the deaths of Drew and the mountaineers. Boorman succeeds in involving us in this situation by presenting the dream in a way that catches us totally off guard while it plays on our fears for Ed: we too do not want any evidence to appear. The discovery that "it was only a dream" works in a complex way to solidify our bond to Ed, for we are all afraid that his secret will be revealed. We are, thus, even more implicated in his guilt and fear than we are in that of the heroes in *The Avenging Conscience* and *The Woman in the Window*, where the "crimes" never really occurred.

The oneiric status of the next four dreams is not established as they begin, but the filmmakers make us aware that we are in fact watching dreams before the dreamlike narratives conclude.

The act of immersing us in another person's dreaming mind at the beginning of a film has been useful to the filmmakers' narrative aims in two works about artists, Fellini's *8 1/2* and Resnais's *Providence*. The filmmakers involve us in the creative act itself by making us sense more fully the dreamlike nature of the operations of the imagination.

Fellini's work begins with the hero Guido (Marcello Mastroianni) trapped in a massive traffic jam. He attempts to escape the suffocating enclosure of his hot car by crawling over car rooftops. We realize that we must be watching a dream or fantasy when the hero finds himself floating in the sky; a point-of-view shot shows that his feet are tethered to a rope that figures below him are pulling down. He falls, the dream ends, and we discover the filmmaker Guido in a bedroom in the combination rest home/spa to which he has come to regain his creative strength.

The action of Resnais's film begins with cuts from various scenes: a forest in which soldiers pursue an old man; a bedroom; and a courtroom. Before the conclusion of this section, we infer that we must be watching something out of the ordinary, a dream or fantasy, since the old man, who appears to be part-werewolf, looks like a creature from a horror movie. The grim opening turns out to have been the dream/creative

fantasy of Clive Langham (John Gielgud), a novelist who is
dying of cancer.

By first involving us in the dreaming fantasies of each artist
and then allowing us to learn where we are, Fellini and
Resnais position us squarely in the consciousness of each
character. We discover we have been watching the dreams
of these creators from their perspectives on our dream screens.
Thus we are bound to them in a special manner. As dreamers,
by definition we are "creative." But now, we are sharing the
screen and being absorbed into the consciousnesses of truly
creative minds. That is, Fellini and Resnais play with the
cinematic nature of dreams and the oneiric quality of film to
include us in the creative act even as they define the experience that links us to the characters. The dreamer is a creator;
the creators in these films are dreamers. We are linked to
them both, given the retroactively discovered dreams.

Anger's *Fireworks* and Fellini's *City of Women* offer special
variants of the retroactive mode. As in *8 1/2* and *Providence*,
we realize that we are watching dreams before the conclusion
of the oneiric sequences. But the sequences themselves constitute almost the entire narrative content. And, unlike the
others, both films begin by tricking us into thinking that we
are watching characters awakening from sleep: Anger's, from
the dream that opens the film; Fellini's, from a momentary
nap. Thus our initial response to the events that occur at the
beginning of each film is belief, for the heroes appear to have
emerged from the state of sleep before our eyes.

Kenneth Anger's complex *Fireworks* explores the homo-
erotic and masochistic longing of its main character (acted
by Anger). The work begins with sounds of a storm and a
view of a torch as it is put in water. This is followed by a
shot of a sailor holding a battered young man (Anger). A cut
takes us to a bedroom where Anger lies in bed asleep. He
seems to awake from his dream of the sailor and appears to
have an erection, an effect caused by raising a statue that he

has underneath the sheet.[7] He rises and the camera watches
attentively as he dresses. As I suggested earlier, the erotic
uses to which the cinematic apparatus can be put are above
sexual distinctions. Here the camera's examination of the
dressing process seems like what Metz describes as a caress,
particularly as it pans slowly up his legs as he buttons his
fly. He discovers photographs of the image we had seen in
his dream and throws them in the unlighted fireplace. Perhaps, we think, these photographs explain the content of the
dream we have been observing.

The man leaves the bedroom through a door marked "Gents"
and appears on the street. In the following sequence, he enters
a room with a painted backdrop of a bar and encounters a
sailor. This scene suggests that we have not left the dreaming
state of the character's mind. What kind of "bar" can this
artificial scene be? The sailor removes his shirt, flexes his
muscles, and walks on his hands. When the man asks for a
light for his cigarette, Anger cuts to a scene in which the
man and sailor, still in the same pose, appear before a fireplace with a fire in it. Alternately shirted or shirtless, the
sailor pummels the man and then leaves. The leap in space
from the setting of the bar to the fireplace and the cutting
pattern which removes and replaces the sailor's shirt confirm
our suspicion that we have not emerged from a dream.

In the next sequence, the man is attacked by a group of
sailors brandishing chains. The violence they inflict on him
is made evident in two grisly shots: one of blood spurting
from his nostrils, and one of his chest, opened by a bottle,
in which appears what seems to be a magnetic needle. More
shots reveal the man being inundated with streams of milk.

The scene shifts to the "Gents" door which opens to allow
the camera to track by empty urinals until it discovers a
naked man sitting on the floor. Then the scene cuts away to
a sailor toward whom the camera dollies as he reaches for
his fly. After a cut, the sailor is exposed, but his "penis" is

a Roman candle; he lights it, and the "fireworks" of the title occur.

We return to the man's room. A Christmas tree, topped by a burning candle, has been strapped to the man's chest and head; he bends down and uses the candle to ignite the pictures seen earlier of the sailor holding him. The camera lingers on a shot of the pictures being consumed by flames in the fireplace, then cuts to a shot of the man asleep in bed, as at the beginning of the film. The camera pans to the right of the sleeper and reveals another sleeping man. This character appears to awake and rise slightly from the bed. It is not possible to see his face clearly because there seems to be a halo-like circle of flames emanating from his head.

The narrative material following the apparent awakening of the man at the beginning of the film has been a dream. Anger describes the overall shape of the film in this way: "A dissatisfied dreamer awakes, goes out in the night seeking a 'light' and is drawn through the needle's eye. A dream of a dream, he returns to a bed less empty than before."[8] Thus the final shot, which reveals another man awaking while the chief character continues to sleep, would signal our first real separation from the oneiric structure of the narrative.

Anger's narrative strategy is to make the audience think that the shots of the sleeper in bed following the initial shots of the sailor holding the boy signal an end to a dream. Given the ontological integrity of the cinematic image, such an effect is easily produced. The apparent emergence from the dream state has the effect of foregrounding the intensity of the experiences which follow. That is, the viewer thinks a dream has just ended, and expects, therefore, a non-oneiric form of reality.

Anger capitalizes on this expectation while creating tension between realistic and the increasingly unreal-seeming events. For example, the repeated shots of the streets and cars and of the sailors' feet as they walk over newspapers lend a realistic element which counters the painted set of the bar, the almost mimelike motions of the sailors during their attack, the ripping open of the man's chest, the Roman candle and the Christmas tree. The man's glances into the camera also add a degree of realism and naturalize the bizarre content by suggesting the character's awareness of the camera and the faces who will watch what the apparatus films. In fact, just before he is attacked, the character actually "falls" into the space of the camera, and, by extension, that of the audience.

Given the hypothesis of the dream screen, viewers become both the objects as well as the mirrors of the man's glances. In one sense, Anger implicates viewers by involving them in the space containing the character's objects of desire and of fear. Although we do not know it at the point of the film immediately after the sleeper has wakened, we are watching his dream screen from his side of the cinematic dream screen. The dream screen has become a mirror revealing the man looking narcissistically back at himself, caught, therefore, in his own gaze.

In other words, if the hypothesis of the dream screen is taken as a perspective by which we examine the operation of this film, the following description seems to be justified. The initial images of the film were a dream projected on the character's dream screen and also the cinematic dream screen which we bring to the viewing experience. When he awakes, we would appear to have a different relationship with the character; he glances at us in the same way that he will later glance at the sailors, beings separate from him. But everything is occurring on a dream screen which continues to receive the projections of the character's dreaming mind, binding us to his psyche which we inhabit on the other side of the screen.

Although Fellini's *City of Women* does not begin with a dream, it too suggests to viewers that a sleeping character is awaking before our eyes. The film opens with a shot of a train emerging from a tunnel and then cuts to a shot of Signor

Snaporaz (Marcello Mastroianni) apparently beginning to fall asleep in a compartment of the train. He snaps back from his sleep and thus appears to be "awake." But, like Anger's character, he only dreams that he has awakened. And, as is the case as we watch *Fireworks*, we sense fairly soon that the events that transpire in the narrative are part of a dream. Our discovery that the adventures that befall the hero are only a dream precedes *his* recognition, an event that occurs at the end of the film.

The controlling action of the film lies in Snaporaz's desire to locate the "perfect woman." He first sees her (Bernice Stegers) sitting across from him in the train when he "awakes." He follows her into the washroom where she gives him a passionate kiss; as they embrace we observe a somewhat phastasmagoric flashing of lights outside the washroom window, our first indication that Snaporaz may be dreaming. The next clue to this condition appears when the woman leaves the train; it stops, apparently in the middle of a field, rather than at a station, and she departs, followed by Snaporaz. She tricks him into holding a ridiculous pose while she takes a picture of him, and then disappears. As he rushes to find her, he stumbles on his coat, falls, and asks, in frustration, "What kind of film am I in?"

If we had any doubt about the oneiric nature of the events thus far, none remains once Snaporaz reaches a hotel which is the scene of a feminists' convention. As he slips from meeting to meeting searching for the perfect woman seen on the train, he becomes involved in increasingly zany and unbelievable adventures. In one particularly bizarre scene, he finds himself roller-skating helplessly; out of control, he plunges unceremoniously down a flight of stairs, the first of three such falls he will experience in the course of the film.

From this point on, he tries desperately to return to the train station, but offers or promises of help from women all turn out to be false. Having escaped from one group of young girls who he believes are trying to run him over with a car, he stumbles into the castle of Xavier Züberkock (Ettore Manni), an aging sybarite who is celebrating his 10,000th sexual conquest this evening. It will, he laments, also be his last, and to honor it, Züberkock is having a celebration. His home includes a gallery with hundreds of pictures of his previous conquests; under each photograph is a button which, when pushed, starts a recording of the woman's comments or cries that occurred during lovemaking and orgasm.

Elena (Anna Prucnal), Snaporaz's "wife," appears at this party, and berates him for his indifference. Later two showgirls (daughters of dancers who were earlier conquests of Snaporaz) appear and dance with him. They put him to bed, and his wife appears in bed, alternately screaming and singing arias. He crawls under the bed and falls into a chute which, as he descends, permits him to re-view past scenes of his sexual activities, beginning with childhood. Among these is a memory of adolescence: a large group of boys on an immense bed masturbating as they watch films of women such as Marlene Dietrich and Mae West who are *literally* projections on his dream screen within the dream.

This descent ends with a drop into a cage, his second fall of the dream. Captured by women, he is taken away and tried for his errors. Acquitted for his behavior, he seems to have been granted a special reward. He enters a large basket carried by a floating balloon figure of a woman wearing a halo (the showgirl seen earlier in the film) and begins what seems to be a paradisiacal flight through heaven. But a woman below (the same showgirl dressed in a military outfit) fires at the balloon and sends the figure, who now looks quite ferocious, crashing down on Snaporaz.

His third and final fall ends as he awakes, back on the train. Seated across from him is the woman who was his wife Elena in the dream. She tells him that he has been snorting for two hours. Other women enter the compartment: the woman he followed earlier and the showgirls. All the women exchange knowing glances and laugh. The bewildered Snaporaz looks at them, the scene cuts to a shot of the train entering a tunnel, and the film ends.

It is understandable that the film has been greeted with scorn by feminists who find the depiction of the convention repellant. And the collective masturbation scene in front of the filmed images of female stars seems to confirm the tenor of the argument cited earlier that film has been used to fragment Woman and make of her a fetish for the male.

But we should put these scenes in the context to which they belong: the dream of Snaporaz. Although the central action of the dream, his search for the perfect woman, involves desire, the underlying theme is his fear of growing old. Everything that occurs during the dream is a projection of a particular dreaming mind that belongs to a man who has begun to anticipate the end of his sexual power. A "City of Women" is a realm that has no place for Snaporaz. The women gathered at the meeting demonstrate their abilities to exist quite happily without men and to subject them to their own desires (for example, the woman with six husbands). The showgirls are daughters of women he knew in his youth. The aging Züberkock's gallery of photographs offers a counterpart to the memory of youthful masturbation. Züberkock's farewell to sex at the party actually embodies Snaporaz's fear about the loss of his own sexual abilities. His helplessness appears throughout the film: in the roller-skating scene, in the attack on him by the furnace stoker, in the chase by the girls, in his trial, and in his final descent.

The unattractive representations of powerful women may thus be seen as projections of the hero's fears just as Züberkock is a projection of his personality. Moreover, the verbal attack he hears from Elena and the trial at which he must defend his behavior suggest that he does, in fact, feel guilt over his failings.

Fellini does not completely alert us to the oneiric nature of the events of the narrative until Snaporaz has entered the City of Women at the convention. Thus the guiding motive of his behavior (to find the perfect woman) and his underlying fear (of being helpless, ridiculous, impotent) are established in a way to suggest their reality to him and to us. Once we are sure that the events transpire in his dream, Fellini presents increasingly inventive variations on the basic theme and situation. In other words, he establishes the "reality" of the issues (desire and fear) early in the film by presenting them in a context that is not completely dreamlike. Once this has been done, he then leads us totally into the dreamlike world of his hero.[9]

An interesting use of retroactivity occurs in Peter Weir's *The Last Wave*, a film that makes extensive use of proleptic dreams. Virtually all of the dreams experienced by the hero, David Burton (Richard Chamberlain), are identified retroactively. Shortly after seeing the first dreams, we become aware that Weir has chosen this mode because it allows him to blur the line between the real and the oneiric worlds. Such a confusion constitutes a major narrative focus of the work. The hero's dreams not only foretell events, such as his encounter with Chris Lee (Gulpilel), but also put him in contact with another kind of reality—the "dreamtime" known only to the Australian aborigines whom he is defending against a charge of murder. At the end of the film, Burton's dreams resolve in a nightmarish but "real" conclusion, as the two temporal modes coalesce and he confronts an immense tidal wave that will obliterate the land.

Closed Oneiric Structures

I have assigned to this group three films that are constituted entirely as dreams. Only toward the end of the viewing experience do we realize that our cinematic dream screen has provided the site for characters' dreams. In *Dead of Night* (1945), our retroactive discovery adds to the horror of the experience we have had. In Buñuel's *Belle de Jour* (1966) and *The Discreet Charm of the Bourgeoisie* (1972), our awareness that we have been locked into oneiric worlds serves the filmmaker's satiric aims brilliantly, for we find that our values have been challenged by films that interrogate us not only as viewers but also as members of society. After watching these films, we discover that our gaze is literally not our own; we have been watching our cinematic/dream screen with another's eyes.

The Endless Dream of Walter Craig in Dead of Night

Dead of Night consists of a frame story and five inserted narratives. Made under the general supervision of producer Michael Balcon, it uses the talents of various directors associated with Ealing Studios, most notably Alberto Cavalcanti.[10]

As the frame story (directed by Basil Dearden) begins under the opening credits, we see architect Walter Craig (Mervyn Johns) arrive at a country house owned by Eliot Foley (Roland Culver); Foley has asked Craig for advice on remodeling the structure. Craig is troubled by a sense of *déjà vu*, for the house and the people he meets in it seem familiar, like elements in a recurring dream he has. He explains his odd sensation to his host and other guests. Most are sympathetic to him, and several discuss strange events of a similar nature from their own pasts. These take the form of independent stories, which are narrated by five persons.

As the afternoon continues, Craig is able to predict accurately what will ensue at the home, a phenomenon explained by the gradual recall of his dream; his predictions are fulfilled uncannily by the events. The one guest who has

24. Walter Craig describes his sense of *déjà vu*.

scoffed at Craig's fears is a psychiatrist, Dr. Van Straaten
(Frederick Valk). He has also offered rational explanations
for the seemingly irrational events described in the stories of
the other guests. But it develops that he is the most important
person in the recurring dream. Craig knows vaguely that at
some point the lights in the house will go out and that something awful will happen. This occurs exactly as he had feared;
the electric power does fail, Van Straaten breaks his glasses,
and Craig strangles the psychiatrist. He then finds himself
in a phantasmagoric world populated by figures from four of
the stories heard earlier in the afternoon. A figure from the
most terrifying of these, the dummy Hugo, begins to strangle
Craig, and then he wakes up from what has been his nightmare; he has his own hands around his throat in his own bed.
So the nightmare is over; it was only a dream. But the tele-

phone rings; Eliot Foley, the host seen earlier in the dream wants him to come down for the weekend. Craig's wife encourages him to go and says that the rest will be good for him. And so the film ends as it began, with shots of Craig arriving in his car at the summer house, the site of his dream.

Very few films manage to generate so many *frissons* as this one. Just when we think we have moved back to some point of stability, the film plays still one more trick on us. Its end is its beginning. We leave Craig about to enter a house in which he will *really* murder someone, as his recurring dream has shown he will. But perhaps the dream has not ended. We may still be in the dreaming mind of Craig at the end; in fact, our very entrapment in such a mind may explain why the film continues to haunt us. We discover that for one hundred minutes our dream screen has belonged to a dreamer who will not let it go, even after the film ends. He still possesses the dream screen he appropriated in the opening moments of the film.

As we reach the end of the film, we realize that all of the stories related by the other characters are themselves parts of Craig's dream. Dr. Van Straaten discounts those of a supernatural nature as useless fears. In contrast, the story the psychiatrist tells the guests is not only true but also admits of a scientific explanation. However, the psychiatrist himself and his denials are also elements in the dream. So too is its endless repetition.

The substance of Craig's dream—the stories and Van Straaten—should be seen as elements that reveal the unconscious of the character. Analysis of these, on the order of a psychoanalytic investigation, may offer some clues as to the nature of the being who has managed to take over our dream screen. To conduct this inquiry, we must observe the content of the various stories in some detail.

The first story, "Hearse Driver" (directed by Dearden), concerns a race-car driver who has an accident that puts him in a hospital. One night he believes he looks out his window and sees a hearse outside on the street below, apparently in the late afternoon. The coachman looks up and says, "Room for just one more, sir." The race-car driver is terrified by the experience, for it seems to have violated temporal laws and occurred at 4:15 in the afternoon when he knows it is really night. His doctor explains it as a result of his obsession with death. But when the driver is released from the hospital and is about to board a bus at 4:15, he encounters the very same coachman on the bus saying, "Room for one more, sir." Frightened, the driver will not enter the bus; moments later it crashes and kills all the occupants. Thus he was wise to heed the warning of the premonitory experience in the hospital; the coachman of the hearse was really associated with death.

The next story, "Christmas Party" (directed by Cavalcanti), relates the experience of Sally O'Hara (Sally Ann Howes), a guest at an old country home. During a game of hide-and-seek she stumbles into a room and encounters Francis Kent, a little boy who is crying because his sister Constance is so cruel to him. When Sally tells her friends about discovering the room and the little boy, her hostess is terrified: Francis Kent was murdered many years ago by his sister Constance, who slit his throat.

Murder is also the theme of the next narrative, "The Haunted Mirror" (directed by Robert Hamer). Peter Cortland (Ralph Michael), a young man about to be married, receives a mirror as a wedding gift from his fiancée Joan (Googie Withers). The mirror is haunted, though, and reflects a place other than the room in which Peter has put it. Years ago, the mirror hung in the home of a jealous man who strangled his wife. Gradually, Peter begins to assume the personality of the killer and tries to strangle Joan. But she has discovered the curse associated with the mirror and smashes it just as Peter is about to kill her.

The fourth tale, "Golfing Story" (directed by Charles Crichton), seems quite out of place in the context of the others. It offers a wryly humorous story about two golfers George and Larry (Basil Radford and Naunton Wayne) in love with the same woman, Mary (Peggy Bryan). They decide that whoever wins a golf match will become Mary's husband. Larry, the loser, commits suicide in anger over having failed to win the game (and Mary). But it turns out his rival George cheated in order to win, and the ghost of the loser comes back to haunt the happy groom. Larry does so by manifesting himself to the groom and following the couple about on their wedding night. George attempts to rid himself of the ghost by helping Larry find the formula that will allow him to dematerialize completely and return to his ghostly realm. But, in the process of trying to make the ghost disappear, George sends himself away, forever. He is not even present as an invisible ghost. As the story ends, Larry, the previously disappointed rival, now looks forward to enjoying the favors of Mary, even though he is invisible to her. (This section was excised from prints for American distribution when it was first released.)

The psychiatrist tells the last story, "The Ventriloquist's Dummy" (directed by Cavalcanti). This concerns Maxwell Frere, a ventriloquist (Michael Redgrave), his dummy Hugo Fitch, and another ventriloquist named Sylvester Kee (Hartley Power). In contrast to the stories told by the other guests, this narrative includes no omens or ghosts, but presents a scientifically explicable phenomenon; Van Straaten calls it "one of the most complex cases of dual identity ever recorded." Maxwell and his dummy meet Sylvester, an American ventriloquist, at a Parisian club, Chez Beulah. When Sylvester sits down at their table, Hugo begins to speak in a veiled manner about the possibility of teaming up with him: "You interest me a lot," he tells him; "you know, Sylvester, I like you a lot." Hugo refuses to "sing" when Maxwell gets on stage to perform their act: "You be the canary tonight, I'd like to talk with Sylvester." Hugo describes Maxwell as his "associate," and claims he is "just about through with this cheap has-been." At this remark, Maxwell slaps the dummy, shocking the audience at the club. Hugo promises to be waiting later for Sylvester: "We've got to talk business."

When Sylvester visits their dressing room, Hugo speaks with him, even though Maxwell, the source of his voice, seems not to be present in the room. Sylvester thinks the trick is clever, but is disconcerted when Maxwell enters and acts as if he had *not* been there for the dialogue; Maxwell wants to know what Hugo has been saying. He spills water on Kee after the latter picks up Hugo; he cannot bear to have anyone else touch the dummy. When Hugo threatens to leave him, Maxwell puts his hand over Hugo's mouth. Horrified, Kee realizes that Hugo has "bitten" his master and actually drawn blood.

When Kee next encounters them in London, Maxwell and Hugo have left a review in which they were performing because Hugo didn't like the producer. Kee witnesses an embarrassing incident in which the drunken Maxwell is knocked down in a bar by a man whose girlfriends Hugo has insulted. The American helps Maxwell to his room and leaves. The shot immediately following their exit from the bar is a dolly toward the bed where Hugo's form sprawls on the coverlet. A medium close-up of Maxwell looking in the mirror as he talks to Kee emphasizes Maxwell's dual image; his face is framed over a photograph of Hugo. Before leaving, Kee helps Maxwell into bed, pulls the coverlet over him, and adjusts Hugo in an upright position at the end of the bed so that the dummy is looking at his owner.

The next scene begins with a banging on the American's door. He awakes and unlocks the door, admitting the frenzied Maxwell, who is searching for Hugo. He accuses Kee of stealing him and, after looking through the room, discovers the dummy under the covers of Kee's bed. Enraged at finding

Hugo there, Maxwell picks up Hugo, holding him so that their faces touch, and shoots Kee, wounding him.

Dr. Van Straaten, the psychiatrist officially called in on the case after Maxwell is arrested, thinks that by bringing the dummy to Maxwell's cell, he will be able to demonstrate that the ventriloquist is mentally ill, and arranges for a meeting. Maxwell seems happy to see the dummy: "I knew you'd come back." But Hugo rejects him: "The hell I will. . . . It looks like I'll be needing a new partner. . . . I have my career to think of." He says he thinks Maxwell is finished; he will be put in a madhouse. At this point, Maxwell strangles Hugo, throws the dummy on the floor and destroys it by stomping on it.

In one last attempt to jolt Maxwell back to reality, Van Straaten brings Kee to the cell. By now, Maxwell, who has not spoken since destroying Hugo, is completely mad. When he sees the American, he speaks in Hugo's voice, his mouth moves like a dummy's, and his eyes focus like a wooden doll's.

We return to the living room of the country home to hear the doctor's rational explanations of Maxwell's dual identity. Then the lights go off, it becomes dark, as Walter Craig had anticipated, and the doctor breaks his glasses. This triggers what had been hidden from Craig's consciousness. He knew only that something terrible would happen; now he knows what that is. As Van Straaten volunteers to help Craig ("My task is to listen to your thoughts"), Craig reveals the end of his dream: he has to kill someone who intends him no harm. He takes a scarf and strangles Van Straaten.

Once this occurs, Craig finds himself in a phantasmagoric nightmare world (a sequence directed by Cavalcanti), which involves him in all but one of the previous narratives he has just heard. He plays hide-and-seek with Sally O'Hara and runs through the same old mansion. When he stumbles into one room, he encounters Peter Cortland, the man who saw a room other than his own in the haunted mirror. In this other room we see the body of Francis Kent, the little boy murdered by his sister. Francis's body is sprawled across the sofa in the same position as Hugo's was on Maxwell's bed. As Craig had predicted, he strikes Sally, flees, and winds up in a nightclub where he encounters Sylvester and Hugo. Craig talks to Hugo as the camera pans the grotesque audience. Unable to hide from the crowd which pursues him, Craig is thrown into jail, after the jailer tells him: "Room for just one more inside, sir"; it is the hearse and bus driver from the first narrative. In the jail cell, Craig observes an enlarged Hugo who moves toward him menacingly and attempts to choke him. During this terrifying shot, we hear a telephone ringing—the call, it turns out, from Eliot Foley asking Craig down for the weekend.

If we view the individual narratives as dreams within the larger dream of Craig, it is possible to speculate on the relationship of their content to his psychic make-up. By denying the reality of the bizarre events in the guests' narratives, Dr. Van Straaten seems to function as the censor of the architect's dreams, in a manner that recalls Freud's description of the censor. For example, Dr. Van Straaten says that the race-car driver's experience of seeing the hearse must have been a dream. The denial of the meaning of a dream, which occurs sometimes when we are conscious as dreamers of the fact of dreaming, is the result of the censor's work. According to Freud: "The contemptuous critical judgment, 'it's only a dream,' appears in a dream when the censorship, which is never quite asleep, feels that it has been taken unawares by a dream which has been allowed through. It is too late to suppress it, and accordingly the censorship uses these words to meet the anxiety of the distressing feeling aroused by it."[11] But the denial is, in fact, a confirmation of the content of the dreamed material which is wished by the dreamer: "The intention is . . . to detract from the importance of what is 'dreamt' in the dream, to rob it of its reality. . . . It is safe to suppose, therefore, that what has been 'dreamt' in the dream is a representation of the reality, the true recollection. . . . In other words, if a particular event is inserted into a dream as a dream by the dream-work itself, this implies the most decided confirmation of the reality of the event—the strongest *affirmation* of it."[12]

Van Straaten considers the story of the hearse as nothing more than a dream. But Craig, who has dreamed the story in the first place, wishes it to be true: heed a premonition and be saved. He tries to do this at the country house; several times he attempts to leave what he fears will be a disastrous setting but is persuaded by his host to stay. The other two stories, which the doctor specifically rejects because they have no basis in reality, concern Sally's discovery of the living Francis Kent and Peter's escape from strangling his wife. These too can be seen as wish fulfillments of Craig, denied by the censorious doctor. In the first, the little boy has not been killed; in the second, Peter is able to avoid strangling his wife. That is, in each story, a character has avoided death.

The exclusion of the golf narrative from the final phantasmagoric dream after Craig strangles Van Straaten bears consideration. Even though this comic story seems out of place in the grim company of the other works, it still plays an important function in the overall dream. It is absurd—precisely for the reason Freud adduces to explain the presence of absurdity in dreams: to disguise and displace as much as possible the actual meaning. When the dream-thoughts include the judgment, "This is absurd," the dream-work accommodates this negative position by rendering an event absurd; "that is to say, if any one of the dreamer's unconscious trains of thought has criticism or ridicule as its motive."[13] In other words, absurdity is a strategy by which the dreamer tries to avoid direct confrontation with criticism. The events as experienced in the dream may be absurd, but not the motive for presenting them in that fashion: "The dream-thoughts are never absurd . . . and . . . the dream-work produces absurd dreams and dreams containing individual absurd elements if it is faced with the necessity of representing any criticism, ridicule, or derision which may be present in the dream-thoughts."[14]

Recall the comic rivalry of the two golfers for the affection of Mary, the loser's suicide, and his final delight as the ghostly survivor who will be able to make invisible advances to the woman. This story presents Craig's attempt to deal with material that in the ventriloquist story will appear in a more straightforward fashion. The story of rivalry for the affection of one person resulting in death and invisibility mirrors in a heterosexual form the essentially homosexual triangle of the next story. In the latter, a dimension of Maxwell is attracted to Kee. As Hugo, he can articulate this feeling, and, indeed, steal into Kee's bed. But as Maxwell, he can be verbally and physically abusive to his rival for the affections of—himself. In killing Hugo, Maxwell is destroying himself.

It is after this story that Craig murders the doctor. Why him, of all people, particularly now that he seems willing to help Craig with his problem of the recurring dream? Perhaps Craig kills the psychiatrist because he alone, of all the guests, is capable of detecting a dual personality, as he has done with Maxwell. It may be that Craig himself is a homosexual who fears the rational methods the doctor will use to examine him; the content of the ventriloquist story makes such an interpretation possible. Even if the latter is not the case, Craig fears being investigated by the psychiatrist. He kills him at a point when the latter's glasses have broken, an instrument that permits clearer vision. Craig kills the one person in the house who can see through him.

The dream about the ventriloquist is a "safe" way of projecting his dual personality. But Hugo, the other side of Craig, will not be denied. He tries to choke Craig at the end of the nightmare; when he awakes, his hands are around his own neck. As Hugo, in the dream, he is trying to kill himself. That is, in a complex manner, the Hugo onto whom he projects his dual psychic and, possibly, sexual identity is the agent of his destruction. But Hugo is part of himself. When Craig murders the censor, Van Straaten, he releases all of the hostile forces that have been controlled in the individual narratives recounted thus far.

If Craig's dream truly ends with the ringing of the telephone, then we are in the position of anticipating the narrative we have just witnessed. The shots of Foley and Craig's arrival at the home indicate that a nightmarish series of events is about to begin. But if we are never out of Craig's dream, the shots of Foley and the architect's arrival can be understood to be images in the dreamer's mind. Craig, like Peter Cortland, is a man looking into a mirror and seeing another place which beckons him to enter. Like Dante's Count Guido de Montefeltrano, used by T. S. Eliot in the epigram for "The Love Song of J. Alfred Prufrock," or John Milton's Satan, Craig is hell himself, and never out of it.

But neither, then, are we. For Craig's dream goes on forever, flickering continually on our dream screen which he has appropriated and refuses to release. Our inability to shake off this film after viewing it arises in part from the sense that it keeps happening, over and over again. Considered in terms of the dream screen, the unending story seems even more appalling, for it is playing out its repeated horrors on a screen that, we discover, belongs to us.

The Dream Worlds of Belle de Jour

Dreams have played a very important part in Buñuel's films. As discussed above, he makes use of the dream mode in *Un Chien Andalou* and inserts a dream in *Los Olvidados*. Other dreams we could mention occur in *Robinson Crusoe* (1952) and *The Exterminating Angel* (1962). In two later works, co-scripted by Jean-Claude Carrière, *Belle de Jour* and *The Discreet Charm of the Bourgeoisie*, Buñuel's use of dreams reaches a level of complexity deserving special attention. To borrow a phrase from Northrop Frye, instead of being contained in films, dreams themselves now become the containers of the films.

Buñuel has said: "A film is the story of a dream. A dream recalled because of the realistic nature of the cinema."[15] This statement is relevant to our analysis of the two films. Even though it suggests one kind of relationship between film and dream, Buñuel as a filmmaker has gone beyond it. Dream, as dream, is seen to be the narrative *given* of the text. Our experience of it is similar to that which we observed in *Dead of Night* where we discover retroactively that we have been watching a dream. But the dreams of these two films must be distinguished from those of the *Dead of Night* because in Buñuel the idea of "dream" is itself charged with moral and political implications. "Dream" refers to the oneiric process, to film, and, simultaneously, to hope, desire, fabrication, illusion, the unreal—as in common parlance we speak of having a dream of achieving this or that goal sometime in our lifetime.

To realize that the entire work we have watched is a dream is to understand that the form Buñuel has chosen to render it is itself a statement about the way he sees the world—and about the way he thinks *we* see it as well. We are implicated by the retroactivity operating in our responses to these films. Although we think we have watched events from our ordinary vantage point, we learn that we are linked to the dreamers. The values that operate in their world constitute their "dreams"—the goals that they wish to achieve and the objects that they seek to attain. Buñuel renders the narratives as dreams which we only fully begin to define at the conclusion of the films. In this way he forces us to confront our own limitations: we too share the values of the dreamers. By using what I call the retroactive mode, Buñuel situates us on the other side of the screen. He uses the nature of the experience to satirize his viewers who find themselves linked to the dreamers whose values the filmmaker laments or deplores. To put this another way, his narrative strategy thus connects us morally and ideologically to the dreaming characters not only by involving us in their adventures but also by binding us to their psychic point of view.

It is instructive to compare these later works to the dream sequence we looked at in *Los Olvidados*. The dream in the earlier film has elements that clearly identify it: shots of the boy going to bed, the superimposition of his body to signal the onset of the dream, and the use of slow motion to evoke a dreamlike state. Such conventions are absent from *Belle de Jour* and *The Discreet Charm of the Bourgeoisie*. With one exception, Buñuel gives no real cues to the presence of the dream states. In fact, what appear to be indicators that we are in one kind of realm rather than another in *Belle de Jour* are nothing of the sort. They seem rather to be Buñuel's equivalents of Henry James's *amusettes*, there to catch those not easily caught.

The narrative of *Belle de Jour* presents the mind of its heroine to us, a mind that appears to manifest itself in day-dreams, fantasies, and memories. One critic has in fact suggested that the entire film is her dream.[16] I would agree, but only with the qualification that we acknowledge the ontolog-ical and symbolic status of the dream itself. Buñuel has chosen to present this story through the medium of film be-cause it is the only form that can define fully the nature of perceptual and moral illusion.

The film's opening credits appear in conjunction with shots of a horse-drawn coach in the Bois de Boulogne carrying a smartly dressed couple, Pierre (Jean Sorel) and Séverine (Catherine Deneuve). We hear the sounds of the horses' bells.

25. Séverine in bondage.

Suddenly the coach stops, and against her will Séverine is dragged out and bound by the coachmen. Pierre directs them to whip her. She pleads with him to stop this: "It's not my fault, I was going to explain everything!" Then, as they begin, she cries, "Pierre, I beg of you, don't let the cats loose!" Pierre watches the proceedings with a malevolent sneer. After they are finished, he leaves her to them to be raped. As one of the men approaches her, we see an ambiguous expression on her face suggestive of ecstasy. Then we hear, "What are you thinking about, Séverine?"[17] And we find ourselves in a plush apartment of the *haute bourgeoisie*; Séverine is lying in bed while Pierre brushes his teeth. It was all a daydream, nothing more. Although Pierre wants to make love, she resists; he complies with her wishes uncompromisingly. This type of abrupt shift from a disturbing fantastic event to an apparently innocuous scene occurs throughout the film. For the moment, though, I would like to describe only those events of a less fantastic nature, saving the others for separate consideration in the context of the initial and final scenes.

Some time has passed and we find the couple in a ski lodge where they encounter Husson (Michel Piccoli), a man whom Séverine detests, and his girlfriend Renée (Macha Meril). Later, Renée tells Séverine about a mutual friend who has been working as a prostitute. Séverine seems appalled at the idea of a woman of their social class working in a brothel. When she returns home, there are flowers awaiting her from Husson. She orders her maid to throw them out but drops the vase in which they have been put. At that point we see what is apparently a flashback to her childhood; she remembers being molested by a plumber.

That evening she asks Pierre about his own experience with prostitutes; he says he has gone to a brothel, but "when you get out, you feel depressed for the rest of the day."[18] At a tennis club, Séverine actually sees the woman who has been working as a prostitute. Husson notices her eyeing the woman and provides the address of the brothel to Séverine. She visits it, timidly, fascinated with the private world of Madame Anaïs (Geneviève Page). As she mounts the stairs, we see her apparent memory of herself as a little girl refusing the communion wafer during the Mass. Although she expresses interest in working for the Madame, she does not immediately follow through. Returning after a week, she manages to win Madame Anaïs's agreement to let her work at the brothel in the afternoons, and she becomes Belle de Jour.

Her clients include a candy salesman who brutalizes her, a Japanese man who evidently brings some kind of viperous bug with him to the bedroom, a masochistic gynecologist, and a gangster named Marcel (Pierre Clementi). This last man falls in love with her and wants to be with her constantly, not just temporarily in the brothel. In the meantime, Husson visits Madame Anaïs's brothel and discovers Séverine at work but does not attempt to have sex with her. His earlier advances to her were made because she was inaccessible; he has, in fact, tried to visit her at home but has been refused entrance. Now that he can have her, he does not want her.

Eventually Marcel follows Séverine to her apartment. When she makes it clear that she will not abandon Pierre for him, Marcel leaves. But he waits outside and shoots Pierre, wounding him critically; Marcel himself is killed by the police. Although Pierre survives, he is left crippled and blind. We see Séverine feeding him as he sits in a wheelchair. Husson arrives, and explains Séverine's other life to Pierre and then leaves the two alone. Pierre's hand shakes, almost as if he were in the throes of death. Tears come from his eyes beneath the dark glasses. But then, he asks: "What are you thinking about Séverine?" We hear again the sound of the horses' bells, and, faintly, the mewing of a cat. He is cured, so it seems, and walks over to her. We see the suggestion, ever so faintly, of the same sneering expression on his face which we observed in the first scene of the film as he watched her being whipped. They prepare drinks, consider vacation plans, and Séverine looks out the window. Below her is the coach we saw in the Bois de Boulogne at the beginning of the film, empty except for the coachmen. It departs, and the film ends.

The events and two memories of her childhood are punctuated with four sequences that seem comparable to the opening sequence in their apparent lack of reality. First, after she has had sex with the candy manufacturer in the brothel, Séverine returns home, burns her underwear, lies in bed, and imagines Pierre and Husson in a field. As we hear the bells from the opening sequence, the men discuss the names of the wild bulls around them. Husson says: "Most of them are called Remorse . . . except for the last one, which is called Expiation."[19] Séverine appears, bound by her hands to a shed. Using stop-action shots, Buñuel shows the men slinging mud at her and verbally assaulting her.

After she encounters the Japanese man at the brothel,

Séverine has a fantasy of being picked up at a café in the Bois de Boulogne by a necrophiliac nobleman. This duke takes her to his palace, has her clothed in a black diaphanous garment, and makes her lie in a coffin. He appears to be using her as a surrogate for his dead daughter. After he takes pictures of her, he tells his butler not to let the cats into the room with them, engages in some form of sexual activity with her, and then throws her out.

Husson, undeterred by her contempt for him, attempts to visit her but is not allowed in the apartment, an event followed immediately by her fantasy of being at the ski lodge again with him and Pierre. Only now, she and Husson lower themselves beneath the table in the middle of the dining room and appear to be having sex under the table. Renée looks under the table at them and reports that Husson has taken out a pack of lily seeds.

The last of such sequences before the end of the film occurs after Husson has discovered that Séverine works in the brothel. Pierre and Husson appear in the Bois de Boulogne, prepared, it seems, to fight a duel. Once the signal to fire is given by the referee, they fire, but their bullets have been aimed at Séverine whom we discover tied to a tree. Blood flows from a wound in her temple.

I may seem to be falling into the same kind of error I think has proved to be a trap for other critics of the film by attempting to differentiate events from memories and from fantasies. Once the film has begun, we think we know whether something actually occurs (the first ski-lodge sequence, for example) or whether it could never have happened (such as the duel and killing of Séverine). The latter sort of event we attribute to Séverine's daydreams; she must be having another fantasy. But, by the time we arrive at the end of the film, and the baffling restoration of Pierre to health, it is impossible to continue making clear distinctions between fact and fantasy. Critics have seized on the presence of the horses' bells and the cat's cry in particular to help distinguish fantasy from reality; but, in the final moments of the film, these no longer avail as helpful signals.

One way of attempting to resolve the confusion is to return to the beginning of the film and consider the opening two scenes paradigmatically. Initially it seems that we have moved from absolute fantasy (the whipping and rape) to reality (the conversation in the bedroom). The film becomes more intelligible if we say these two scenes set the pattern for the rest of the narrative we are about to watch. We are not shifting from a fantasy to a real event; rather, we are moving from one kind of reality to another, *both* of which exist on the level of dream. Buñuel's point, I believe, is that the "reality" to which we move after the whipping is as much a product of dream and wishful desire as the first fantastic reality. That a good and understanding husband respects his wife's temporary reluctance to have sex and does not force her into it because he loves her is *also* a fantasy. This man and this world in which Séverine's wishes can be honored do not exist. It is the kind of dream I mentioned at the beginning of this section: the hope, the illusion that somehow the impossible may be true. This hope is presented to us as a reality. We are deceived into thinking that the well-appointed apartment, and the considerate, tooth-brushing husband somehow represent what is real. Not so, Buñuel seems to be saying. What we think is reality is only the surface of the dream, the film which is "the story of a dream. A dream recalled because of the realistic nature of the cinema."

Adopting the hypothesis that the opening two scenes establish a pattern for the rest of the film, we can make sense of its progression and resolution in a new way. Essentially the agon that drives the film is an internalized one in Séverine. We watch the shifting of her mind from one kind of "reality" to another as she attempts to control and order her own moral and psychic world.

If we assume that the primary nature of the film is a dream, then, rather as in the previous discussion of *Dead of Night*, those events that seem to be genuine dreams or fantasies can be viewed as dreams within the larger dream which is the constitutive structure and container of the film. The line that Pierre speaks in their apartment, "What are you thinking about, Séverine?" draws her back from a daydream. But if the world figured in association with Pierre is also unreal, then her fantasy can be seen to be very real, the wish that the censor has attempted to negate with the claim, "It was only a dream." These fantasies do, in fact, assume virtually the same status as some of the other dreams we have been speaking of throughout this study, at least in Freudian terms. Freud thinks daydreams "share a large number of their properties with night-dreams"; "like dreams, they are wish-fulfillments; like dreams, they are based to a great extent on impressions of infantile experiences; like dreams, they benefit by a certain degree of relaxation of censorship."[20] Thus the call back to reality by Pierre in the apartment can be seen as *affirming* rather than denying the nature of her daydream of being whipped. What is "real" is her vision of herself as an object who feels guilt, who fights off attempts to brutalize her, but who, at the same time, enjoys the horrible treatment at the hands of her husband and the coachmen. Perhaps she knows the reasons for her own mixed feelings and for their behavior. They depend on her for their pleasure; Man is incomplete without Woman. Her existence is a constant reminder to them that they need her. The rape asserts their power and reveals their contempt.

Buñuel wants to convey through Séverine's story a dark picture of the status of sexual relationships. This contempt for Woman appears elsewhere in the narrative. For example, when Husson discusses the brothel with her early in the film, he speaks of the "special atmosphere" in it: "The women are completely enslaved."[21] Pierre's admission, cited earlier, about feeling depressed the rest of the day after visiting a brothel, may be understood not as an admission of guilt, but, rather, as a comment on his own frustration as one who is sexually dependent on women.

Consider the fantasies in light of this argument about Séverine's sense of value. The scene of mud-slinging and verbal attack as Pierre and Husson tend the bulls expresses her complex feelings of self-contempt and remorse: contempt for herself which society has engendered in her and remorse because nothing can be changed.

The necrophiliac duke asks her forgiveness, even as she had asked it earlier of Pierre. But he rejects her immediately after he uses her in the coffin. The fantasy does not exist to reveal her desire for perverse sex so much as it does to suggest her desire to be dead. Indeed, as a sexual object for this man, she *is* dead.

The ski-lodge fantasy includes a report that Husson gives her lily seeds from a packet. Buñuel may be saying that what the male "plants" in the woman is death, or the awareness of it. Perhaps this fantasy explains in part her reluctance to have a child with Pierre. She may be afraid to continue the process by which humanity perpetuates its bondage of women. The presence of death is even more overt in the next fantasy when Pierre and Husson have their duel and kill Séverine. Now she is really dead, not just pretending to be dead as she did earlier for the duke.

The brothel scenes, taken as one more aspect of her existence, are no more "real" or "false" than the other events we witness. They are somewhere in between the extremes of the "good" fantasy (the Paris apartment) and the "bad" ones (the whipping, etc.). In dialectical terms, they are a compromise between the alternatives of the pure mother Pierre would like her to be, and the absolute whore she feels herself to be. Perhaps we might view these as her attempts to act out in her mind a kind of behavior that will allow her to adjust to the view of women she finds operating in the world.

Her descent into brothel life is slow. As she climbs the stairs at Madame Anaïs's for the first time, Buñuel pictures her in a low-angle shot through the stair rails, emphasizing her entrapment. With her first encounter, the candy manufacturer, she is again reluctant, at least until he slaps her; he knows she wants to be brutalized. The Japanese man with the insect finds her more accommodating. The shot of her in bed after he has left, sprawled next to the bloodied towel, suggests her pleasure in a new kind of abuse. And when she meets the vicious Marcel, she is so overcome by their sexual encounter that she shakes.

One of Madame Anaïs's clients is not pleased with her. Others have observed that the gynecologist is in some ways a mirror of Séverine. He has come to the brothel for self-abasement and masochistic pleasure. Buñuel emphasizes their linkage by reference to the vases. Séverine breaks one earlier in the apartment. The gynecologist, dressed as a servant, pleads for forgiveness for his incompetence; he too has broken a vase. In addition, Buñuel suggests a parallel between the two by having Séverine look at him through a peephole in an adjoining room. Madame Anaïs observes *her* through just such a peephole when Séverine first appears at the brothel. But Séverine cannot see how similar she is to the gynecologist. As she watches him being whipped and stepped on by a prostitute, she says: "How can anyone get so low? . . . [I]t disgusts me."[22] Buñuel has established the mise-en-scène in such a way that the light from within the room occupied by the gynecologist passes through the peephole and falls on Séverine's hair. Perhaps we should understand the lens of Buñuel's camera as offering another aperture through which we watch behavior that seems unconnected to our lives. In other words, Buñuel may be asking us to consider whether Séverine's inability to recognize herself in the masochist may

26. Séverine observes her mirror image.

be a mirror of our own lack of understanding; are we represented on the screen we watch through the lens of the projector?

The early experiences in the brothel seem to help Séverine; she no longer denies Pierre's requests for sex, and even seems to encourage them. "You don't frighten me any more," she says, because she is beginning to be able to inhabit several worlds of fantasy simultaneously.[23] The meaning of the sexual experience, embodied in the brutalizations, can be kept separate from the act itself. By repetition, she can adjust to the divided nature of her sexual status as a woman.

But the entrance of Marcel changes everything. He wants to monopolize her, and refuses to have her only as Belle de Jour. Psychologically, in relation to the fantasies, I think we can interpret this as a sign that the psychic censoring process she maintains has begun to break down. She has attempted to live in two fantasy worlds in such a way that one (the brothel) enhances the other (life with Pierre). But she fails. Marcel's invasion of her apartment signals the passage of one kind of fantasy across both a psychic and physical threshold she and the censoring process have established.

Curiously, though, after Marcel wounds Pierre, life seems to be simpler. Séverine tends him like a mother, feeding the helpless man as if he were an infant. But Husson enters and spoils this world too by telling Pierre the truth and healing him. "What are you thinking about, Séverine"—we are back to the line from the second scene of the film.

Now things are different. When she looks out the window and sees the coach they were riding in at the beginning of the film, it contains only the coachmen. The coach appears where we had seen it before, in the Bois de Boulogne. But the point-of-view shot of the coach is an impossible one, since Séverine and Pierre live in an apartment that does not over-look the park. When Buñuel follows Séverine's glance with the shot of the coach, he is not only providing an example of what Lev Kuleshov called creative geography; he is also creating mental geography. Her "sight" of the coach suggests that its previous occupants have departed and will no longer return. But its occupants have come to this apartment. Séverine and Pierre are at home. The fantasy world of brutalization she experienced with Pierre has come indoors, just as Husson and Marcel were able to penetrate the last bastion of her dream life.

Belle de Jour is a tragedy. Séverine feels guilty because she cannot please Pierre as the perfect wife and mother, the role associated with the ideal world embodied in their wealth, their grand apartment, and their class. Her earliest experience with a man, the plumber who molests her, has made her feel unclean, defiled. Yet society asks her to behave as if she did not suspect men viewed her only as a means of satisfying their own sexual desires. Her visions of degradation and life in the brothel permit her to experience her own sexuality in situations that are robbed of the illusions maintained about women's purity. Perhaps she thinks that if she can be a whore outside and satisfy her needs in a totally abasing context, then she can be a mother inside, safe in the idealized world represented by the dream world of their apartment.

What cures Pierre, I suggest, is the knowledge that Séverine is like all the rest, another whore, no better and no worse, rather than the mother who has been feeding him and satisfying his bodily needs. Pierre rises from his wheelchair, restored. Séverine awakes from her "dream," her hope that it might be possible to be viewed as a woman who is not a whore.

We are implicated in her tragedy. The surfaces of her life, the warm tones in the mise-en-scène of their apartment, the attractive world she inhabits are part of a dream which disguises as much as any dream we could imagine.

In *Belle de Jour* we discover retroactively that what appears to be one kind of reality is, in fact, a dream. Buñuel relies on our willingness to accept as reality the comfortable world of the *haute bourgeoisie*. We think, "This world *must* be real; the fantasies are defined as unreal by their apparent departure from such an attractive representation." Buñuel uses our acceptance of such a world to demonstrate that we are trapped ideologically in a framework of assumptions about values and human behavior. He seems to be telling us that the only reality we believe in is an illusion, a dream. But this dream is as much an illusion as the fantasies that inhere in Séverine's mind. Along with her, we watch this dream from the other side of the screen, and discover at the end of the film that we are as vulnerable to its appeal as she is.

The Collective Dream in The Discreet Charm of the Bourgeoisie

In *The Discreet Charm of the Bourgeoisie*, Buñuel exploits the potential of retroactivity even more, and involves us in a collective dream. If it bears any affinity to what Jung defines as a collective dream, though, it is not in the expected sense of presenting archetypal symbols which belong to the consciousness of the race. Rather, it is as an ironic depiction of shared desires and fears that haunt the minds of those who control the corrupt society Buñuel wishes to condemn. By the end of the film, we realize that the various narrative tricks Buñuel has played on us through his use of retroactively recovered dreams are designed to expose our own culpability as members of a society that has allowed the charming dreamers we meet to prosper. We are surprised to find ourselves in the position of sharing their dreams since we did not think we had any relation to such forces in society. Dope runners, an oppressive banana republic emissary, individuals for whom a good meal is the most important element in life—surely these beings are not like us. But, given my hypothesis, the retroactive mode has the effect of situating us on the other side of the screen. Buñuel thus employs a narrative technique which simultaneously links us to the characters and demonstrates that we share their perspective. To watch the film we must literally see the world through their dreaming angle of vision as their dream plays on our cinematic/dream screen which they have appropriated. By letting us discover we have been involved in the collective dreaming mind of such people, Buñuel argues that we most certainly *are* a part of their existence.[24]

The narrative line of the film concerns a number of characters: Raphael, the ambassador from Miranda (Fernando Rey); the Thévenots (Delphine Seyrig, Paul Frankeur, and Bulle Ogier); the Sénéchals (Stéphane Audran and Jean-Pierre

Cassel); and the Colonel (Claude Piéplu). Thévenot, Sénéchal, and Raphael are involved in smuggling dope, aided by
the ambassador's travel connections with South America. The
ambassador is having an affair with Thévenot's wife. They
are all very good friends and try to dine with each other as
often as possible.

In fact, the central conflict in the film involves their attempt
to eat a first-rate meal even though they are constantly frustrated in this activity. The film opens with the arrival of the
ambassador and Thévenots at the Sénéchals' for dinner, but
they discover that there has been a mix-up. This is the wrong
night; Sénéchal is not at home. They take Mme. Sénéchal
with them to an *auberge*, but they leave quickly after discovering that the body of the owner who has recently died is
resting in state at the back of the restaurant.

The friends try to assemble for lunch at the Sénéchals',
but this gathering fails to produce satisfaction because the
host and hostess have decided to have intercourse shortly
before the arrival of their guests. Their absence seems ominous to the expectant diners, who flee the house in alarm.
On another occasion, the ladies meet at a tearoom. But every
item they order (including tea) is, unfortunately, unavailable.

Another attempt to have dinner at the Sénéchals' is somewhat more successful. At least they are able to consume food.
But the dinner is interrupted by the arrival of the Colonel
and his troops who are practicing war games in the neigh-
borhood. Although Mme. Sénéchal finds a way to feed the
army, the continuation of the meal is partially spoiled by the
fact that the diners have to contend with the noise of booming
guns from the games. The Colonel asks them all to come to
his home for dinner later.

They try to have meals at the Sénéchals' on two more
occasions. The first is ruined by the arrival of the police who
arrest them all and take them to jail for smuggling. The second
is marred by gunmen who burst in (gangsters? Mirandan

27. The endless road and dream.

nationalists? it is not clear) and assassinate all the diners except the ambassador. He has been hiding under the dining room table. But, hungry for the *gigot d'agneau*, he slips his hand up to the table for one more piece and is exposed. Now he too will be shot. But then he wakes up from a nightmare and goes to raid the refrigerator in his apartment.

The last sequence, it seems, has been a dream. But we cannot determine when the dream begins. As we attempt to work our way back from this retroactively recovered dream, we find ourselves lost in an interlocking network of dreams which suggests that this last dream is not solely the property of Raphael. Rather, it and his recovery of it are parts of a larger, more extensive collective dream of all the characters. They share this oneiric experience and the fears and values that inform it just as they share the road on which we see them walking aimlessly three times in the film.

The first time the narrative openly addresses the subject of dreams occurs at the Sénéchals' dinner party which is interrupted by the arrival of the army. A sergeant who has brought in a message asks if he can tell the group his dream. The dream, which is accompanied by the sound of a slowly tolling bell, first pictures his experience encountering the ghost of his dead *copain* in an eerily lighted and partially destroyed building. In the second part of the dream, the sergeant explains how he tried to find his dead mother, and, after meeting her (a beautiful young woman), saw her being buried. The dream ends; its mournful and haunting tone provide a sharp contrast to the activities that have preceded it at the Sénéchals': pot-smoking, a defense of Frenchmen drinking wine in the trenches but condemnation of Americans in Vietnam who take dope, the priest's flurry to bring adequate chairs to this secular assemblage, and so on. One of the sergeant's comrades asks him to tell his dream about the train, but he has no time to share that one with the group.

The remaining dreams in the film are all recovered retroactively. The first presents dinner at the Colonel's. We see the Thévenots, Sénéchals, and the priest arriving for a meal, but no one seems to be about. They find the dining room and sit at the table to which a waiter brings what is clearly rubber chicken. In the midst of this strange event, the "drapes" behind them open to reveal an audience out beyond the footlights. They discover that they are on a stage in a theater. A prompter tries to help Sénéchal, but even with this assistance, he cannot remember his lines.[25] At this point, Sénéchal awakes with a start; he has been having a nightmare in which he is incapable of maintaining the illusion called for by the stage on which he finds himself.

He and Mme. Sénéchal then proceed to the Colonel's. There they appear to find all their friends at a real dinner party. But some tension exists to spoil the occasion. Various guests taunt Raphael about the repressive regime in Miranda: students are picked off like flies; guerrillas still try to overthrow the government; problems exist in administering "justice." The angry ambassador claims that Miranda is a true democracy, and, affronted, tries to leave. Although the Colonel wants him to stay, he too insults Raphael. The ambassador warns him that, were he not his guest, he would "demand satisfaction." When the Colonel issues an even more provocative insult, the ambassador takes out a gun and shoots him.

This scene is also a nightmare, one belonging to Thévenot. In fact, his nightmare of the shooting of the Colonel has *included* Sénéchal's nightmare of being on stage. We have recovered a dream which itself recovered a dream: retroactivity within retroactivity. At the end of Sénéchal's dream, Buñuel would appear to be indulging our sophistication as cinephiles: we *know* the convention of the retroactively recovered dream; Buñuel had us fooled for a moment. But then he undercuts our complacency and smugness as informed viewers by revealing that we were in someone else's dream all along.

The next dream is even more problematic. It too grows out of the texture of the events and simply happens, rather than being announced. But it is not clear when it begins. The events leading up to the revelation that there has been another dream involve the arrest of the Thévenots and Sénéchals at the next-to-last of the dinners. They are taken to prison where we see two policemen talking about "the bloody sergeant," a member of the force noted for his oppression of students; he was killed on this very date some years ago. In a flashback, we see one of his achievements in particular: the torturing of a young radical who refuses to talk. The sergeant has him put in a piano wired with electricity and then turns on the current; large, ugly bugs are shaken loose from their hiding

28. The aftermath of the massacre-nightmare.

place within the piano by the jolt. Then we see the sergeant's
bloody ghost walking the halls among the cells and hear a
tolling bell such as we heard earlier in the army sergeant's
dream. He releases the Thévenots and Sénéchals from their
bondage. But this event is also a dream. Now, though, we
find that the dreamer is someone we have not previously met
in the narrative, a police lieutenant who most certainly does
not want them released. His nightmare that they escape comes
true, for various important contacts of the ambassador's in
the higher echelons of the French government arrange for the
release of the prisoners.

The next event in the film is the final dinner party. Conversation focuses on the rather innocuous topic of astrology,
but also on the fact that Miranda seems to be a country
populated by Nazis who have found it a sanctuary. The as-
sassins enter and mow down the terrified guests. The am-

bassador temporarily escapes, but he too seems destined for liquidation until the sequence is concluded when he awakens from his nightmare. But we are unsure where his dream begins. With the dinner party? Does it include the lieutenant's dream? How do we know, in effect, when to differentiate dreamed from lived experience?

In fact, some things presented to us as facts seem as fantastic as any dream. For example, the young army lieutenant who introduces himself to the ladies in the tearoom tells them the story of his life. Visually, the narrative has the appearance of a dream. He explains to them that at the prompting of the ghost of his mother, he poisoned his father, a dour, military disciplinarian; actually the man was not his real father. That man had been shot by the man whom the lieutenant poisons. Consider also the bishop. He was left an orphan when both of his parents were poisoned some years ago. After a life as a clergyman, he became a gardener for the Sénéchals. One day he is asked to perform last rites for a man. The latter confesses that many years ago he had worked as a gardener for a family (the bishop's) and poisoned his employers. The bishop offers absolution to the man, and then picks up a rifle and shoots him. The murdered man's wound in the head links him visually to the army lieutenant's real father and to the bloody sergeant.

The lines between reality and dream, and between dream and dream are very faint. Perhaps we might sort out some aspects of the dreams within the dreams by returning again to comments cited earlier. To repeat, when the censor finds some element in a dream it wishes to repress, the dreamer will have the sense that what is being experienced is only a dream. But the elements denied as being "only" a dream, are, for Freud, what the unconscious really does affirm. With this in mind, we might consider the way Thévenot's dream denies the reality of Sénéchal's dream of being exposed. It did not happen; it was only a dream. But the fears of exposure evinced there are real. This is not an ordinary wish-fulfillment dream, obviously, but an anxiety dream on the order of an examination dream. The dreamer tries to cope with fears by generating a dream in which anxiety turns out *not* to have been justified in reality. Thévenot's container dream also displays anxiety, not about himself, but about the social world that he inhabits. His nightmare presents an event in which assassination ruptures the convenient link between the military establishment and a corrupt government official. On the one hand, then, the anxiety dreams can be seen to afford the dreamers a way of dealing with their fears. On the other hand, the denial of this dream within a dream has the effect of emphasizing *how* real the fears of the bourgeoisie are.

The police lieutenant's dream is more complex. In one sense we might say that his dream of losing his prisoners performs the same function as Sénéchal's dream does in Thévenot's. That is, the lieutenant and his dream are elements in a dream in the mind of the ambassador; the lieutenant represents a force that would retain him and his friends in prison. When the lieutenant's dream of the bloody (and repressive) sergeant turns out to be a dream, we can see something like the following scheme at work: the police lieutenant is happy because he has not, as he dreamed, lost his prisoners. If his dream and awakening are part of a larger dream, then the police lieutenant's experience, "this was only a dream," would make the content of it true for the *ultimate* dreamer, Raphael, who can deny the denial that this was only a dream.

But why Raphael alone? Those shots of the walkers on the road suggest they are linked forever. The film has been the collective dream of them all. Their collective fear is of exposure. The dinner table at which generally pleasant conversation can occur becomes Buñuel's equivalent of the shower in Hitchcock's *Psycho*. Of all places in the world, the characters would expect to be safe here. But this is not the case. The activity they associated with pleasure is subject to disturbances. First, they arrive for a dinner, but it turns out to be the wrong night. When they try to find a suitable place to dine out, the *auberge* has an air of death about it. Seated in a gracious *salon de thé*, they must struggle to be served a glass of water. Another time, when they arrive for a meal on the right date, the host and hostess are having intercourse and are not ready to entertain. Once, the appearance of an army intrudes on their pleasure. They begin to dream that their food is not real and that they are actors seated in front of rubber chicken. Then the meals themselves become increasingly frightening. An angry guest shoots his host. They are arrested. Worse, they are assassinated.

As with *Belle de Jour*, we do not escape this world simply by discovering, retroactively, that it is a dream. We must confront the reality underlying the manifest dream, a reality we have experienced with them on the other side of the screen. Our perceptual bonding to the characters, a phenomenon that is a result of their appropriation of our cinematic dream screen, thus creates a moral linkage. Buñuel proves that we actually see the world in the same way as the deceptively charming characters. Even though we thought we were above them, we too are ideologically tainted. Observe how we want the meals to be consumed. Reflect on the fact that we are tempted by the sight of Mme. Sénéchal's *gigot d'agneau*.

Buñuel's narrative strategy is brilliant. He catches us up in the minor aspects of his characters' lives. Our concern for the trivialities deflects from the larger concerns he is aiming at: corruption and complacency. He wants us to recognize that our tacit, silent complicity permits such beings to dominate society. The vehicle of this righteous indignation is the very nature of film, which is, as he says, "a dream recalled."

Conclusion

OUR RELATIONSHIP to the physical screen in the theater as we watch any film owes much to our experience as nurtured infants and to our earliest dreams. Films in general seem both real and dreamlike because they appear to us in a way that activates the regressive experience of watching dreams on our psychic dream screens. The actual screen in the theater functions as a psychic prosthesis of our dream screen, a structure constituted by the mother's breast, or a surrogate for it, and by our own ego.

When films present actual dreams of characters, our relationship to the narrative material is potentially even more intense. In dreams for which narrative cues and preparation are provided, our cinematic dream screens become doubly charged sites of that part of the oneiric narrative. Many techniques used by filmmakers to convey certain sensations in dreams can appeal with special force to us as viewers who know how we feel when we fall in dreams; when we are paralyzed; when we appear ridiculous or childish; when we are terrified; or when we desire.

At times, filmmakers choose to depict characters' dreams on a cinematic screen or its equivalent that is engrafted onto our cinematic dream screen. In such circumstances, we find ourselves watching dreams on a complex structure: in part physical—the actual screens; in part psychical—the dream screens. In some cases we learn that artists withhold information about the dreamlike status of parts or all of the narrative. Our retroactive discovery that our cinematic dream screen has been the location of another's dream results in various effects: some psychological and some satirical.

The development of cinematic technology has made it possible for us to watch films that seem to imitate reality very accurately. Included in this reality is an approximation of our own experience as dreamers. Part of the pleasure that cinema gives us derives from our sense that we are, like Wordsworth's infant, at one with our perceptions. But when the film ends, the revival of visionary unity is lost. We must leave the theater, separated from its extraordinary screen, and emerge into the light of common day.

Notes

Part One
THE
DREAM
SCREEN

1. Albert Benderson reminds us of another important consideration in this regard: the manner in which psychoanalytic theories have become "givens": "Psychoanalysis, whether Freudian or Jungian, has frequently proved a valuable tool in film scholarship, not by virtue of its scientific validity but rather by virtue of its pervasive influence in modern intellectual life. One of the major ironies of twentieth century aesthetics surely must reside in the fact that the psychoanalytical critical perspective has become progressively more useful largely because important writers, dramatists, and filmmakers, influenced by psychoanalytical concepts, began to create fictional worlds in which characters were motivated as if the hypothetical drives and forces posited by psycho-therapy really existed. Thus, in the narrative arts of our century, psychoanalysis has become a kind of self-fulfilling prophecy." "An Archetypal Reading of *Juliet of the Spirits*," *Quarterly Review of Film Studies* 4, No. 2 (Spring 1979), 193.

2. Specific references to Freud's theory of dreams occur throughout the text where they are fully annotated.

3. Carl G. Jung, "Symbols and the Interpretation of Dreams," *The Symbolic Life, Miscellaneous Writings*, in *The Collected Works of C. G. Jung*, trans. R.F.C. Hull, ed. Sir Herbert Read, Michael Fordham, Gerhard Adler, and William McGuire, 20 vols. (Princeton, N.J.: Princeton University Press, 1953-1979), 18: 183-264; "The Practical Use of Dream Analysis,"

The Practice of Psychotherapy, in *The Collected Works of C. G. Jung*, 16: 139-161. All quotations from Jung are taken from the *Collected Works*, hereafter *CW*.

4. Frederick Snyder notes that William Griesinger advanced a similar hypothesis in 1867: "The Physiology of Dreaming," in *Dream Psychology and the New Biology of Dreaming*, ed. Milton Kramer (Springfield, Ill.: Charles C. Thomas, 1969), p. 7.

5. Eugene Aserinsky and Nathaniel Kleitman, "Regularly Occurring Periods of Eye Motility and Concomitant Phenomena, during Sleep," *Science* 118 (4 September 1953), 273-274; "Two Types of Ocular Motility Occurring during Sleep," *Journal of Applied Physiology* 8 (1955), 1-10. Two helpful overviews of the development of modern dream research are offered by Rosalind D. Cartwright, *Nightlife: Explorations in Dreaming* (Englewood Cliffs, N.J.: Prentice-Hall, 1977); and William C. Dement, *Some Must Watch While Some Must Sleep* (New York: W. W. Norton and Co., Inc., 1978).

6. William C. Dement and Nathaniel Kleitman, "The Relation of Eye Movements during Sleep to Dream Activity: An Objective Method for the Study of Dreaming," *Journal of Experimental Psychology* 53 (1957), 339-346; William C. Dement and Edward A. Wolpert, "The Relation of Eye Movements, Bodily Motility, and External Stimuli to Dream Content," *Journal of Experimental Psychology* 55, No. 6 (1958), 543-553; Howard P. Roffwarg, William C. Dement, Joseph N. Muzio, and Charles Fisher, "Dream Imagery: Relation to Rapid Eye Movements of Sleep," *Archives of General Psychiatry* 7 (1962), 235-258.

7. W. David Foulkes, "Dream Reports from Different Stages of Sleep," *Journal of Abnormal and Social Psychology* 65, No. 1 (1962), 14-25. For a fuller view of Foulkes's theory of dreaming, see *A Grammar of Dreams* (New York: Basic Books, 1978). Foulkes has been influenced by the work of Noam Chomsky on linguistics and the earlier work of Calvin S. Hall;

see the latter's "A Cognitive Theory of Dreams," *The Journal of General Psychology* 49 (1953), 273-282.

8. Ralph J. Berger and Eric Moscowitz, "Rapid Eye Movements and Dream Imagery: Are They Related?" *Nature* 224 (8 November 1969), 613-614. See also Berger's argument that REM sleep may exist to help innervate the oculomotor system and "maintain facilitation of binocularly coordinated eye movements into subsequent wakefulness"; "Oculomotor Control: A Possible Function of REM Sleep," *Psychological Review* 76, No. 2 (1969), 144-163.

9. William C. Dement, "Experimental Dream Studies," in *Science and Psychoanalysis: Scientific Proceedings of the Academy of Psychoanalysis*, Vol. 7, ed. J. Masserman (New York: Greene and Stratton, 1964), pp. 129-162; Mardi Jon Horowitz, *Image Formation and Cognition* (New York: Appleton Century Crofts, 1970), pp. 35, 205; Richard M. Jones, *The New Psychology of Dreaming* (New York: Greene and Stratton, 1970), pp. 168-187; Michel Jouvet, "The States of Sleep," *Scientific American* (February 1967), 62-72; and Snyder, "The Physiology of Dreaming," pp. 7-31.

10. Robert W. McCarley and J. Allan Hobson, "The Neurobiological Origins of Psychoanalytic Dream Theory," *American Journal of Psychiatry* 134, No. 11 (November 1977), 1211-1221; "The Brain as a Dream State Generator: An Activation-Synthesis Hypothesis of the Dream Process," *American Journal of Psychiatry* 134, No. 12 (December 1977), 1335-1348; "The Form of Dreams and the Biology of Sleep," in *Handbook of Dreams: Research, Theories and Applications*, ed. Benjamin B. Wolman (New York: Van Nostrand Reinhold Co., 1979), pp. 76-130. Their theory is rejected by Foulkes, *A Grammar of Dreams*, p. 99; and by Harry Fiss, "Current Dream Research: A Psychobiological Perspective," in *Handbook of Dreams*, p. 49. Rosalind D. Cartwright accepts their hypothesis about neurophysiological activity but continues to maintain the importance of the dreamer's psychic make-up, desires, and wishes in the formation of dreams; *A Primer on*

Sleep and Dreaming (Reading, Mass.: Addison-Wesley Publishing Co., 1978), p. 131.

11. J. Allan Hobson, "Film and the Physiology of Dreaming Sleep: The Brain as Camera-Projector," *Dreamworks* 1, No. 1 (Spring 1980), 9-25; "Dream Image and Substrate: Bergman's Films and the Physiology of Sleep," in *Film and Dreams: An Approach to Bergman*, ed. Vlada Petrić (South Salem, N.Y.: Redgrave Publishing Co., 1981), pp. 75-95.

12. "A Dream Dialogue, Allan Hobson's Reply," *Dreamworks* 2, No. 1 (Fall 1981), 84.

13. André Bazin, "The Myth of Total Cinema," in *What is Cinema?*, vol. i, trans. and ed. Hugh Gray (Berkeley and Los Angeles: University of California Press, 1971), p. 21.

14. For related commentary dealing with the appeal of cinema, see Stanley Cavell, *The World Viewed: Reflections on the Ontology of Film*, enlarged ed. (Cambridge, Mass., and London: Harvard University Press, 1979), pp. 101-102. Also relevant is Annette Michelson's discussion of the wax museum, a kind of "proto-cinema," and its attraction to spectators: "Film and the Radical Aspiration," in *The New American Cinema*, ed. Gregory Battock (New York: E. P. Dutton and Co. Inc., 1967), p. 85.

15. F. E. Sparshott, "Vision and Dream in the Cinema," *Philosophic Exchange* 1 (Summer 1971), 120-121. Elsewhere, Sparshott refers to a suggestion by J. Rabkin who "pointed out that a factor contributing to the ready acceptance of inconsequentialities in film narrative techniques might be, not as I had tentatively suggested the familiarity of the inconsequentialities of actual dreams, but rather the well-established literary genre of dream-narrations whose stock in trade was just those shifts of place and identity that constitute my stereotype of the dream": in "Retractions and Reiterations on Films and Dreams," *Journal of Aesthetics and Art Criticism* 33, No. 1 (Fall 1974), 92. Marsha Kinder reminds us helpfully of the obverse of Sparshott's comment as she notes that our experience of film and other media inevitably affects the

style of our dreams: "The Adaptation of Cinematic Dreams," *Dreamworks* 1, No. 1 (Spring 1980), 54.

16. Sigmund Freud, *Civilization and Its Discontents*, in *The Standard Edition of the Complete Psychological Works of Sigmund Freud*, trans. and ed. James Strachey, 24 vols. (London: The Hogarth Press, 1953-1974), 21: 90-91. All quotations from Freud are taken from the *Standard Edition*, hereafter *SE*.

17. "A Note upon the Mystic Writing Pad," *SE*, 19: 228.

18. *Civilization and Its Discontents*, *SE*, 21: 91-92.

19. Bertram Lewin, *The Image and the Past* (New York: International Universities Press, Inc., 1968), p. 39.

20. Jean-Louis Baudry, "The Apparatus," trans. Jean Andrews and Bertrand Augst, *Camera Obscura* 1 (Fall 1976), 107-113; Frank D. McConnell, *The Spoken Seen: Film and the Romantic Imagination* (Baltimore: The Johns Hopkins University Press, 1975), pp. 88-91.

21. Baudry, "The Apparatus," p. 111.

22. Ibid., pp. 112-113.

23. Ibid., p. 119.

24. Ibid., p. 121. Christian Metz speaks in similar terms as he describes "a general tendency . . . to perceive as true and external the events and the heroes of the fiction rather than the images and sounds belonging purely to the screening process (which are, nonetheless, the only real impression): a tendency, in short, to perceive as real the represented and not the representer (the technological medium of the representation). . . .": "The Fiction Film and Its Spectator: A Metapsychological Study," trans. Alfred Guzzetti, *New Literary History* 8 (August 1976), 85.

25. Baudry has referred to Lewin's dream screen but has not fully explained its potential in relation to the apparatus, "The Apparatus," pp. 116-117. As far as I have been able to determine, the first film theorist to mention Lewin is Edgar Morin. In "Rêve et film," a section of *Le Cinéma ou l'homme imaginaire* (Paris: Editions Gonthier, 1958), pp. 67-68, he

discusses psychoanalysts' reports of patients who claimed their dreams were like films; at this point he indicates that he has heard about (but apparently not read) Lewin's work. See also "Les Attributes du rêve, la Précision du réel" (pp. 127-128) in the chapter entitled "La Complexe de rêve et de réalité" (pp. 126-142). Others who speak of Lewin's work are: Daniel Dervin, "Filmgoing and Bertram Lewin's Three Worlds of Experience," *Psychocultural Review* 1, No. 2 (Spring 1977), 247-249; Stephen Heath, "Narrative Space," *Screen* 17, No. 3 (Autumn 1976), 68-112; T. Jefferson Kline, "Endymion's Wake: Oneiric Projection and Protection in Bertolucci's Cinema," *Dreamworks* 2, No. 1 (Fall 1981), 26-34; and Guy Rosolato, "Souvenir-écran," *Communications* 23 (1975), 79-87. See also J. B. Pontalis, "Dream as an Object," trans. Carol Martin-Sperry and Masud Khan, *International Review of Psychoanalysis* 1, Nos. 1-2 (1974), 125-133.

26. Thierry Kuntzel compares Freud's mystic writing pad, a model of memory, consciousness, and perception, to the filmic apparatus in "A Note upon the Filmic Apparatus," *Quarterly Review of Film Studies* 1, No. 3 (August 1976), 266-271.

27. Freud, *The Interpretation of Dreams*, SE, 5: 565.

28. Ibid., p. 566.

29. *Civilization and Its Discontents*, SE, 21: 67.

30. Ibid., p. 64.

31. "Negation," SE, 19: 237.

32. *Civilization and Its Discontents*, SE, 21: 68.

33. "Metapsychological Supplement to the Theory of Dreams," SE, 14: 222.

34. "Project for a Scientific Psychology," SE, 1: 336.

35. "The Sexual Life of Human Beings," *Introductory Lectures on Psychoanalysis*, SE, 16: 314.

36. Paul Federn, "Some Variations in Ego-Feeling," *International Journal of Psycho-Analysis* 7 (1926), 434, 438.

37. Otto Isakower, "A Contribution to the Patho-Psychol-

ogy of Phenomena Associated with Falling Asleep," *International Journal of Psycho-Analysis* 19 (1938), 337-338.

38. Ibid., p. 338.

39. Ibid., p. 331.

40. Ibid., p. 334.

41. Truett Allison and Henry Van Twyver, "The Evolution of Sleep," *Natural History* 79, No. 2 (February 1970), 60.

42. Howard P. Roffwarg, Joseph N. Muzio, and William C. Dement, "Ontogenetic Development of the Human Sleep-Dream Cycle," *Science* 152 (29 April 1966), 609.

43. Ibid., p. 610.

44. René Spitz, "The Primal Cavity," *The Psychoanalytic Study of the Child* 10 (1955), 220.

45. Isakower, "A Contribution to the Patho-Psychology . . . ," p. 339. See also Eric Aronson and Shelley Rosenbloom, "Space Perception in Early Infancy: Perception within a Common Auditory-Visual Space," *Science* 172 (11 June 1971), 1161-1163. For more on the infant's relationship to space, see Robert L. Fantz, "The Origin of Form Perception," in *Perception: Mechanisms and Models*, ed. Richard Held and Whitman Richards (San Francisco: W. H. Freeman and Co., 1971), pp. 334-340; and T.G.R. Bower, "The Visual World of the Infant," pp. 349-357 in the same collection. Also by T.G.R. Bower and worth seeing is "The Object in the World of the Infant," in *Recent Progress in Perception*, ed. Richard Held and Whitman Richards (San Francisco: W. H. Freeman and Co., 1976), pp. 221-229.

46. Jean Piaget, *Play, Dreams, and Imitation in Childhood*, trans. C. Gattegno and F. M. Hodgson (New York: W. W. Norton and Co., Inc., 1962), p. 185.

47. Jean Piaget and Bärbel Inhelder, *The Child's Conception of Space*, trans. F. J. Langdon and J. L. Lunzer (New York: W. W. Norton and Co., Inc., 1967), p. 6.

48. Ibid., p. 7.

49. *Play, Dreams, and Imitation in Childhood*, p. 200.

50. Ibid., p. 201.

51. Leon S. Roudiez, "Introduction" to Julia Kristeva, *Desire in Language: A Semiotic Approach to Literature and Art*, trans. Thomas Gora, Alice Jardine, and Leon S. Roudiez (New York: Columbia University Press, 1980), p. 6.

52. Plato, *Timaeus*, trans. Benjamin Jowett, in *The Collected Dialogues of Plato including the Letters*, ed. Edith Hamilton and Huntington Cairns (New York: Pantheon, 1961), p. 1176.

53. Ibid., pp. 1177-1178.

54. Julia Kristeva, "Place Names," trans. Thomas Gora and Alice Jardine, *October*, No. 6 (Fall 1978), p. 102.

55. Ibid., p. 103.

56. Ibid., p. 104.

57. D. W. Winnicott, *Playing and Reality* (London: Tavistock Publications, 1971), p. 11.

58. Jacques Lacan, "The Mirror Stage as Formative of the Function of the I," in *Ecrits*, trans. Alan Sheridan (New York: W. W. Norton and Co., Inc., 1977), pp. 1-7.

59. Winnicott, *Playing and Reality*, p. 12.

60. Ibid., p. 107.

61. Bertram Lewin, "Sleep, the Mouth, and the Dream Screen," *Psychoanalytic Quarterly* 15 (1946), 420. An earlier version of the following argument first appeared in my article, "Reflections on the Breast," *Wide Angle* 4, No. 3 (1981), 48-53.

62. "Sleep, the Mouth, and the Dream Screen," pp. 421-422.

63. Bertram Lewin, "The Forgetting of Dreams," in *Drives, Affects, Behavior*, ed. Rudolph M. Lowenstein (New York: International Universities Press, Inc., 1953), p. 193.

64. Isakower, "A Contribution to the Patho-Psychology . . . ," pp. 341-342.

65. Bertram Lewin, "Inferences from the Dream Screen," *The Yearbook of Psychoanalysis* 6 (1950), 107.

66. Bertram Lewin, "Reconsideration of the Dream Screen," *Psychoanalytic Quarterly* 22 (1953), 184.

67. Ibid., p. 186.

68. Spitz, "The Primal Cavity," p. 218.

69. See "A Voyage to Brobdingnag," in Book 2, Chapter 1, of *Gulliver's Travels*.

70. Spitz, "The Primal Cavity," p. 219.

71. Ibid., p. 222.

72. René Spitz, *No and Yes: On the Genesis of Human Communication* (New York: International Universities Press, Inc., 1957), pp. 77-78.

73. Ibid., p. 113.

74. Ibid., pp. 113-114.

75. Lewin, "Sleep, the Mouth, and the Dream Screen," p. 427.

76. Bertram Lewin, *The Psychoanalysis of Elation* (New York: The Psychoanalytic Quarterly, 1961), p. 172.

77. Ibid., p. 174.

78. Lewin, *The Psychoanalysis of Elation*, pp. 146-147; he is citing William James, *Varieties of Religious Experience* [1902] (New York: Longmans, Green and Co., 1928).

79. Hugo Mauerhofer, "Psychology of Film Experience," in *Film: A Montage of Theories*, ed. Richard Dyer MacCann (New York: E. P. Dutton and Co., Inc., 1966), p. 232; Bruce F. Kawin, "Creative Remembering and Other Perils of Film Study," *Film Quarterly* 32, No. 1 (Fall 1978), 62-65.

80. George W. Linden, *Reflections on the Screen* (Belmont, Cal.: Wadsworth Publishing Co., 1970), p. 174.

81. David R. Hawkins, "A Freudian View," in *Dream Psychology and the New Biology of Dreaming*, ed. Kramer, pp. 48-49.

82. See "The Forgetting of Dreams," *SE*, 5: 512-532.

83. Harry Fiss, "Current Dream Research: A Psychobiological Perspective," in *Handbook of Dreams*, ed. Wolman, p. 46. See also Carl A. Meier, "A Jungian View," in *Dream Psychology and the New Biology of Dreaming*, ed. Kramer, p. 105.

84. Bruce F. Kawin, "Right-Hemisphere Processing in Dreams and Films," *Dreamworks* 2, No. 1 (Fall 1981), 14.

85. Lewin, "Inferences from the Dream Screen," p. 106.

86. Lewin, "The Forgetting of Dreams," p. 193.

87. Ibid., p. 197. Lewin's comment on "writing" the remembered dream warrants our attention in another connection. Lewin suggests that when the awakened dreamer attempts to write down the dream on a blank piece of paper, it is as if "the blank page . . . represented the blank dream screen and (more deeply) blank, undisturbed infantile sleep; the recorded dream is the equivalent of a new version of the dream, which, since it proves unanalyzable is equal to 'no dream at all' or only to the paper on which it is written. That is to say, the paper itself is the main addition to the new manifest version, and it stands for the 'background' of the dream, that is, the dream screen or the breast, as an indicator of the wish for more, uninterrupted sleep"; Ibid., pp. 198-199. The implications of this observation might profitably be connected with the argument offered by Jacques Derrida on the nature of "writing" in dreams: "The overall writing of dreams exceeds phonetic writing and puts speech back in its place. As in hieroglyphics or rebuses, voice is circumvented": "Freud and the Scene of Writing," in *Writing and Difference*, trans. Alan Bass (Chicago: University of Chicago Press, 1978), p. 218.

88. Susanne Langer, "A Note on the Film," in *Film: A Montage of Theories*, ed. MacCann, p. 203.

89. Robert Curry, "Films and Dreams," *Journal of Aesthetics and Art Criticism* 33, No. 1 (Fall 1974), 85.

90. Sparshott, "Vision and Dream in the Cinema," pp. 115-116.

91. Ibid. On the topic of the spectator's identification with the screen, see Jean-Louis Baudry, "Ideological Effects of the Cinematic Apparatus," trans. Alan Williams, *Film Quarterly* 28, No. 2 (Winter 1974-75), 39-47; Nick Browne, "The Spectator in the Text," *Film Quarterly* 29, No. 2 (Winter

1975-76), 26-38; Daniel Dayan, "The Tutor-Code of Classical Cinema," *Film Quarterly* 28, No. 1 (Fall 1974), 22-31; Christian Metz, "The Imaginary Signifier," trans. Ben Brewster, *Screen* 16, No. 2 (Summer 1975), 14-76 and "Metaphor/ Metonomy, or the Imaginary Referent," in *The Imaginary Signifier*, trans. Celia Britton, Annwyl Williams, Ben Brewster, and Alfred Guzzetti (Bloomington: Indiana University Press, 1982), pp. 149-314; and my "Spectator-Viewer," *Wide Angle* 2, No. 2 (1978), 4-9.

92. Piaget and Inhelder, *The Child's Conception of Space*, p. 212.

93. Ibid., p. 217.

94. Ibid., pp. 233, 209-210, 245, 452.

95. Ibid., pp. 242-243.

96. On the topic of "suture" see Dayan, "The Tutor-Code of Classical Cinema"; William Rothman, "Against the System of the Suture," *Film Quarterly* 29, No. 1 (1975), 45-50; Stephen Heath, "Cinema and Suture" and "Notes on Suture," in *Screen* 18, No. 4 (Winter 1977-78), 35-47 and 48-76; and Noël Carroll, "Address to the Heathen," *October*, No. 23 (Winter 1982), 125-135.

97. Lewin, "Reconsideration of the Dream Screen," p. 176.

98. See *The Interpretation of Dreams*, *SE*, 5: 488-508.

Part Two
WATCHING THE DREAM SCREEN

Section 1
A TAXONOMY OF DREAMS

1. Compare F. E. Sparshott, "Vision and Dream in the Cinema," *Philosophic Exchange* 1 (Summer 1971), 120-121.

2. Carl G. Jung, "Symbols and the Interpretation of Dreams,"

The Symbolic Life, Miscellaneous Writings, CW, 18: 183-264; see especially "The Language of Dreams," pp. 203-215.

3. For an excellent description of Murnau's technique in this sequence, see Lotte H. Eisner, *The Haunted Screen: Expressionism in the German Cinema and the Influence of Max Reinhardt*, trans. Roger Greaves (Berkeley and Los Angeles: University of California Press, 1973), pp. 216-217.

4. The identification of the devil with the succubus and incubus of nightmares has a long tradition. See Ernest Jones, *On the Nightmare* (London: The Hogarth Press, 1949), especially pp. 82-83. Recently Noël Carrol has questioned the exclusive importance that Jones attaches to sexuality in the nightmare and has argued that "the plot structures and fantastic beings of the horror film correlate with nightmares and other repulsive materials"; Carroll, "Nightmare and the Horror Film: The Symbolic Biology of Fantastic Beings," *Film Quarterly* 34, No. 3 (Spring 1981), 24. The tiny demons who poke the aching head of the rarebit fiend are not in the same league with the devil who interrupts the sleep of the hero in Porter's *Uncle Josh's Nightmare* (1902). Uncle Josh spends part of his nightmare grappling with the satanic figure who first materializes in a dissolve and then disappears and reappears with monotonous regularity.

5. See Beverle Houston and Marsha Kinder, "*Rosemary's Baby*," *Sight and Sound* 38, No. 1 (Winter 1968-69), 19. They note that, "ironically, the events which trigger the uncertain reality of Rosemary's response are just as fantastic as the images themselves."

6. Porter's *Jack and the Beanstalk* (1900) also depicts a character who experiences a dream that is actually a visitation. The sleeping Jack dreams that a beautiful woman appears and offers him various gifts, including money. In reality, a good fairy is predicting to him what he will take from the giant. As such the dream also has affinities with the proleptic dreams discussed at the end of this section.

7. Freud, *Beyond the Pleasure Principle*, *SE*, 18: 32-33. For a fuller discussion of *Ordinary People* see my "The Structure of *Ordinary People*," *Literature/Film Quarterly* 11, No. 1 (1983), 9-15.

8. For commentary on this important film, see Bernard Chodorkoff and Seymour Baxter, "*Secrets of a Soul*: An Early Psychoanalytic Film Venture," *American Imago* 31 (1974), 319-334; and Nick Browne and Bruce McPherson, "Dream and Photography in a Psychoanalytic Film: *Secrets of a Soul*," *Dreamworks* 1, No. 1 (Spring 1980), 35-45.

9. See S. M. Eisenstein, "A Dialectical Approach to Film Form," and "The Structure of the Film," in *Film Form*, trans. and ed. Jay Leyda (New York: Harcourt, Brace and World, 1949), pp. 45-63 and 150-178. He explains how the cutting pattern and the alternation of long and close shots in the Odessa Steps sequence of *Potemkin* are designed to create a sense of conflict in the viewer.

10. Alan Rudolph and Robert Altman, *Buffalo Bill and the Indians or Sitting Bull's History Lesson* (New York: Bantam Books, 1976), pp. 139-140.

11. Robert T. Self, personal communication.

12. George W. Linden, *Reflections on the Screen* (Belmont, Cal.: Wadsworth Publishing Co., 1970), p. 171.

13. See David Bordwell's discussion of the dream in his excellent study, *The Films of Carl Theodor Dreyer* (Berkeley and Los Angeles: University of California Press, 1981), 107-116. He explores the dream in connection with Dreyer's use of space and narrative structure. Also worth consulting is Mark Nash's study, "*Vampyr* and the Fantastic," *Screen* 17, No. 3 (Autumn 1976), 29-67.

14. Bergman has explained: "Suddenly about a year ago while making *Hour of the Wolf*, I discovered that all of my pictures were dreams. Of course I understood that some of my films were dreams, that part of them were dreams. . . . But that *all* of my pictures were dreams was a new discovery

to me"; "Introduction to Ingmar Bergman," a television documentary produced by Lewis Freedman, 1967, cited by Marsha Kinder, *"From the Life of the Marionettes* to *The Devil's Wanton*: Bergman's Creative Transformation of a Recurrent Nightmare," *Film Quarterly* 34, No. 3 (Spring 1981), 26. See also Vlada Petrić, "Bergman and Dream," *Film Comment* 17, No. 2 (March-April 1981), 57. He suggests that in Bergman's films "the emphasis is on similarity—not sameness—between film and dreams, or more specifically, on the fact that cinema provides a much stronger dreamlike experience than any other medium." Essential reading on this topic is *Film and Dreams: An Approach to Bergman*, ed. Vlada Petrić (South Salem, N.Y.: Redgrave Publishing Co., 1981).

15. Maya Deren, "Writings of Maya Deren and Ron Rice," *Film Culture*, No. 39 (Winter 1965), p. 1, cited by Lucy Fischer in "Notes for Program 1," *A History of the American Avant-Garde Cinema*, ed. American Federation of the Arts (New York: American Federation of Arts, 1976), p. 70.

16. For a fuller treatment of the film, see my "Looking for Mister Hermann: Fassbinder's *Despair*," *University of Dayton Review* 14, No. 2 (Spring 1980), 112-120.

17. *The Interpretation of Dreams*, *SE*, 4: 322-323.

18. Ibid., p. 318.

19. Jean-Paul Sartre, *L'Imaginaire: Psychologie phénoménologique de l'imagination* (Paris: Librairie Gallimard, 1948), pp. 162-163; my translation.

20. Marshall Deutelbaum, *"And the Villain Still Pursued Her*: Vitagraph's 1906 Dream Burlesque of Melodramatic Conventions," paper presented at the Midwest Modern Language Association Meeting, Oconomowoc, Wis., November 1981; and personal communication.

21. Vincente Minnelli, *I Remember It Well* (London: Angus and Robertson, 1975), p. 157.

22. Patricia Mellencamp, "Spectacle and Spectator: Look-

ing Through the American Musical," *Ciné-Tracts* 1, No. 2 (Summer 1977), 33.

23. Parker Tyler, *Magic and Myth of the Movies* (London: Secker and Warburg, 1971), p. 119. Also see "The Daylight Dream," in Tyler's *The Hollywood Hallucination* (New York: Simon and Schuster, 1970), pp. 230-246.

24. For example, see Leo Braudy, *The World in a Frame: What We See in Films* (Garden City, N.Y.: Anchor Books, 1977), pp. 139-155.

25. The dream sequence in musicals has not received the attention it deserves. Nothing of a detailed nature about it appears in John Russell Taylor and Arthur Jackson, *The Hollywood Musical* (New York: McGraw-Hill, 1971); in Timothy E. Scheurer, "The Aesthetics of Form and Convention in the Movie Musical," *Journal of Popular Film* 3, No. 4 (Fall 1974), 307-324; in J. P. Telotte, "A Sober Celebration: Song and Dance in the 'New' Musical," *Journal of Popular Film* 8, No. 1 (Spring 1980), 2-13; or in *Genre: The Musical*, ed. Charles [Rick] F. Altman (London: Routledge & Kegan Paul, 1981). Thomas Schatz discusses various aspects of musicals, including individual dream sequences, as he develops his definition of what he calls "the integrated musical," one which "manipulates the tension between object and image, between reality and illusion"; such a musical "is therefore among the most cinematic of Hollywood films": *Hollywood Genres: Formulas, Filmmaking, and the Studio System* (New York: Random House, 1981), pp. 216-217. See his illuminating discussion of the musical film, pp. 186-220. Jane Feuer provides an excellent analysis of dream sequences from a psychoanalytical perspective in *The Hollywood Musical* (Bloomington: Indiana University Press, 1982), pp. 73-76.

26. Carlos Rebolledo, "Buñuel and the Picaresque Novel," in *The World of Luis Buñuel*, ed. Joan Mellen (New York: Oxford University Press, 1978), pp. 147-148. See also Michael Gould, *Surrealism and Film (Open-Eyed Screenings)*

(South Brunswick and New York: A. S. Barnes and Co., 1970), p. 74.

27. See Bruce F. Kawin's review of *The Elephant Man*, *Film Quarterly* 34, No. 4 (Summer 1981), 21-25.

28. André Breton, "The First Surrealist Manifesto," in *What is Surrealism? Selected Writings*, ed. Franklin Rosemont (New York: Moriad Press, 1978), p. 122.

29. Breton, "The Second Surrealist Manifesto," in *What is Surrealism?*, p. 138.

30. Luis Buñuel, cited by David Curtis, *Experimental Cinema* (New York: Delta Books, 1971), p. 30. Jean Cocteau takes a similar position in regard to the form of *Le Sang d'un poète* (1930-1932): "*The Blood of a Poet* draws nothing from either dreams or symbols. As far as the former are concerned, it initiates [for imitates?] their mechanism, and by letting the mind relax, as in sleep, it lets memories entwine, move and express themselves freely": "Preface to *The Blood of a Poet*," in *Two Screenplays*, trans. Carol Martin-Sperry (New York: The Orion Press, 1968), p. 4.

31. Buñuel, "Cinema, Instrument of Poetry," in Francisco Aranda, *Luis Buñuel: A Critical Biography*, trans. and ed. David Robinson (New York: Da Capo Press, 1976), pp. 274-275.

32. See Linda Williams, "The Prologue to *Un Chien Andalou*: A Surrealist Film Metaphor," *Screen* 17, No. 4 (Winter 1976-77), 26. The prologue "is rather like Freud's description in *The Interpretation of Dreams*, of certain kinds of 'introductory dreams' that establish a certain state of affairs out of which the 'principal clause' dreams develop." See also her fine book on Surrealism which contains extensive discussions of dreams: *Figures of Desire: A Theory and Analysis of Surrealist Film* (Urbana: University of Illinois Press, 1981).

33. An equally demanding film that rejects traditional narrative form to concentrate on creating an impression of a mental state is Germaine Dulac's *La Coquille et le clergyman*

(1928). The work grew out of a collaboration between Dulac and Antonin Artaud. Artaud claimed that the film "does not tell a story but develops a succession of states of minds." Like *Un Chien Andalou* it rejects traditional modalities of space and time, operating with the energy of dream. But Artaud rejected Dulac's decision to call the entire film "a dream." Instead, he stated: "I will not seek to find excuse for its apparent incoherence through the facile loophole of the dream." Rather, according to J. H. Matthews, his aim was "to display the motives of our actions 'in their original and profound barbarity' and to transmit them visually"; *Surrealism and Film* (Ann Arbor: University of Michigan Press, 1971), pp. 78-79.

34. Robert Desnos, "Eroticism," in *The Shadow and Its Shadow: Surrealist Writings on Cinema*, ed. Paul Hammond (London: British Film Institute, 1978), p. 122.

35. Laura Mulvey, "Visual Pleasure and Narrative Cinema," *Screen* 16, No. 3 (Autumn 1975), 6-18. For a fuller examination of the complex issues involved in the depiction of women, see Stephen Heath, "Difference," *Screen* 19, No. 3 (Autumn 1978), 51-112. Relevant psychoanalytic writings on this topic are Sigmund Freud, "Fetishism," *SE*, 21: 152-157; and Jacques Lacan, "Of the Gaze as *objet petit a*," in *The Four Fundamental Concepts of Psycho-Analysis*, trans. Alan Sheridan, ed. Jacques-Alain Miller (New York: W. W. Norton and Co., Inc., 1978), pp. 67-119.

36. Stanley Cavell, *The World Viewed: Reflections on the Ontology of Film*, enlarged ed. (Cambridge, Mass., and London: Harvard University Press, 1979), p. 45.

37. Christian Metz, "The Imaginary Signifier," trans. Ben Brewster, *Screen* 16, No. 2 (Summer 1975), 64.

38. Ibid., p. 74.

39. Maurice Merleau-Ponty, "The Film and the New Psychology," in *Sense and Non-Sense*, trans. Hubert L. and Pa-

tricia Allen Dreyfuss (Evanston: Northwestern University Press, 1964), p. 58.

40. Stan Brakhage, *Metaphors on Vision* (New York: Film Culture Inc., 1963), unnumbered. Excerpts have been reprinted in *The New American Cinema*, ed. Gregory Battock (New York: E. P. Dutton and Co., Inc., 1967), pp. 211-226. See Paul S. Arthur, "Notes for Program 3," in *A History of the American Avant-Garde Cinema*, ed. American Federation of the Arts, p. 106 for a comment on Brakhage's oneiric aim in the film. For a detailed examination of the entire film, see P. Adams Sitney's important *Visionary Film: The American Avant-Garde*, 2nd ed. (New York: Oxford University Press, 1979), especially pp. 173-200.

41. Siegfried Kracauer, *Theory of Film: The Redemption of Physical Reality* (New York: Oxford University Press, 1971), p. 164.

42. Paul M. Jensen describes an unusual kind of proleptic dream that occurs in Fritz Lang's *Siegfrieds Tod*, the first part of *Die Niebelungen* (1923-1924). Kriemhild has a symbolic dream in which she sees a white dove set upon by two black hawks. Unlike the other works discussed here, the dream appears in the form of an animated sequence. See Paul M. Jensen, *The Cinema of Fritz Lang* (New York, A.S. Barnes and Co., 1969), p. 50. See the commentary on *The Last Wave* in Part Two, section 3.

Section 2
MANIFEST DREAM SCREENS

1. For a discussion of this practice, see my "Comedy and the Film within a Film," *Wide Angle* 3, No. 2 (1979), 12-17.

2. Bruce F. Kawin, *Mindscreen: Bergman, Godard, and First-Person Film* (Princeton, N.J.: Princeton University Press, 1978), p. 9. See also Hugo Münsterberg, *The Film: A Psy-*

chological Study (New York: Dover Publishing Company, 1970), pp. 43-44.

3. *SE*, 8: 9-236.

4. Marsha Kinder, "The Adaptation of Cinematic Dreams," *Dreamworks* 1, No. 1 (Spring 1980), 55. For a discussion of the film in terms of narrative technique, see my "The Filmic Dream and Point of View," *Literature/Film Quarterly* 8, No. 3 (1980), 197-203.

5. Daniel Dervin has been exploring the topic of the primal scene in a number of essays: "The Primal Scene and the Technology of Perception in Theatre and Film: A Historical Perspective with a Look at *Potemkin* and *Psycho*," *The Psychoanalytic Review* 62, No. 2 (1975), 269-304; "The Primal Scene and the Technology of Perception in Antonioni's *Blow-Up*," *Psychocultural Review* 1, No. 1 (Winter 1977), 77-95; "Splitting and Its Variants in Four Films Plus *Ten*," *Film/Psychology Review* 4, No. 2 (Summer-Fall 1980), 251-266.

6. Christian Metz, "The Fiction Film and Its Spectator: A Metapsychological Study," trans. Alfred Guzzetti, *New Literary History* 8 (Autumn 1976), 77.

7. Freud, "Negation," *SE*, 19: 237.

8. Ibid., p. 236.

9. Raymond Durgnat, *The Strange Case of Alfred Hitchcock, or the Plain Man's Hitchcock* (Cambridge, Mass.: MIT Press, 1978), p. 193.

10. Eric Rohmer and Claude Chabrol, *Hitchcock: The First Fifty Films*, trans. Stanley Hochman (New York: Frederick Ungar Publishing Co., 1979), p. 80.

11. William F. Van Wert, "Compositional Analysis: Circles and Straight Lines in *Spellbound*," *Film Criticism* 3, No. 3 (Spring 1979), 42.

12. Ibid., p. 47.

13. Durgnat, *Strange Case of Alfred Hitchcock*, p. 194. For a survey of films about psychiatrists see Glen O. and Krin Gabbard, "From *Psycho* to *Dressed to Kill*: The Decline and

Fall of the Psychiatrist in Movies," *Film/Psychology Review* 4, No.2 (Summer-Fall 1980), 157-168. Also worth consulting is Parker Tyler's earlier discussion of psychoanalytic films, dreams, and illusions in *Spellbound* and *The Seventh Veil*, "Supernaturalism at Home," and "Finding Freudism Photogenic," in *Magic and Myth of the Movies* (London: Secker and Warburg, 1971), pp. 86-109 and 111-122.

14. Royal S. Brown, "Hitchcock's *Spellbound*: Jung versus Freud," *Film/Psychology Review* 4, No. 1 (Winter-Spring 1980), 35.

15. Ibid., p. 56.

16. Ben Hecht, *Spellbound* (script), in *Best Film Plays*, ed. John Gassner and Dudley Nichols (New York: Crown Publishers, 1946), p. 97.

17. Ibid., p. 67.

18. Ibid, pp. 98-99.

19. Ibid., p. 100.

20. Bertram Lewin, "Sleep, the Mouth, and the Dream Screen," *Psychoanalytic Quarterly* 15 (1946), 420.

21. Ibid., p. 422.

22. Bertram Lewin, "Inferences from the Dream Screen," *The Yearbook of Psychoanalysis* 6 (1950), 107.

23. Hecht, *Spellbound*, p. 63.

24. Ibid., p. 66.

25. Ibid., p. 102.

26. Ibid., p. 98.

27. Ibid., p. 113. Robert Benton's *In the Still of the Night* (1982) offers an interesting collection of references to Hitchcock's films, including *Spellbound*. At the film's climax, the hero, a psychiatrist (Roy Scheider), finds himself literally in the "scene" of his former patient's dream. His interpretation of the meaning of various details allows him to identify the killer of his patient.

28. Interview conducted by Gideon Bachmann, "Federico

Fellini: The Cinema Seen as a Woman," *Film Quarterly* 34, No. 2 (Winter 1980-81), 8.

29. I am very grateful to Professor Stubbs for providing this insight and for his helpful commentary on Fellini.

30. Melanie Klein, *The Psycho-Analysis of Children*, 3rd ed., trans. Alix Strachey (London: The Hogarth Press, 1959), pp. 179-180.

31. Klein, "The Emotional Life of the Infant," in Melanie Klein, Paula Heimann, Susan Isaacs, and Joan Riviere, *Developments in Psycho-Analysis*, ed. Joan Riviere (London: The Hogarth Press, 1952), p. 200.

32. Another example that I believe qualifies as an occurrence of the dream screen in Fellini's films is found in *Juliet of the Spirits* (1965). Early in the film, after demonstrating her abilities to call up fantasies at will, Juliet (Giulietta Masina) appears before us sitting in a chair near the water and wearing an enormous white hat. As the camera moves closer to her, she falls asleep; her head moves down in such a way that the white hat overwhelms the entire screen. Fellini then cuts to her dream, a frightening narrative in which she sees bizarre figures and decrepit horses emerge from the sea. She feels threatened by the figures who seem to be ill, but calls in vain for aid from her doctor who refuses to help her. As the dream concludes, she sees a particularly menacing figure with a club, but then is awakened by the sound of a jet plane. The last object that Juliet sees before going to sleep is the white hat, the object that precedes *our* vision of the dream she is having. This seems very much to be a case where a surrogate object has functioned as a character's dream screen, especially since the object takes over the cinematic dream screen that we are watching.

33. Quotation in Peter Cowie, *Sweden 2*, cited by John Simon, *Ingmar Bergman Directs* (New York: Harcourt Brace Jovanovich, 1972), p. 239.

34. Ibid., p. 39.

35. Stan Björkman, Torsten Manns, and Jonas Sima, *Bergman on Bergman*, trans. Paul Britten Austin (New York: Simon and Schuster, 1973), p. 198.

36. Oswald Stack, *Pasolini on Pasolini* (Bloomington: Indiana University Press, 1970), p. 150. This conception informs Pasolini's theory of *im-signs*: "in man, an entire world is expressed by means of significant images—shall we therefore propose, by analogy, the term 'im-signs' (*imsegni*, i.e. image signs). *This is the world of memory and of dreams.* Every attempt at memorization is a series of im-signs, that is primarily a cinema sequence. . . . And thus, all dreams are a series of im-signs which have all the characteristics of the cinematic sequence: close-ups, long shots, etc."; "The Cinema of Poetry," *Cahiers du Cinéma in English* 6 (December 1966), 36.

37. Marsha Kinder, "The Penetrating Dream Style of Ingmar Bergman," in *Film and Dreams: An Approach to Bergman*, ed. Vlada Petrić (South Salem, N.Y.: Redgrave Publishing Co., 1981), p. 69. Kinder acknowledges the presence of the "dream screen" but does not develop it, p. 71. James C. Manley also refers to it in "Artist and Audience, Vampire and Victim: The Oral Matrix of Imagery in Bergman's *Persona*," *Psychocultural Review* 3 (Spring 1979), 137.

38. Susan Sontag, "*Persona*, the Film in Depth," in *Styles of Radical Will* (New York: Delta Books, 1978), p. 137. Two other critics have discussed our identification with the boy: Simon, *Ingmar Bergman Directs*, pp. 238-239; and Robin Wood. The latter suggests: "We are not only what the boy sees, we are the boy seeing": *Ingmar Bergman* (New York: Praeger, 1970), p. 158.

39. Kinder, "The Penetrating Dream Style of Ingmar Bergman," p. 71. For general commentary on the relationship between film viewing and REM, see David Thomson, *America in the Dark: Hollywood and the Gift of Unreality* (New York: William Morrow, 1977), pp. 102-105.

40. Thierry Kuntzel, "The Film-Work, 2," trans. Nancy Huston, *Camera Obscura* 5 (Spring 1980), 20. Also see the first part of Kuntzel's study: "The Film-Work," trans. Lawrence Crawford, Kimball Lockhart, and Claudia Tysdal, *Enclitic* 2, No. 1 (Spring 1978), 39-62.

41. Kawin, *Mindscreen*, p. 125. Kawin suggests that the face seen by the boy in the prologue "is looking at him as if it were a withdrawn mother" (p. 112).

42. Ingmar Bergman, *Persona* (script), in *Persona and Shame*, trans. Keith Bradfield (New York: Grossman Publishers, 1972), p. 41.

43. "The Shadow," *Aion: Researches into the Phenomenology of Self*, *CW*, 9, Part Two: 9.

44. Bergman's practice here might be described in the same terms used by Roman Jakobson in reference to the poetic function. He explains: "*the poetic function projects the principle of equivalence from the axis of selection into the axis of combination*"; "Linguistics and Poetics," in *The Structuralists from Marx to Lévi-Strauss*, ed. Richard T. and Fernande De George (Garden City, N.Y.: Anchor Books, 1972), p. 95. Also see his essay, "The Metaphoric and Metonymic Poles," in *Critical Theory since Plato*, ed. Hazard Adams (New York: Harcourt Brace Jovanovich, 1971), pp. 1113-1116. Jakobson connects metaphor and metonymy to Freud's theory of the operation of the dream-work in *The Interpretation of Dreams*.

45. *The Interpretation of Dreams*, *SE*, 4: 320.

46. Ibid., p. 324.

47. Keith Cohen, *Film and Fiction: The Dynamics of Exchange* (New Haven and London: Yale University Press, 1979), p. 77.

48. Related to this are discussions by I. Lloyd Michaels, "The Imaginary Signifier in Bergman's *Persona*," *Film Criticism* 2, Nos. 2-3 (1978), 72-77; Christian Metz, "The Imaginary Signifier," trans. Ben Brewster, *Screen* 16, No. 2 (Summer 1975), 52-54; and Jacques Lacan, *The Four Fundamental*

Concepts of Psycho-Analysis, trans. Alan Sheridan, ed. Jacques-
Alain Miller (New York: W. W. Norton and Co., Inc., 1978),
pp. 105-108.

49. Bergman, *Persona,* pp. 58-59.

Section 3

THE RETROACTIVE MODE

1. Siegfried Kracauer, *From Caligari to Hitler: A Psychological Study of German Cinema* (Princeton, N.J.: Princeton
University Press, 1974), pp. 61-76. Kracauer thinks the story
is "a madman's fantasy" (p. 70). So also does Lotte H. Eisner,
*The Haunted Screen: Expressionism in the German Cinema
and the Influence of Max Reinhardt,* trans. Roger Greaves
(Berkeley and Los Angeles: University of California Press,
1973), p. 20.

2. Those who call the interior sequence a dream include
David Thomson, *Movie Man* (New York: Stein and Day, 1967),
p. 34; Paul M. Jensen, *The Cinema of Fritz Lang* (New York:
A. S. Barnes and Co., 1969), p. 24; Frank D. McConnell,
The Spoken Seen: Film and the Romantic Imagination (Bal-
timore: The Johns Hopkins University Press, 1975), p. 29;
Leo Braudy, *The World in a Frame: What We See in Films*
(Garden City, N.Y.: Anchor Books, 1977), p. 52; and Bruce
F. Kawin, *Mindscreen: Bergman, Godard, and First-Person
Cinema* (Princeton, N.J.: Princeton University Press, 1978),
p. 50.

3. John Frazer, *Artificially Arranged Scenes: The Films of
Georges Méliès* (Boston: G. K. Hall and Co., 1979), pp. 193-
194. Frazer's invaluable book provides descriptions of a number of obscure or no longer extant Méliès films.

4. Freud, "Revision of the Theory of Dreams," in *SE,* 22:
27-28.

5. For another discussion of the film, see Vlada Petrić,

"Griffith's *The Avenging Conscience*: An Early Dream Film," *Film Criticism* 6, No. 2 (Winter 1982), 5-27.

6. Braudy, *The World in a Frame*, pp. 52-53. Also see Kristin Thompson's helpful study, "Closure within a Dream: Point-of-View in *Laura*," *Film Reader* 3 (1978), 90-105. She examines Otto Preminger's film (1944) as an example of "duplicitous structures" of Hollywood film. Here the question of whether the second half of the film is or is not a dream of the detective Mark McPherson (Dana Andrews) is never resolved, thus denying closure to the dream (if it is one) that is not withheld from the plot.

7. See P. Adams Sitney's discussion of the film in *Visionary Film: The American Avant-Garde*, 2nd ed. (New York: Oxford University Press, 1979), pp. 97-101. See also Lucy Fischer, "Notes for Program 1," in *A History of the American Avant-Garde Cinema*, ed. American Federation of the Arts (New York: American Federation of the Arts, 1976), pp. 75-79. For commentary on the phenomenon of penile erection during the REM state, see David R. Hawkins, "A Freudian View," in *Dream Psychology and the New Biology of Dreaming*, ed. Milton Kramer (Springfield, Ill.: Charles C. Thomas, 1969), p. 51.

8. Kenneth Anger, "Filmography," *Film Culture* 31 (Winter 1963-64), 8, cited by Sitney, *Visionary Film*, p. 97.

9. See Marie Jean Lederman, "Dreams and Vision in Fellini's *City of Women*," *Journal of Popular Film and Television* 9, No. 3 (Fall 1981), 114-122.

10. See Charles Barr, *Ealing Studios* (London: Cameron and Tayleur, 1977) for the place of *Dead of Night* in relation to the history of the studio. He sees the framework structure of the narrative as a possible reflection of the activities of the Ealing Round Table (p. 187).

11. *The Interpretation of Dreams*, SE, 5: 489.

12. Ibid., p. 338.

13. Ibid., p. 434.

14. Ibid., pp. 444-445.

15. Quoted by Penelope Gilliatt in her profile of Buñuel, "Long Live the Living," *The New Yorker*, 5 December 1977, p. 53.

16. This critic, unnamed, is cited by Andrew Sarris in an introductory essay to *Belle de Jour* (script), by Luis Buñuel and Jean-Claude Carrière, trans. Robert Adkinson (New York: Simon and Schuster, 1971), p. 20. Sarris thinks she is still dreaming at the end of the film. The following are also worth consulting, particularly for the light they cast on the ending: J. H. Matthews, *Surrealism and Film* (Ann Arbor: University of Michigan Press, 1971), p. 174 (the whole film is a "fantasy"). Freddy Buache, *The Cinema of Luis Buñuel*, trans. Peter Graham (New York: A. S. Barnes and Co., 1973), pp. 166-167 (the film is a "kaleidoscope" in which meaning cannot be pinned down); Roy Armes, *The Ambiguous Image: Narrative Style in Modern European Cinema* (Bloomington: Indiana University Press, 1976), pp. 32-41 (the entire film seems to be taking place in the heroine's mind); Raymond Durgnat, *Luis Buñuel*, rev. ed. (Berkeley and Los Angeles: University of California Press, 1977), pp. 139-144 (there are four possible interpretations, some better than others); and Virginia Higginbotham, *Luis Buñuel* (Boston: Twayne Publishers, 1979), p. 137 (the film works with the motif of beauty and the beast).

17. *Belle de Jour* (script), pp. 36-39.

18. Ibid., p. 52.

19. Ibid., p. 86.

20. Freud, *The Interpretation of Dreams*, *SE*, 5: 492.

21. *Belle de Jour* (script), p. 55.

22. Ibid., p. 97.

23. Ibid., p. 116.

24. Compare this observation with that of Jonathan Rosenbaum: "Their myths, behaviour and appearance—a seductive, illusory surface—carry us (and them) through the

film with a sense of unbroken continuity and logic, a con-
sistency that the rest of the universe and nature itself seem
to rail against helplessly. Despite every attempt at annihi-
lation, the myths of the bourgeoisie and of conventional narrative survive and prevail, a certainty that Buñuel reconciles
himself to by regarding it as the funniest thing in the world":
"*Le Charme discret de la bourgeoisie,*" *Sight and Sound* 42,
No. 1 (Winter 1972-73), 3. See also Raymond Durgnat's
discussion of the film in *Luis Buñuel,* pp. 159-166.

25. In a personal communication, Dolores Burdick notes:
"The prompter is whispering lines from a play about Don
Juan. There is a reference in those lines to the invitation to
the Stone Guest—another ominous dinner reference."

Bibliography

Allison, Truett, and Henry Van Twyver. "The Evolution of Sleep." *Natural History* 79, No. 2 (February 1970), 56-65.

Altman, Charles [Rick] F. *Genre: The Musical*. London: Routledge & Kegan Paul, 1981.

————. "Psychoanalysis and Cinema: The Imaginary Discourse." *Quarterly Review of Film Studies* 2, No. 3 (August 1977), 257-272.

American Federation of the Arts. *A History of the American Avant-Garde Cinema*. New York: American Federation of the Arts, 1976.

Anderson, Barbara. "Eye Movement and Cinematic Perception." *Journal of the University Film Association* 32 (1980), 23-26.

Aranda, Francisco. *Luis Buñuel: A Critical Biography*. Translated and edited by David Robinson. New York: Da Capo Press, 1976.

Armes, Roy. *The Ambiguous Image: Narrative Style in Modern European* Cinema. Bloomington: Indiana University Press, 1976.

Aronson, Eric, and Shelley Rosenbloom. "Space Perception in Early Infancy: Perception within a Common Auditory-Visual Space." *Science* 172 (11 June 1971), 1161-1163.

Arthur, Paul S. "Notes for Program 3." In *A History of the American Avant-Garde Cinema*, edited by American

Federation of the Arts, pp. 99-108. New York: American Federation of the Arts, 1976.

Aserinsky, Eugene, and Nathaniel Kleitman. "Regularly Occurring Periods of Eye Motility and Concomitant Phenomena, during Sleep." *Science* 118 (4 September 1953), 273-274.

————. "Two Types of Ocular Motility Occurring during Sleep." *Journal of Applied Psychology* 8 (1955), 1-10.

Bachmann, Gideon. "Federico Fellini: The Cinema Seen as a Woman." *Film Quarterly* 34, No. 2 (Winter 1980-81), 2-9.

Barr, Charles. *Ealing Studios.* London: Cameron and Tayleur, 1977.

Battock, Gregory, ed. *The New American Cinema.* New York: E. P. Dutton and Co., Inc., 1967.

Baudry, Jean-Louis. "The Apparatus." Translated by Jean Andrews and Bertrand Augst. *Camera Obscura* 1 (Fall 1976), 97-126.

————. "Ideological Effects of the Cinematic Apparatus." Translated by Alan Williams. *Film Quarterly* 28, No. 2 (Winter 1974-75), 39-47.

Bazin, André. *What is Cinema?* Vol. 1. Translated and edited by Hugh Gray. Berkeley and Los Angeles: University of California Press, 1971.

Benderson, Albert. "An Archetypal Reading of *Juliet of the Spirits.*" *Quarterly Review of Film Studies* 4, No. 2 (Spring 1979), 193-206.

Berger, Ralph J. "Oculomotor Control: A Possible Function of REM Sleep." *Psychological Review* 76, No. 2 (1969), 144-163.

————, and Eric Moscowitz. "Rapid Eye Movements and Dream Imagery: Are They Related?" *Nature* 224 (8 November 1969), 613-614.

Bergman, Ingmar. *Persona and Shame.* Translated by Keith Bradfield. New York: Grossman Publishers, 1972.

Björkman, Stan, Torsten Manns, and Jonas Sima. *Bergman on Bergman*. Translated by Paul Brittin Austin. New York: Simon and Schuster, 1973.

Bordwell, David. *The Films of Carl Theodor Dreyer*. Berkeley and Los Angeles: University of California Press, 1981.

Bower, T.G.R. "The Object in the World of the Infant." In *Recent Progress in Perception*, edited by Richard Held and Whitman Richards, pp. 221-229. San Francisco: W. H. Freeman and Co., 1976.

————. "The Visual World of the Infant." In *Perception: Mechanisms and Models*, edited by Richard Held and Whitman Richards, pp. 349-357. San Francisco: W. H. Freeman and Co., 1971.

Boyer, L. Bryce. "A Hypothesis Regarding the Time of Appearance of the Dream Screen." *International Journal of Psycho-Analysis* 41 (1960), 114-122.

Brakhage, Stan. *Metaphors on Vision*. New York: Film Culture Inc., 1963.

Braudy, Leo. *The World in a Frame: What We See in Films*. Garden City, N.Y.: Anchor Books, 1977.

Breton, André. *What is Surrealism? Selected Writings*. Edited by Franklin Rosemont. New York: Moriad Press, 1978.

Brown, Royal S. "Hitchcock's *Spellbound*: Jung versus Freud." *Film/Psychology Review* 4, No. 1 (Winter-Spring 1980), 35-58.

Browne, Nick. "The Spectator in the Text." *Film Quarterly* 29, No. 2 (Winter 1975-76), 26-38.

————, and Bruce McPherson. "Dream and Photography in a Psychoanalytic Film: *Secrets of a Soul*." *Dreamworks* 1, No. 1 (Spring 1980), 35-45.

Buache, Freddy. *The Cinema of Luis Buñuel*. Translated by Peter Graham. New York: A. S. Barnes and Co., 1973.

Buñuel, Luis, and Jean-Claude Carrière. *Belle de Jour*. Translated by Robert Adkinson. New York: Simon and Schuster, 1971.

Carroll, Noël. "Address to the Heathen." *October*, No. 23 (Winter 1982), 89-163.

————. "Nightmare and the Horror Film: The Symbolic Biology of Fantastic Beings." *Film Quarterly* 34, No. 3 (Spring 1981), 16-25.

Carterette, E. C., and M. P. Friedman. *Handbook of Perception*. Vol. 1. New York: Academic Press, 1974.

Cartwright, Rosalind D. *Nightlife: Explorations in Dreaming*. Englewood Cliffs, N.J.: Prentice-Hall, 1977.

————. *A Primer on Sleep and Dreaming*. Reading, Mass.: Addison-Wesley Publishing Co., 1978.

Cavell, Stanley. *The World Viewed: Reflections on the Ontology of Film*. Enlarged edition. Cambridge, Mass., and London: Harvard University Press, 1979.

Chodorkoff, Bernard, and Seymour Baxter. *"Secrets of a Soul*: An Early Psychoanalytic Film Venture." *American Imago* 31 (1974), 319-334.

Cocteau, Jean. *Two Screenplays*. Translated by Carol Martin-Sperry. New York: The Orion Press, 1968.

Cohen, Keith. *Film and Fiction: The Dynamics of Exchange*. New Haven and London: Yale University Press, 1979.

Curry, Robert. "Films and Dreams." *Journal of Aesthetics and Art Criticism* 33, No. 1 (Fall 1974), 83-89.

Curtis, David. *Experimental Cinema*. New York: Delta Books, 1971.

Dayan, Daniel. "The Tutor-Code of Classical Cinema." *Film Quarterly* 28, No. 1 (Fall 1974), 22-31.

DeGeorge, Richard T. and Fernande, eds. *The Structuralists from Marx to Lévi-Strauss*. Garden City, N.Y.: Anchor Books, 1972.

Dement, William C. "Experimental Dream Studies." In *Science and Psychoanalysis: Scientific Proceedings of the Academy of Psychoanalysis*. Vol. 7, edited by J. Masserman, pp. 129-162. New York: Greene and Stratton, 1964.

————. *Some Must Watch While Some Must Sleep.* New York: W. W. Norton and Co., Inc., 1978.

————, and Nathaniel Kleitman. "The Relation of Eye Movements during Sleep to Dream Activity: An Objective Method for the Study of Dreaming." *Journal of Experimental Psychology* 53 (1957), 339-346.

————, and Edward A. Wolpert. "The Relation of Eye Movements, Bodily Motility, and External Stimuli to Dream Content." *Journal of Experimental Psychology* 55, No. 6 (1958), 543-553.

Derrida, Jacques. *Writing and Difference.* Translated by Alan Bass. Chicago: University of Chicago Press, 1978.

Dervin, Daniel. "Filmgoing and Bertram Lewin's Three Worlds of Experience." *Psychocultural Review* 1, No. 2 (Spring 1977), 247-249.

————. "The Primal Scene and the Technology of Perception in Antonioni's *Blow-Up.*" *Psychocultural Review* 1, No. 1 (Winter 1977), 77-95.

————. "The Primal Scene and the Technology of Perception in Theatre and Film: A Historical Perspective with a Look at *Potemkin* and *Psycho.*" *The Psychoanalytic Review* 62, No. 2 (1975), 269-304.

————. "Splitting and its Variants in Four Films Plus *Ten.*" *Film/Psychology Review* 4, No. 2 (Summer-Fall 1980), 251-266.

Desnos, Robert. "Eroticism." In *The Shadow and Its Shadow: Surrealist Writings on Cinema,* edited by Paul Hammond, pp. 122-123. London: British Film Institute, 1978.

Deutelbaum, Marshall. "*And the Villain Still Pursued Her*: Vitagraph's 1906 Dream Burlesque of Melodramatic Conventions." Paper presented at Midwest Modern Language Association Meeting, Oconomowoc, Wis., November 1981.

Dunlop, Charles E. M., ed. *Philosophical Essays on Dream-*

ing. Ithaca, N.Y., and London: Cornell University Press, 1977.

Durgnat, Raymond. "A Dream Dialogue: The Hunting of the Dream-Snark." *Dreamworks* 2, No. 1 (Fall 1981), 76-82.

————. *Luis Buñuel.* Rev. ed. Berkeley and Los Angeles: University of California Press, 1977.

————. *The Strange Case of Alfred Hitchcock, or the Plain Man's Hitchcock.* Cambridge, Mass.: MIT Press, 1978.

Eberwein, Robert T. "Comedy and the Film Within a Film." *Wide Angle* 3, No. 2 (1979), 12-17.

————. "The Filmic Dream and Point of View." *Literature/ Film Quarterly* 8, No. 3 (1980), 197-203.

————. "Looking for Mister Hermann: Fassbinder's *Despair.*" *University of Dayton Review* 14, No. 2 (Spring 1980), 112-120.

————. "Reflections on the Breast." *Wide Angle* 4, No. 3 (1981), 48-53.

————. "Spectator-Viewer." *Wide Angle* 2, No. 2 (1978), 4-9.

Edelson, Marshall. "Language and Dreams: "The Interpretation of Dreams Revisited." *The Psychoanalytic Study of the Child* 27 (1973 [for 1972]), 203-282.

Eisenstein, S. M. *Film Form.* Translated and edited by Jay Leyda. New York: Harcourt, Brace and World, 1949.

Eisner, Lotte H. *The Haunted Screen: Expressionism in the German Cinema and the Influence of Max Reinhardt.* Translated by Roger Greaves. Berkeley and Los Angeles: University of California Press, 1973.

Fantz, Robert L. "The Origin of Form Perception." In *Perception: Mechanisms and Models,* edited by Richard Held and Whitman Richards, pp. 334-340. San Francisco: W. H. Freeman and Co., 1971.

Federn, Paul. "Some Variations in Ego-Feeling." *International Journal of Psycho-Analysis* 7 (1926), 434-444.

Fellini, Federico. *Three Screenplays*. Translated by Judith Green. New York: The Orion Press, 1970.

Feuer, Jane. *The Hollywood Musical*. Bloomington: Indiana University Press, 1982.

Fischer, Lucy. "Notes for Program 1." In *A History of the American Avant-Garde Cinema*, edited by American Federation of the Arts, pp. 69-83. New York: American Federation of the Arts, 1976.

Fiss, Harry. "Current Dream Research: A Psychobiological Perspective." In *Handbook of Dreams: Research, Theories and Applications*, edited by Benjamin B. Wolman, pp. 20-75. New York: Van Nostrand Reinhold Co., 1979.

Fliess, Robert. *The Revival of Interest in the Dream: A Critical Study of Post-Freudian Psychoanalytic Contributions*. New York: International Universities Press, Inc., 1953.

Foulkes, W. David. "Children's Dreams." In *Handbook of Dreams: Research, Theories and Applications*, edited by Benjamin B. Wolman, pp. 131-167. New York: Van Nostrand Reinhold Co., 1979.

———. "Dream Reports from Different Stages of Sleep." *Journal of Abnormal and Social Psychology* 65, No. 1 (1962), 14-25.

———. *A Grammar of Dreams*. New York: Basic Books, 1978.

Frazer, John. *Artificially Arranged Scenes: The Films of Georges Méliès*. Boston: G. K. Hall and Co., 1979.

Freud, Sigmund. *The Standard Edition of the Complete Psychological Works of Sigmund Freud*. Translated and edited by James Strachey. 24 vols. London: The Hogarth Press, 1953-1974.

Gabbard, Glen O. and Krin. "From *Psycho* to *Dressed to Kill*: The Decline and Fall of the Psychiatrist in Movies." *Film/Psychology Review* 4, No. 2 (Summer-Fall 1980), 157-168.

Gilliatt, Penelope, "Long Live the Living." *The New Yorker*, 5 December 1977, 53-72.

Gould, Michael. *Surrealism and Film (Open-Eyed Screenings)*. South Brunswick and New York: A. S. Barnes and Co., 1970.

Gregory, R. L. "Eye Movements and the Stability of the Visual World." *Nature* 182 (1958), 1214-1216.

————. *The Intelligent Eye*. New York: McGraw-Hill, 1970.

Hall, Calvin S. "A Cognitive Theory of Dreams." *The Journal of General Psychology* 49 (1953), 273-282.

Hammond, Paul, ed. *The Shadow and Its Shadow: Surrealist Writings on Cinema*. London: British Film Institute, 1978.

Hawkins, David R. "A Freudian View." In *Dream Psychology and the New Biology of Dreaming*, edited by Milton Kramer, pp. 39-56. Springfield, Ill.: Charles C. Thomas, 1969.

Heath, Stephen. "Cinema and Suture." *Screen* 18, No. 4 (Winter 1977-78), 35-47.

————. "Difference." *Screen* 19, No. 3 (Autumn 1978), 51-112.

————. "Narrative Space." *Screen* 17, No. 3 (Autumn 1976), 68-112.

————. "Notes on Suture." *Screen* 18, No. 4 (Winter 1977-78), 48-76.

Hecht, Ben. *Spellbound*. In *Best Film Plays*, edited by John Gassner and Dudley Nichols. New York: Crown Publishers, 1946.

Held, Richard, and Whitman Richards, eds. *Perception: Mechanisms and Models*. San Francisco: W. H. Freeman and Co., 1971.

————. *Recent Progress in Perception*. San Francisco: W. H. Freeman and Co., 1976.

Higginbotham, Virginia. *Luis Buñuel*. Boston: Twayne Publishers, 1979.

Hobson, J. Allan. "A Dream Dialogue, Allan Hobson's Reply." *Dreamworks* 2, No. 1 (Fall 1981), 83-86.

————. "Dream Image and Substrate: Bergman's Films and the Physiology of Sleep." In *Film and Dreams: An Approach to Bergman*, edited by Vlada Petrić, pp. 75-95. South Salem, N.Y.: Redgrave Publishing Co., 1981.

————. "Film and the Physiology of Dreaming Sleep: The Brain as Camera-Projector." *Dreamworks* 1, No. 1 (Spring 1980), 9-25.

Horowitz, Mardi Jon. *Image Formation and Cognition.* New York: Appleton Century Crofts, 1970.

Houston, Beverle, and Marsha Kinder. *"Rosemary's Baby." Sight and Sound* 38, No. 1 (Winter 1968-69), 17-19.

————. *Self and Cinema: A Transformationalist Perspective.* Pleasantville, N.Y.: Redgrave Publishing Co., 1980.

Isakower, Otto. "A Contribution to the Patho-Psychology of Phenomena Associated with Falling Asleep." *International Journal of Psycho-Analysis* 19 (1938), 331-345.

Jakobson, Roman. "Linguistics and Poetics." In *The Structuralists from Marx to Lévi-Strauss*, edited by Richard T. and Fernande De George, pp. 85-122. Garden City, N.Y.: Anchor Books, 1972.

————. "The Metaphoric and Metonymic Poles." In *Critical Theory Since Plato*, edited by Hazard Adams, pp. 1113-1116. New York: Harcourt Brace Jovanovich, 1971

Jensen, Paul M. *The Cinema of Fritz Lang.* New Y... A. S. Barnes and Co., 1969.

Jones, Ernest. *On the Nightmare.* London: The Hogarth Pr... 1949.

Jones, Richard M. *The New Psychology of Dreaming.* ... York: Greene and Stratton, 1970.

Jouvet, Michel. "The States of Sleep." *Scientific Ameri...* (February 1967), 62-72.

Jung, Carl G. *The Collected Works of C. G. Jung.* Transla... by R.F.C. Hull. Edited by Sir Herbert Read, Mic...

Fordham, Gerhard Adler, and William McGuire. 20 vols. Princeton, N.J.: Princeton University Press, 1953-1979.

Kawin, Bruce F. "Creative Remembering and Other Perils of Film Study." *Film Quarterly* 32, No. 1 (Fall 1978), 62-65.

————. *Mindscreen: Bergman, Godard, and First-Person Film.* Princeton, N.J.: Princeton University Press, 1978.

————. "Review of *The Elephant Man.*" *Film Quarterly* 34, No. 4 (Summer 1981), 21-25.

————. "Right-Hemisphere Processing in Dreams and Films." *Dreamworks* 2, No. 1 (Fall 1981), 13-17.

Kelman, Harold. "A Phenomenological Approach to Dream Interpretation. Part I: Phenomenology—An Historical Perspective." *American Journal of Psychoanalysis* 25, No. 2 (1965), 188-202.

————. "A Phenomenological Approach to Dream Interpretation. Part II: Clinical Examples." *American Journal of Psychoanalysis* 27, No. 1 (1967), 75-94.

Kerr, Walter. *The Silent Clowns.* New York: Alfred A. Knopf, 1975.

Kinder, Marsha. "The Adaptation of Cinematic Dreams." *Dreamworks* 1, No. 1 (Spring 1980), 54-68.

————. "The Art of Dreaming in *Three Women* and *Providence*: Structures of the Self." *Film Quarterly* 31, No. 1 (Fall 1977), 10-18.

————. "*From the Life of the Marionettes* to *The Devil's Wanton*: Bergman's Creative Transformation of a Recurrent Nightmare," *Film Quarterly* 34, No. 3 (Spring 1981), 26-37.

————. "The Penetrating Dream Style of Ingmar Bergman." In *Film and Dreams: An Approach to Bergman*, edited by Vlada Petrić, pp. 57-73. South Salem, N. Y.: Redgrave Publishing Co., 1981.

Klein, Melanie. *The Psycho-Analysis of Children.* 3rd ed.

Translated by Alix Strachey. London: The Hogarth Press, 1959.

———, Paula Heimann, Susan Isaacs, and Joan Riviere. *Developments in Psycho-Analysis*, edited by Joan Riviere. London: The Hogarth Press, 1952.

Kline, T. Jefferson. "Endymion's Wake: Oneiric Projection and Protection in Bertolucci's Cinema." *Dreamworks* 2, No. 1 (Fall 1981), 26-34.

Kracauer, Siegfried. *From Caligari to Hitler: A Psychological Study of German Cinema*. Princeton, N.J.: Princeton University Press, 1974.

———. *Theory of Film: The Redemption of Physical Reality*. New York: Oxford University Press, 1971.

Kramer, Milton, ed. *Dream Psychology and the New Biology of Dreaming*. Springfield, Ill.: Charles C. Thomas, 1969.

Kristeva, Julia. *Desire in Language: A Semiotic Approach to Literature and Art*. Translated by Thomas Gora, Alice Jardine, and Leon S. Roudiez. New York: Columbia University Press, 1980.

———. "Place Names." Translated by Thomas Gora and Alice Jardine. *October*, No. 6 (Fall 1978), 93-111.

Kuntzel, Thierry. "A Note upon the Filmic Apparatus." *Quarterly Review of Film Studies* 1, No. 3 (August 1976), 266-271.

———. "The Film-Work." Translated by Lawrence Crawford, Kimball Lockhart, and Claudia Tysdal. *Enclitic* 2, No. 1 (Spring 1978), 39-62.

———. "The Film-Work, 2." Translated by Nancy Huston. *Camera Obscura* 5 (Spring 1980), 7-69.

Lacan, Jacques. *Ecrits*. Translated by Alan Sheridan. New York: W. W. Norton and Co., Inc., 1977.

———. *The Four Fundamental Concepts of Psycho-Analysis*. Translated by Alan Sheridan. Edited by Jacques-Alain Miller. New York: W. W. Norton and Co., Inc., 1978.

Langer, Susanne. "A Note on the Film." In *Film: A Montage of Theories*, edited by Richard Dyer MacCann, pp. 199-204. New York: E. P. Dutton and Co., Inc., 1966.

Laurendeau, Monique, and Adrien Pinard. *The Development of the Concept of Space in the Child*. New York: International Universities Press, Inc., 1970.

Lederman, Marie Jean. "Dreams and Visions in Fellini's *City of Women*." *Journal of Popular Film and Television* 9, No. 3 (Fall 1981), 114-122.

Lewin, Bertram. "The Forgetting of Dreams." In *Drives, Affects, Behavior*, edited by Rudolph M. Lowenstein, pp. 191-202. New York: International Universities Press, Inc., 1953.

―――. "Inferences from the Dream Screen." *The Yearbook of Psychoanalysis* 6 (1950), 104-117.

―――. *The Image and the Past*. New York: International Universities Press, Inc., 1968.

―――. *The Psychoanalysis of Elation*. New York: The Psychoanalytic Quarterly, 1961.

―――. "Reconsideration of the Dream Screen." *Psychoanalytic Quarterly* 22 (1953), 174-199.

―――. "Sleep, the Mouth, and the Dream Screen." *Psychoanalytic Quarterly* 15 (1946), 419-434.

Linden, George W. *Reflections on the Screen*. Belmont, CA: Wadsworth Publishing Co., 1970.

MacCann, Richard Dyer, ed. *Film: A Montage of Theories*. New York: E. P. Dutton and Co., Inc., 1966.

McCarley, Robert W., and J. Allan Hobson. "The Brain as a Dream State Generator: An Activation-Synthesis Hypothesis of the Dream Process." *American Journal of Psychiatry* 134, No. 12 (December 1977), 1335-1348.

―――. "The Form of Dreams and the Biology of Sleep." In *Handbook of Dreams: Research, Theories and Applications*, edited by Benjamin B. Wolman, pp. 76-130. New York: Van Nostrand Reinhold Co., 1979.

————. "The Neurological Origins of Psychoanalytic Dream Theory." *American Journal of Psychiatry* 134, No. 11 (November 1977), 1211-1221.

McConnell, Frank D. *The Spoken Seen: Film and the Romantic Imagination.* Baltimore: The Johns Hopkins University Press, 1975.

Mahony, Patrick, and Rajendra Singh. "*The Interpretation of Dreams*, Semiology, and Chomskian Linguistics: A Radical Critique." *The Psychoanalytic Study of the Child* 30 (1975), 221-241.

Manley, James C. "Artist and Audience, Vampire and Victim: The Oral Matrix of Imagery in Bergman's *Persona*." *Psychocultural Review* 3 (Spring 1979), 117-139.

Matthews, J. H. *Surrealism and Film.* Ann Arbor: University of Michigan Press, 1971.

Mauerhofer, Hugo. "Psychology of Film Experience." In *Film: A Montage of Theories*, edited by Richard Dyer MacCann, pp. 229-235. New York: E. P. Dutton and Co., Inc., 1966.

Meier, Carl A. "A Jungian View." In *Dream Psychology and the New Biology of Dreaming*, edited by Milton Kramer, pp. 101-111. Springfield, Ill.: Charles C. Thomas, 1969.

Mellen, Joan, ed. *The World of Luis Buñuel.* New York: Oxford University Press, 1978.

Mellencamp, Patricia. "Spectacle and Spectator: Looking Through the American Musical." *Ciné-Tracts* 1, No. 2 (Summer 1977), 27-35.

Merleau-Ponty, Maurice. *Sense and Non-Sense.* Translated by Hubert L. and Patricia Allen Dreyfuss. Evanston: Northwestern University Press, 1964.

Metz, Christian. "The Fiction Film and its Spectator: A Metapsychological Study." Translated by Alfred Guzzetti. *New Literary History* 8 (August 1976), 75-105.

————. "The Imaginary Signifier." Translated by Ben Brewster. *Screen* 16, No. 2 (Summer 1975), 14-76.

Metz, Christian. *The Imaginary Signifier*. Translated by Celia Britton, Annwyl Williams, Ben Brewster, and Alfred Guzzetti. Bloomington: Indiana University Press, 1982.

Michaels, I. Lloyd. "The Imaginary Signifier in Bergman's *Persona.*" *Film Criticism* 2, Nos. 2-3 (1978), 72-77.

Michaels, John. "Film and Dream." *Journal of the University Film Association* 32 (1980), 85-87.

Michelson, Annette. "Film and the Radical Aspiration." In *The New American Cinema*, edited by Gregory Battock, pp. 83-102. New York: E. P. Dutton and Co., Inc., 1967.

Minnelli, Vincente. *I Remember It Well*. London: Angus and Robertson, 1975.

Morin, Edgar. *Le Cinéma ou l'homme imaginaire*. Paris: Editions Gonthier, 1958.

Mulvey, Laura. "Visual Pleasure and Narrative Cinema." *Screen* 16, No. 3 (Autumn 1975), 6-18.

Münsterberg, Hugo. *The Film: A Psychological Study*. New York: Dover Publishing Co., 1970.

Nash, Mark. "*Vampyr* and the Fantastic." *Screen* 17, No. 3 (Autumn 1976), 29-67.

Pasolini, Pier Paolo. "The Cinema of Poetry." *Cahiers du Cinéma in English* 6 (December 1966), 34-43.

Penley, Constance. "The Avant-Garde and Its Imaginary." *Camera Obscura* 2 (1978), 3-33.

Petrić, Vlada. "Bergman and Dream." *Film Comment* 17, No. 2 (March-April 1981), 57-59.

—————, ed. *Film and Dreams: An Approach to Bergman*. South Salem, N.Y.: Redgrave Publishing Co., 1981.

—————. "Griffith's *The Avenging Conscience*: An Early Dream Film." *Film Criticism* 6, No. 2 (Winter 1982), 5-27.

Piaget, Jean. *Play, Dreams, and Imitation in Childhood*. Translated by C. Gattegno and F. M. Hodgson. New York: W. W. Norton and Co., Inc., 1962.

—————, and Bärbel Inhelder. *The Child's Conception of Space*.

Translated by F. J. Langdon and J. L. Lunzer. New York: W. W. Norton and Co., Inc., 1967.

Pontalis, J. B. "Dream as an Object." Translated by Carol Martin-Sperry and Masud Khan. *International Review of Psychoanalysis* 1, Nos. 1-2 (1974), 125-133.

Rebolledo, Carlos. "Buñuel and the Picaresque Novel." In *The World of Luis Buñuel*, edited by Joan Mellen, pp. 139-148. New York: Oxford University Press, 1978.

Roffwarg, Howard P., Joseph N. Muzio, and William C. Dement. "Ontogenic Development of the Human Sleep-Dream Cycle." *Science* 152 (29 April 1966), 604-619.

————, and Charles Fisher. "Dream Imagery: Relation to Rapid Eye Movements of Sleep." *Archives of General Psychiatry* 7 (1962), 235-258.

Rohmer, Eric, and Claude Chabrol. *Hitchcock: The First Fifty Years*. Translated by Stanley Hochman. New York: Frederick Ungar Publishing Co., 1979.

Rosenbaum, Jonathan. *"Le Charme discret de la bourgoisie."* *Sight and Sound* 42, No. 1 (Winter 1972-73), 2-4.

Rosolato, Guy. "Souvenir-écran." *Communications* 23 (1975), 79-87.

Rothman, William. "Against the System of the Suture." *Film Quarterly* 29, No. 1 (1975), 45-50.

Rudolph, Alan, and Robert Altman. *Buffalo Bill and the Indians or Sitting Bull's History Lesson*. New York: Bantam Books, 1976.

Rycroft, Charles. *Imagination and Reality: Psycho-Analytical Essays*. London: The Hogarth Press, 1968.

————. *The Innocence of Dreams*. New York: Pantheon Books, 1979.

Sarris, Andrew. *"Belle de Jour."* In *Belle de Jour*, by Luis Buñuel and Jean-Claude Carrière, translated by Robert Adkinson, pp. 21-28. New York: Simon and Schuster, 1971.

Sartre, Jean-Paul. *L'Imaginaire: Psychologie phénoménologique de l'imagination*. Paris: Librairie Gallimard, 1948.

Schatz, Thomas. *Hollywood Genres: Formulas, Filmmaking, and the Studio System*. New York: Random House, 1981.

Scheurer, Timothy E. "The Aesthetics of Form and Convention in the Movie Musical." *Journal of Popular Film* 3, No. 4 (Fall 1974), 307-324.

Simon, John. *Ingmar Bergman Directs*. New York: Harcourt Brace Jovanovich, 1972.

Sitney, P. Adams. *Visionary Film: The American Avant-Garde*. 2nd ed. New York: Oxford University Press, 1979.

Snyder, Frederick. "The Physiology of Dreaming." In *Dream Psychology and the New Biology of Dreaming*, edited by Milton Kramer, pp. 7-31. Springfield, Ill.: Charles C. Thomas, 1969.

Sontag, Susan. *Styles of Radical Will*. New York: Delta Books, 1978.

Sparshott, F. E. "Retractions and Reiterations on Films and Dreams." *Journal of Aesthetics and Art Criticism* 33, No. 1 (Fall 1974), 91-93.

————. "Vision and Dream in the Cinema." *Philosophic Exchange* 1 (Summer 1971), 111-121.

Spitz, René. "Autoeroticism Re-Examined: The Role of Early Sexual Behavior Patterns in Personality Formation." *The Psychoanalytic Study of the Child* 17 (1962), 283-315.

————. *The First Year of Life*. New York: International Universities Press, Inc., 1965.

————. *No and Yes: On the Genesis of Human Communication*. New York: International Universities Press, Inc., 1957.

————. "The Primal Cavity." *The Psychoanalytic Study of the Child* 10 (1955), 215-240.

Stack, Oswald. *Pasolini on Pasolini*. Bloomington: Indiana University Press, 1970.

Stein, Eliot. "Buñuel's *Golden Bowl*." In *Belle de Jour*, by Luis Buñuel and Jean-Claude Carrière, translated by

Robert Adkinson, pp. 12-20. New York: Simon and Schuster, 1971.

Taylor, John Russell, and Arthur Jackson. *The Hollywood Musical*. New York: McGraw-Hill, 1971.

Telotte, J. P. "A Sober Celebration: Song and Dance in the 'New' Musical." *Journal of Popular Film* 8, No. 1 (Spring 1980), 2-13.

Thompson, Kristin. "Closure within a Dream: Point-of-View in *Laura*." *Film Reader* 3 (1978), 90-105.

Thomson, David. *America in the Dark: Hollywood and the Gift of Unreality*. New York: William Morrow, 1977.

————. *Movie Man*. New York: Stein and Day, 1967.

Tyler, Parker. *The Hollywood Hallucination*. New York: Simon and Schuster, 1970.

————. *Magic and Myth of the Movies*. London: Secker and Warburg, 1971.

Van Wert, William F. "Compositional Analysis: Circles and Straight Lines in *Spellbound*." *Film Criticism* 3, No. 3 (Spring 1979), 41-47.

Webb, Wilse B. *Sleep: The Gentle Tyrant*. Englewood Cliffs, N.J.: Prentice-Hall, 1975.

Williams, Linda. *Figures of Desire: A Theory and Analysis of Surrealist Film*. Urbana: University of Illinois Press, 1981.

————. "The Prologue to *Un Chien Andalou*: A Surrealist Film Metaphor." *Screen* 17, No. 4 (Winter 1976-77), 24-33.

Winnicott, D. W. *Playing and Reality*. London: Tavistock Publications, 1971.

Wolman, Benjamin B., ed. *Handbook of Dreams: Research, Theories and Applications*. New York: Van Nostrand Reinhold Co., 1979.

Wood, Robin. *Ingmar Bergman*. New York: Praeger, 1970.

Woods, Ralph L., and Herbert B. Greenberg, eds. *The New World of Dreams*. New York: Macmillan Publishing Co., Inc., 1974.

Index

Library of Congress Cataloging in Publication Data

Eberwein, Robert T., 1940-
Film and the dream screen.

Bibliography: p.   Includes index.
1. Moving-pictures—Psychological aspects. 2. Moving-picture plays—History
and criticism. 3. Dreams. 4. Psychoanalysis. I. Title.
PN1995.E32 1984   791.43'01'5   84-42583
ISBN 0-691-06619-1 (alk. paper)

Robert T. Eberwein is Professor of English at
Oakland University in Rochester, Michigan.